AF522365

Research in Social Work

Research in Social Work

Dr. Poonam Rani

RANDOM PUBLICATIONS
NEW DELHI (INDIA)

Research in Social Work

ISBN 978-93-5111-623-3

Published in 2015 in India by

RANDOM PUBLICATIONS

4376-A/4B, Gali Murari Lal, Ansari Road
New Delhi-110 002
Phone : +9111-43580356, 011-23289044, 011-43142548
e-mail: sales@randompublications.com,
info@randompublications.com, randomexports@gmail.com

Reprinted 2025

Type Setting by : Friends Media, Delhi-110089
Digitally Printed at: Replika Press Pvt. Ltd.

Preface

Social work research is shown to be both a distinctive academic enterprise and a task that can be accomplished effectively in line with the values and ethical principles that lie at the disciplines core.

Social work is, quite simply, the act of investigating a certain factor or problem that clients are facing. It could involve the societal causes of homelessness, or the root problems behind substance or alcohol abuse. Social work is a diverse and complex field, and research not only allows social work professionals to expand their personal knowledge within a practice area, but it can also benefit their clients and even society from a policy or legislative level.

Researchers within the social work profession are crucial in determining the true effect of human services programs. From measuring the impact of societal causes of child abuse to assessing the true extent of homelessness in light of the economic crisis, social work researchers are making a difference every day by providing insight into the numbers behind the problems.

Research and social work practice with regard to families and parenting have traditionally focused on mothers, with fathers becoming increasingly recognized over the past three decades. The lack of attention to fathers is inconsistent with social work practice frameworks, e.g., the ecological theory and family systems perspectives that are inclusive of all aspects of the family. Fatherhood became a topic of political focus with the Fatherhood Initiative in the 1990s and has recently become a widely recognized sub-specialty across a number of fields. Despite this recent growth in father-focused research, the very conceptualization of fathering as a sub-specialty reflects that fathers are still not considered as central to parenting as mothers.

This book exposes social workers, practitioners, and researchers to research methods that can be alternative or complementary to the largely quantitative methods that have dominated social work research.

I would like to thank my team for standing beside me throughout my career and writing this book. My special thanks go to "Random Publications" who have published the book.

– Dr. Poonam Rani

Contents

1

Introduction

In 1984, in the aftermath of early enthusiasm about the promise of single-case evaluation for integrating research and practice, the Council on Social Work Education (CSWE) adopted new accreditation standards implying the need for all schools of social work to prepare students to evaluate their own practice.

Although the standards did not explicitly specify the use of singlecase evaluation techniques as the only way for practitioners to evaluate their own practice, the emergence of the notion of empirically evaluating one's own practice coincided with the advent of single-case evaluation, and the two concepts are generally associated with one another.

Throughout the 1980s, as more schools of social work began teaching single-case evaluation as a way to conform to the new accreditation standards, studies consistently reported disappointing findings about the extent to which practitioners who learn about single-case evaluation as students eventually use it in their professional practice. In light of these studies, social work educators currently disagree as to whether single-case evaluation has lived up to its promise.

Nevertheless, the 1992 CSWE Curriculum Policy Statement contains language that is likely to foster a continued emphasis on single-case evaluation, such as in provision M5.7.11, requiring M.S.W. programmes to prepare students to &dquo; conduct empirical evaluations of their own practice interventions&dquo;. So far, the debate about the prospects for greater practitioner use of single-case evaluation methods has tended to focus on motivating more practitioners to use them or finding ways to give practitioners the agency supports and resources they need to use them. This article identifies problems in the analysis of single-case evaluation data that are likely to confront practitioners conducting single-case evaluations. Although some of the technical literature on single-case evaluation discusses data analysis problems, the problems to be identified in this article have been neglected as issues influencing the extent to which practitioners are likely to conduct single-case evaluations.

The authors postulate that these data analysis problems pose a serious barrier to efforts to promote increased use of single-case evaluation by practitioners and have implications for the way schools of social work are educating practitioners about research. Some readers might anticipate that this will be another one of the attacks on single-case evaluation and quantitative methods that have appeared in the social work literature since the early 1980s. It is not. The authors value quantitative research and single-case evaluation, and would like to see more of it. Our focus is limited exclusively to the prospects for increased use of single-case evaluation by practitioners, and whether too much emphasis is being placed on single-case evaluation at the expense of other approaches to quantitative evaluation.

MAIN DATA ANALYSIS AND DATA PATTERNS

The main data analysis problem to which we refer involves ambiguity in visually interpreting graphed data patterns. Graphs are deemed visually significant when they clearly imply that the most plausible explanation for improvement in the target problem is the effectiveness of the tested intervention. To rule out the plausibility of alternative explanations, graphs must depict a pattern of unlikely coincidences.

These coincidences should show that the target problem begins to improve in a stable manner consistently after the onset of intervention, and not at other times. Ideally, these unlikely coincidences should be replicated. The more successive replications, the less likely are alternative explanations and the more plausible becomes the hypothesis that the intervention is the real cause of the improvements that occur in the target problem. These replications can be done within one study, such as in ABAB or multiple baseline designs, or across studies. Replicating across studies can entail using a simple AB design for different clients with similar target problems who receive the same intervention. Although there is a rich literature on successful applications of single-case evaluation by clinical researchers in other fields, within-study replications are difficult for social work practitioners to conduct, due to practical constraints, such as heavy caseloads, inadequate agency support, and clients who do not stay in treatment very long. To date, the field has not succeeded in generating widespread social work practitioner use of AB designs without replication, let alone with replication.

AB designs are recognized as much more feasible for practitioners to use than are ABAB designs or multiple baseline designs. However, when AB designs are used, we seek to attribute improvement in the target problem to the effects of an intervention based on only one baseline phase and one intervention phase. This is doable, but precarious. To reduce the plausibility of history, cyclicity, or similar alternative explanations in an AB design, the improvement in the B phase must commence almost immediately at the start of that phase and after the end of the A (baseline) phase. Suppose improvement occurs during the intervention phase, but does not start until long after intervention begins.

What would this mean? Would it imply that the intervention was working, but with delayed effects? Perhaps. On the other hand, it might mean that something else happened to cause the improvement. That something might be an extraneous event, perhaps a cyclical change, or something else that coincided with the B phase.

Unless the improvement commences almost immediately after the onset of intervention, we cannot call the change a sufficiently dramatic coincidence to enable us to rule out the plausibility of these alternative explanations. There is simply too much time for something else to happen to permit us to conclude that improvement at any point during the B phase means that our intervention caused the improvement. And yet, it remains entirely plausible that the improvement indeed does reflect the delayed effects of our intervention. The point here is that we simply would not know what to conclude. If we have conducted a series of replications, then it may not be necessary for improvement in the target problem to commence immediately after the onset of intervention to infer that the intervention is effective. That is, the improvement can commence later during the intervention period.

But the timing of the improvement would have to occur in a consistent manner from case to case to establish the principle of unlikely successive coincidences and thereby imply that the most plausible explanation is one of delayed treatment effects (as opposed to the far-fetched speculation that extraneous variables are operating at the same time across different, independent replications).

Single-case evaluation graphs also might seem to have clear implications if virtually no sustained improvement occurs during the intervention phase. This might suggest the ineffectiveness of an intervention. If some improvement appears early during intervention, but then tails off later during intervention, we may wonder whether some extraneous factor is causing just a temporary setback. But even when there is no improvement during the intervention phase, we may wonder whether the study lasted long enough to detect delayed treatment effects. Thus the types of data patterns that permit practitioners to draw conclusive inferences about their efficacy are rather limited. Based on the authors' experience in conducting single-case evaluations, which we shall illustrate in the next part, we postulate that practitioners will often fail to obtain clear-cut findings as to the effects of their interventions, and that this experience will limit the value they are likely to perceive in continuing to conduct single-case evaluations.

CASE ILLUSTRATION

A study that evaluated the effectiveness of cognitive-behavioural group therapy with male adolescent sex offenders illustrates the types of ambiguous data patterns that can be found in single-case evaluation. That study, which is reported in depth elsewhere, provided single-case evaluation graphs on 23 offenders, who were distributed among three therapy groups. All the subjects had already been participating in outpatient group therapy that had been court-ordered as part of their probation for a sexual offence in Travis County, Texas. They ranged in age from 13 to 18, with a mean age of 15. Slightly more than half of them were Hispanic; the remainder were about evenly divided between African Americans and Caucasians. None of them had ever been incarcerated in a correctional facility. Most of the offences involved siblings or other relatives, and none involved strangers. The age of the victims ranged from 3 to 14 years. Only two of them were repeat offenders.

The baseline on each group started at the same time, and the intervention was introduced in a staggered fashion, producing a multiple baseline design. The baseline lengths for the three groups were 14 days, 21 days, and 28 days. The data were analysed separately for each of the 23 cases, for the purpose of obtaining numerous replications. Outcome for each case was measured according to whether there was a decrease in antisocial behaviours, an increase in prosocial behaviours or both.

Each indicator was self-monitored by the adolescent offenders and reported on a checklist devised for this study. The checklist included 21 antisocial behaviours and 19 prosocial behaviours. The antisocial behaviours ranged from milder forms such as arguing, cussing, and so forth to more extreme forms such as fighting, being sexually inappropriate, being truant, or substance abuse. Where possible, the adolescents' selfreports were triangulated with parental reports of the same behaviours. For the purpose of this article, we focused on the extent of ambiguity in the study's graphs. We found ambiguous outcomes in 6 of the 23 graphs displaying data on self-monitoring of antisocial behaviours and in 7 of the 23 graphs displaying data on self-monitoring of prosocial behaviours.

For the parental reports, we found ambiguous outcomes in 7 of the 16 graphs on antisocial behaviours and 6 of the 16 graphs on prosocial behaviours. The remaining graphs, with only a few exceptions, did not support treatment efficacy. (Because most of our graphs clearly failed to support treatment efficacy, and most of the rest were ambiguous, it can be argued that our study results, overall, were not ambiguous; that is, they unambiguously failed to provide much support for the effectiveness of the intervention. However, it is not our thesis that our overall results were ambiguous. Rather, it is our thesis that practitioners conducting single-case evaluation on a single case are likely to come up with an ambiguous graph. A different report focuses on the overall report of the study.) Due to space limitations, we cannot present all of the ambiguous graphs.

This provides some evidence that the intervention may be responsible for the improvement. But this evidence is limited because of the unclear, and somewhat unstable, pattern during baseline-in which the days when antisocial behaviour was reported fall in between periods of no antisocial behaviour. Those days, therefore, may represent just a temporary blip up rather than a pattern representative of the adolescent's functioning before intervention. But that improvement may have begun on the 10th through 14th days of baseline, and therefore, despite the near absence of antisocial behaviours during B, we cannot conclusively attribute the drop to the effects of the intervention.

A complete disappearance of antisocial behaviours coinciding with the onset of intervention. This, plus the fact that we see no antisocial behaviours during the final 11 days of the study, supports the notion that the intervention may be having powerful effects. But during the middle of the B phase we see a pattern of antisocial behaviours that is not much better than during baseline. We are therefore left unsure as to whether this is just a cyclical pattern in which the better parts of the cycle just happened to coincide with the beginning and ending weeks of the B phase.

A temporary increase of antisocial behaviours at the onset of the intervention, followed by an improvement to levels below baseline at the end of the B phase. What does this mean? One possibility is that the intervention worked. Perhaps the bad start of the B phase reflects just a temporarily adverse reaction to the intervention, or perhaps it reflects a coming out of denial. The stable improvement later on supports the notion that the intervention worked, but that it just took a while for its effects to appear. The alternative, and equally plausible, explanation, however, is that this is an unstable or possibly cyclical pattern. The improvement that started more than midway through the B phase did not coincide with the onset of intervention, and therefore may be due to extraneous factors having nothing to do with the intervention. In other words, we just do not know-the results are ambiguous.

An immediate improvement at the start of B, after a worsening at the end of baseline, may influence some practitioners to suppose that the intervention may be working. But this improvement is followed by a worsening, which in turn is followed by a trend towards improvement at the end of B. Although the improvements at the beginning and end of B offer some hope that the intervention may be effective, the worsening in between suggests that this may simply be a cyclical pattern, having nothing to do with the intervention.

And yet again, hopeful practitioners might look at the steady improvement at the end of B and wonder whether this would have continued down to zero had the study lasted longer. We do not find this graph to be visually significant. Its pattern does not offer the level of unlikely coincidence needed to conclude that intervention effectiveness is the most plausible explanation. But we think most practitioners obtaining findings like this on their own interventions will find enough hopeful signs in this graph to conclude that its implications regarding their effectiveness are unclear.

It is unclear whether the treatment has caused the improvement at the start of the B phase or whether the decline in prosocial behaviours near the middle of the B phase means that a similar decline in the second half of baseline is simply a cyclical fluke, in which the poorer part of the cycle just happened to occur at that time. But at the end of the intervention phase there is a precipitous decline in the frequency of these desired behaviours. Does this mean that the improvement at the start of intervention can be attributed to a honeymoon period, cyclicity, or some other extraneous factor? Or does it merely reflect a temporary setback during the course of effective treatment, perhaps due to some extraneous event that temporarily disrupted the ongoing trend of improvement? We do not know.

Finding the answer would require monitoring the client over a much longer period. Sometimes clinicians can monitor behaviours over much longer periods. Sometimes they cannot. An additional three graphs showed an increase in selfreported antisocial behaviours throughout the intervention period. Typically, graphs that appear to be visually significant, but in the unanticipated (*i.e.*, harmful) direction, would not be called ambiguous. Instead, they would be interpreted as rather conclusively showing that the intervention was harmful. Yet one of the major short-term treatment objectives of the tested intervention was to overcome the offender's denial and refusal to recognize or admit to his behaviour as antisocial. Thus, despite the obvious plausibility of harmful treatment effects (such as through group contagion, for example) as an explanation for these findings, practitioners can also argue that it is plausible that these findings do not mean that the intervention is harmful. That is, they can argue that the results could mean that short-term objectives are being reached and that if the study lasted longer, the antisocial behaviours of these offenders would diminish significantly.

It is important to recognize here that even if one thinks the practitioners' argument is implausible, it is their perception of what these data mean that will influence how valuable they find single-case evaluation. If they perceive data patterns like these to be inconclusive, rather than perceiving them as indicative of a harmful or ineffectual intervention, then regardless of what readers think of their interpretations, those practitioners may become less inclined to employ single-case evaluation. (In the same vein, practitioners might deem as inconclusive those graphs showing no change whatsoever in the intervention period, in that they may wonder whether the study lasted long enough to detect delayed treatment effects.)

STRATEGIES FOR REDUCING AMBIGUITY

One way to attempt to reduce ambiguity and sort out whether the intervention or some alternative explanation seems to be the most plausible explanation is by extending our evaluation of a particular case over a much larger number of data points and then replicating the evaluation over a large number of similar cases. But practitioners are likely to encounter significant practical obstacles to obtaining many data points and many similar cases. Also, replications across many cases may find that improvement commences at very different points after intervention begins for many cases, while many others do not improve. Consider what would be implied by an evaluation using a one-group pretest-posttest design, in which some cases improved and others did not.

We would conclude that the target problems may have improved without treatment, due to a variety of potential factors other than the intervention being evaluated. We would not infer that the intervention was effective just because some of the cases improved. To make such causal inferences, and to rule out the plausibility of alternative explanations, we would need a control group. But in single-case evaluation, we rely on obtaining numerous data points and replication rather than on obtaining a control group. We hope to find unlikely coincidences in which sustained improvement in the target behaviour commences at about the same time after the onset of intervention across replications.

But what if improvement commences at very different points after the onset of intervention for some cases? And what if many other cases do not improve? Under these conditions we will not have established a sufficiently consistent series of unlikely coincidences to support the argument that the observed improvements are not plausibly due to alternative explanations. Continuing this line of thought, suppose that a slight majority of cases improve at various points during intervention. It is quite plausible that a similar percentage of untreated controls may have improved to the same extent. Unlike a single-case evaluation, in a design using a control group we would be able to assess how much improvement occurred among untreated controls and be able to compare it to the extent of improvement among treated cases.

If the improvement among treated cases significantly exceeded the improvement among controls, the results would support the efficacy of the evaluated intervention. In other words, the precise timing of the onset of improvement from case to case would not matter. Neither would it matter whether all or even most of the treated cases improved. Even if most of the treated cases did not improve, treatment efficacy might be indicated if a much smaller proportion of untreated controls improved. But in single-case evaluation we lack comparison rates. Therefore, we are forced to look for dramatic unlikely coincidences in the timing of stable improvement. Moreover, these coincidences must replicate consistently from case to case. How reasonable is the implicit expectation in single-case evaluation that when evaluating effective interventions dramatic coincidences in the timing of stable improvement can be found across cases? With some types of target populations and target problems that expectation may seem realistic, such as when behavioural modification and social skills training interventions are applied to problems that respond quickly to them, and, as noted earlier, there is a rich literature in allied fields showing this to be so.

But social workers often work with problems or populations that do not respond so quickly to intervention. For example, in a study of an outreach group work programme for battered women, Rubin (1991) found ambiguous data patterns similar to the ambiguity discussed in the graphs illustrated previously, patterns in which questions about delayed treatment effects and overcoming denial complicated the interpretation of graphs across cases. Numerous other types of interventions and target populations would seem to pose similar concerns about the likelihood of obtaining unambiguous graphed data patterns. For example, consider play therapy interventions with children who have been abused or the treatment of adult survivors of sexual abuse.

In light of variability across cases in overcoming denial, in building trust, and so on, it does not seem realistic, even when we are assessing effective interventions, to suppose that single-case evaluations will consistently yield graphs showing stable improvement coinciding with the onset of treatment or commencing at about the same time from case to case. Neither does it seem particularly realistic to suppose that practitioners will be able to sustain the duration of monitoring nor the extent of replications needed to sort out intervention effects when results are ambiguous and inconsistent.

AMBIGUITY ON STATISTICAL SIGNIFICANCE TESTING

Another strategy that has been proposed to offset visual ambiguity is through the use of statistical techniques designed for practitioners conducting single-case evaluations. Those advocating this strategy argue that testing whether the data in the graph are statistically significant can be used as the criterion for deciding whether visually ambiguous results support treatment efficacy. But this argument has several problems.

One is that statistical significance refers only to ruling out chance, not to determining whether it was the intervention or some extraneous factor that caused the statistically significant change. For example, in an uncontrolled pre-experimental design we would not conclude that the intervention caused an improvement in the target problem just because there was a statistically significant improvement from pretest to posttest. Despite our ability to rule out chance as the explanation for the improvement, we would recognize the need for a more internally valid design to draw causal inferences about intervention effects, and we would not let statistical conclusion validity obviate our doubts about internal validity.

For the same reason, a statistically significant improvement during the B phase of an AB design does not obviate the need for unlikely coincidences in the timing and stability of the improvement. Another problem is the low statistical power inherent in single-case evaluations. Texts on this topic designed for social workers suggest that practitioners often find it unfeasible to obtain more than 10 data points in each phase of an AB design.

The power of a two-tailed significance test with a significance level of. 05, assuming a moderately effective intervention, is only about. 25 in an AB design with 10 data points in each phase. This means that we take a huge risk of a Type II error when we conduct significance testing in such studies. If practitioners understand this, then they will know that statistical significance tests are unlikely to help them develop more conclusive, clinically useful implications from visually ambiguous data patterns. Moreover, the statistical techniques that have been designed for practitioners conducting single-case evaluations can come up with results that are contradictory and which defy logic.

Consider, for example, which come from the sex offender treatment evaluation study discussed previously. We see a visually ambiguous data pattern regarding the intervention's effect on antisocial behaviours. Using the two standard deviation procedure to test for statistical significance in this graph, we would find a baseline mean of 7.21.Two standard deviations equals 6.65. Two consecutive data points during intervention (points 36 and 37) fall more than two standard deviations above the baseline mean. Thus, they are in the undesirable zone, because the desired effect is a reduction in antisocial behaviours.

Because Bloom and Fischer (1982) recommend as a criterion for significance finding two consecutive data points during intervention that fall more than two standard deviations away from the baseline mean, relying on this significance test to resolve the graph's visual ambiguity would influence us to conclude that the intervention had statistically significant harmful effects. Yet the visual pattern in this graph shows that such a conclusion would be ludicrous, because a similarly bad cycle can be found at the end of baseline, and because the remaining data during intervention show a consistently improving trend. Furthermore, using the celeration line approach to test for the statistical significance of these data would yield the opposite conclusion.

That is, the proportion of data points in the desired zone (under the celeration line) during intervention is significantly greater than the proportion during baseline, indicating that the intervention had statistically significant beneficial effects. This, too, would not be logical. A visual analysis reveals that the only reason that the celeration line approach yields statistical significance is the blip up at the end of baseline. Because of this blip, practitioners might be unsure as to which of the foregoing two statistical significance approaches to use with these data. Imagine their reaction if they tried both approaches and found that they yield contradictory conclusions. Of course, inconclusive statistical results can be found in all kinds of research, not just single-case evaluation. But the focus of this article is on practitioners producing single-case evaluations. In that proponents of singlecase evaluation, such as Bloom and Fischer (1982), often find it unfeasible to obtain more than 10 data points in each phase of an AB design, it seems reasonable to suppose that practitioners are particularly vulnerable to having low statistical power, and therefore inconclusive results, when they conduct single-case evaluation.

Moreover, the problems in the statistical procedures developed for practitioners doing single-case evaluation further suggest that this kind of evaluation is more likely to produce inconclusive findings than are other types of evaluation.

COUNTERARGUMENTS

The foregoing argument is built around the need to obtain clear-cut results that permit causal inferences. Some may counter that single-case evaluations with ambiguous results can have value as exploratory steps in the process of accumulating many replications and using inductive logic to tease out working hypotheses about the conditions required for a particular intervention to be effective and how long it takes for its effects to begin appearing. We would agree, but would argue that it is more realistic to expect practice-based researchers to carry out that very long-range and time-consuming research agenda than it is to expect practitioners to do it.

The extensive resources and data-gathering time that would be required would probably far exceed that required of many research strategies involving traditional group designs. Is it realistic to suppose that practitioners will find its elusive long-range payoff sufficient inducement to motivate them to use single-case techniques to evaluate their own practice? Another counterargument is that practitioners may find value in collecting and graphing repeated measurements because it gives them more clinical information and a better empirical basis for assessing when a target problem has been adequately alleviated or when a different intervention should be tried.

But visually ambiguous graphs complicate such clinical decisions. If it is unclear from the graph whether the intervention is working, or has had enough time to work, it is difficult to rely on the data for clinical decisions about when to abandon the intervention and try something new. Likewise, without clear, stable data patterns collected over a long period, it is unclear whether the graphed improvement in the target problem is only a temporary cycle. A related counterargument maintains that single-case designs serve a sufficient purpose if they merely show, from a clinical standpoint, that adequate change has taken place, regardless of what caused it.

Thus it can be argued that the fact that graphs can show whether target behaviours seem to have been attained is a sufficient benefit to augur well for the prospects of increased practitioner conducting of single-case evaluation. We would note, however, that this argument represents a vision of the benefits of single-case evaluation that is considerably scaled down from the original vision of single-case evaluation, the vision that captured the imagination of many social work educators by promoting single-case evaluation as a way to evaluate one's practice effectiveness. Moreover, if single-case evaluation means little more than monitoring whether there is any change in clients, and does not focus on attempting to ascertain what caused the change, then this raises questions about whether it really represents a significant way to integrate practice and research.

This vision of single-case evaluation seems to see it more as a clinical assessment tool than as a way for practitioners to answer research questions about their own practice. Perhaps the most seductive counterargument to this article's thesis is to assert that the interventions social workers are using have already been shown to be effective in group level evaluations and to argue that therefore practitioners do not need unambiguous, conclusive, visually significant graphs to rule out the plausibility of alternative explanations for the data patterns they observe.

If the interventions they are using have already been shown to be effective in group studies, practitioners would not need to worry as much about the timing of the improvement. The improvement could commence at almost any point during intervention. As long as the data pattern was merely consistent with the plausibility of intervention efficacy, practitioners might conclude that the intervention appeared to be working with this particular case.

This argument presumes that practitioners would not be conducting single-case evaluations to test the general effectiveness of an intervention; instead, they would use them to see whether the probabilistic findings of group research supporting the effectiveness of interventions apply to a particular case. This counterargument correctly notes that group research gives us only probabilities, that each case-practitioner dyad is unique, and that different cases will respond to tested interventions in different ways. But if this is so, then it would seem to support this article's point that single-case evaluations of effective interventions are not likely to produce graphs that are consistent across cases in the timing of improvement.

Therefore, the strength of this counterargument would appear to depend on whether the interventions that social workers use have already had sufficient group research support of their efficacy. Some interventions, particularly some behavioural ones, have had considerable support.

But many others have not. Moreover, even if practitioners assume they are applying an intervention that group research has found to be effective, they may have to further assume that the beneficial effects will emerge on their graphs near the onset of intervention. If the treatment effects are delayed, then they may need to conduct lengthy monitoring to ensure that they do not prematurely decide that the intervention is not working with their particular case. How realistic is it to suppose that practitioners will want to continue this type of data collection from case to case? If they are assuming that group research has already established the efficacy of their intervention, are they not more likely to rely on traditional forms of clinical feedback to make decisions about how well particular clients are responding to the intervention?

FOR SOCIAL WORK PRACTICE AND EDUCATION

The foregoing analysis suggests the need to reconsider whether substantial increases in the conducting of single-case evaluation among social work practitioners can be achieved and sustained through educational or motivational strategies.

It suggests that although the possibility of obtaining inconclusive findings inheres in all research and evaluation designs, the likelihood of obtaining inconclusive findings is particularly problematic for social work practitioners using single-case designs to evaluate their own, non-behavioural forms of practice.

We postulate two reasons why it is particularly problematic for them:

- Because they are more likely to obtain inconclusive findings than are researchers employing single-case or other designs; and
- Because inconclusive findings are more likely to sap practitioner enthusiasm for sustained investment in employing single-case evaluation than they are to sap researcher enthusiasm for sustained involvement in conducting research.

If this thesis is correct, then efforts to increase agency supports and resources for single-case evaluation may, in the long run, yield disappointing returns, as those practitioners and administrators who are persuaded to invest in single-case evaluation encounter findings that do not give them the degree of guidance for practice that they expected. Likewise, our thesis suggests that the current emphasis on single-case evaluation in the social work curriculum may be overdone.

This in turn implies the need to reconsider the wording of CSWE curriculum policy and accreditation standards that may be influencing schools of social work to pursue a heavy emphasis on single-case evaluation in both their research and practice curricula. Reducing the amount of emphasis on single-case evaluation in the research curriculum would free up time to try to enhance students' grasp of other research content areas. Some M.S.W. programmes also may want to reduce the emphasis on single-case evaluation in the practice curriculum.

For example, like some other M.S.W. programmes, the master's programme with which the authors are associated requires a large portion of the second-year field practicum and practice seminar to be devoted to conducting a singlecase evaluation on a case the student has in the field. Deleting that requirement would provide more room to work on improving practice competence, which some research suggests is sorely in need of improvement or on using the research of others to guide practice.

We are not arguing for less research curriculum or for less researchpractice curriculum integration; we are just questioning whether those curricular areas are overrelying on single-case evaluation to achieve their aims. Neither are we recommending that single-case evaluation be deleted from social work education. Some researchers have published useful single-case evaluation studies, most commonly but not exclusively involving behavioural and/or cognitive interventions. (We wonder how many other single-case evaluation studies produced findings that were so ambiguous that their investigators deemed them not worth submitting for publication.) We believe that students should learn about using or producing single-case evaluation studies to the same extent to which they learn about useful surveys, group experiments, quasi-experiments, and so on.

In other words, rather than going overboard in emphasizing single-case evaluation as some sort of panacea for integrating research and practice, we should treat it the same way we treat other research methods and designs. A second, and different, implication of this analysis pertains to how we teach students or social work practitioners about single-case evaluation.

We should make sure they are taught about the foregoing data analysis problems. We should not oversell single-case evaluation or, by neglecting data analysis problems, implicitly foster the notion that single-case evaluations are likely to produce conclusive findings that will provide clear implications for practice. We should prepare students and practitioners to encounter and deal with these data analysis problems. Forewarning them and forearming them about these problems seems more likely to help them sustain a commitment to conducting single-case evaluations in the long run than is neglecting these problems. Likewise, we should not teach in a simplistic, mechanistic fashion the statistical significance tests designed for practitioners conducting single-case evaluations.

Neither should we imply that the results of these tests can be relied on to determine which rival explanations are to be inferred from visually ambiguous graphs. We should demonstrate the hazards of such reliance. Practitioners and students should understand the large risk of Type II errors taken in many single-case evaluation studies, and they should understand the difference between internal validity and statistical conclusion validity. Regardless of whether we are teaching about group research or single-case evaluation, we should make sure students understand that if design considerations do not permit drawing conclusive causal inferences, statistical significance should not overrule design considerations in interpreting causality, regardless of how statistically significant a study's findings are. Practitioners and students should also learn that the data analysis problems inherent in single-case evaluations can require long-range, labour intensive, inductive research efforts to sort out when and under what conditions certain interventions are effective. This applies particularly to target problems that are not likely to respond immediately to effective interventions.

Finally, this analysis implies the importance of teaching students about group research studies and how to critique them. This implication is particularly important if a heavy emphasis on single-case evaluation is retained, based on the assumption that group research has already demonstrated the probabilistic efficacy of social work interventions. Students should be prepared to understand and to critically evaluate that assumption. Social work has had a long history of going overboard in embracing and overemphasizing new research modalities as panaceas, dating back to the social survey movement at the turn of this century. Eventually, as the limitations of these modalities become better understood, we teach about them in a more realistic, critical manner, giving them about the same emphasis as other research modalities that have both advantages and disadvantages. The single-case evaluation movement seems to fit this historical pattern.

RESEARCH AS A SOCIAL ACTIVITY

In the final analysis, social research, like all other scientific enquiry, is a social practice. What does this mean? In essence it means that, like all the worlds of everyday life, the world of science is part of the social world. Although the world of research views the world of everyday life as an object of enquiry, it is part of the social world.

This implies the following:

- Researchers are social beings with specific beliefs, values and interests.
- Researchers follow certain implicit and explicit rules.
- The activities of researchers are conducted within more or less organised and institutionalised frameworks, which impose certain constraints on what is acceptable.
- Researchers stand in different relations of power to each other. This implies that access to resources differs across the research community.

RESEARCH COMMUNITIES AND MECHANISMS OF CONTROL

Sociologists of science maintain that scientists usually operate within clearly defined 'scientific communities' or 'invisible colleges' and that they belong to identifiable disciplinary matrices or are linked in research networks. It is only relatively recently that we have witnessed the large-scale institutionalisation of the empirical social sciences. It was only in the second half of the nineteenth century that departments of psychology and sociology were established in Germany and the USA.

In the early twentieth century, scientific societies were established to cater exclusively for the social sciences. Various other developments contributed to the growth of the social sciences in the twentieth century. These included the interest in public opinion polling in the twenties and thirties, the use of social science research during World War II and the rise of quantitative social science methods like sampling and statistics, both of which were reinforced by developments in the area of computerisation in the sixties.

All of these developments have led to the establishment of what may justifiably be called the 'social sciences industry'. This has resulted in a proliferation and a concommitant increase in competition for resources such as funds, computers and infrastructure in a continually expanding industry.

However, the social dimension of science should not be limited to its tangible or material elements. Although social science has become 'big business' and extensive research programmes and surveys can no longer be conducted without the availability of extensive material resources, there are also social resources involved in scientific research.

These are the intangible and non-material resources that are part and parcel of scientific networks and institutions. Examples are support networks formed by scientific societies and institutions, the role played by social science organisations in lobbying on behalf of social scientists, the role of journals, scientific societies and computer networks in linking researchers who share common interests, and the role played by national data archives and scientific databases in information exchange. Social rules and conventions regulate social life.

This is equally true of science as a social system. It is impossible to list all the potential ways in which social rules such as norms, principles, regulations and laws affect social scientists in general. Because social scientists are citizens of countries, they are already subject to the laws and regulations of their countries, of which laws on freedom of information, copyright and libel are examples. However, there are two categories of social rules that impact directly on the manner in which social research is conducted, namely the rules that pertain to the allocation of social resources within the scientific community and the rules that pertain to the relationship between researchers and participants in research projects.

This issue is usually dealt with in discussions on research ethics. The domain of research ethics is concerned with protection of the rights and interests of research participants. Rules of research conduct regulate the behaviour of social scientists and ensure protection of the rights of participants in research projects. These rights include the right to privacy, informed consent and confidentiality. But social rules also regulate the behaviour of members of the scientific community in their interaction with each other. Depending on the nature of the activities and the resources, various kinds of rules will apply.

In The scientific community, Hagstrom depicts a research community as one that is characterised by the exchange of information for the sake of community- specific rewards. A researcher who produces acceptable scientific information is rewarded by having his findings accepted for publication, by being elected to the editorial boards of learned journals, and so on. Störer advocates a similar model, except that he interprets 'scientific information' as 'creative products' which are exchanged for academic recognition. A characteristic of both of these models is the degree of social control with which scientific communities are credited. Because scientists seek recognition they tend to accept not only the goals but also the rules, sometimes tacit, of the research community.

This system of social control is institutionalised in many forms:

- Review systems for either research grants or objects in scientific journals incorporate rules such as blind refereeing and peer evaluation.
- Rules of promotion within research organisations would include reference to the academic track records of candidates, their teaching records and community work.
- Rules of membership of various kinds of scientific organisations and societies include reference to degrees, publications and other achievements.
- Rules of dissemination require that due recognition be given to the works of cited authors when quoting authors and that dissemination must be effected through public means and should not be limited to select groups.

These are all examples of ways in which the interrelationships within the scientific community are organised and controlled at both local and global levels. Underlying these rules are values such as excellence, quality, fairness, openness, equity and justice. It should be emphasised that the application of these rules carries with it a sanction which is no less severe than in other social systems. Professional societies have codes of conduct and scientific institutions have disciplinary codes in accordance with which any transgression of rules is punished. Consequently, those who are in positions of authority wield immense control and power within a specific community. When power is abused through plagiarism, favouritism, nepotism and elitism, inequity and injustice will be manifested in the science system. There are enough examples of scientific fraud and favouritism to dispel any notion of the value-free and clinically objective scientist!

CRITICAL REFLECTION AND ASSIGNMENT

A policy embodies a range of 'rules' or 'normative principles' that regulate the conduct of a certain group of people. In our daily life we regularly encounter various policies such as policies for affirmative action, education and development. Read the following four examples of statements of editorial policy. The first two are from overseas journals and the other two are from South African journals.

THE SOCIAL WORLD AS AN OBJECT OF ENQUIRY

The term 'ontology' literally means the study of 'being' or 'reality'. I will also use the term 'social ontologies' to refer to conceptions of the ontology of social reality. How we define 'social reality' is, of course, a contestable matter. The history of social science is also the history of different theories of the social world. Theories such as behaviourism and constructivism represent different 'pictures' or 'accounts' of the social world. An even more fundamental question dominates many of the debates about the nature of the social world: namely, to what extent, if at all, are the natural and social worlds similar or comparable? It is not surprising that the seventeenthand eighteenth-century scholars, Francis Bacon, Thomas Hobbes, David Hume and Adam Smith, who first reflected on the possibility of a social science, looked to their colleagues in the natural sciences and to their successes and posed the following question: Are there not enough similarities between the social world and the natural world that we could, at least in principle, follow the methodological rules that have proved so successful in the natural sciences?

This has indeed become the key issue just as to which one can classify the main ontological approaches in the social sciences. Those who agree that there are sufficient similarities between the social and natural worlds are known as 'ontological naturalists' or 'positivists'. They believe, usually on the basis of theories such as evolutionary theory or systems theory, that there are enough similarities in the behaviour of all beings to justify the pursuit of a similar epistemology and methodology in all the sciences. Those who disagree with the naturalists or positivists can be broadly classified into two categories: the anti-positivists and the realists.

1. The anti-positivists believe that the differences between the social world and the natural world are so fundamental that there can be no basis for using the same methods and techniques in the human sciences. Antipositivists would include, inter alia, constructivists, interpretivists and phenomenologists.
2. Realists, on the other hand, believe that, although there are fundamental differences between the social and natural world, there are also certain similarities, or at least continuities, which justify the adoption of similar approaches in epistemology and methodology.

However, one should avoid creating the impression that most social researchers have explicit social ontologies. This is clearly not the case. On the whole, social scientists hold very implicit beliefs about the social world and most of them would see no point in making such beliefs explicit. Wellarticulated and systematic ontologies are really only encountered in the World of Metascience. The fact of the matter is that philosophers of science usually debate issues on the ontology of the social world. In their reflection on World 2 they make explicit what is only implicitly held by the scientists.

But the question that interests all social scientists is: what kinds of entities do we encounter in the social world? Even if they do differ about the 'nature' of these entities, most researchers will agree that there are certain basic categories or classes of social phenomena. We identify seven categories of 'social entities', namely individuals, collectives, organisations, institutions, actions, interventions and cultural objects.

A TYPOLOGY OF THE 'FURNITURE' IN THE SOCIAL WORLD

The social world is 'populated' by various kinds of 'entities' and social 'objects'. The lines along which social science disciplines have developed, especially since the late nineteenth century, provide the first indication of the wide range of subject matter in the social sciences. Broad distinctions between social and human sciences, or between the behavioural and cultural sciences, suggest one way of demarcating the social world. Disciplinary differences between disciplines that primarily study texts such as literary theory, theology and history and the ones that study social action like sociology and anthropology, suggest an alternative classification, namely one based respectively on hermeneutic and social sciences.

However, it would be inappropriate to try and develop an 'encyclopaedia' of the human sciences at this stage. The purpose of the classification of 'social objects' provided below is to list the broad categories and not to compile a complete list. The idea is to show how different definitions of what is also referred to as 'the unit of analysis' influence other decisions in the research process. It also aims to show how a broad classification of units of analysis will help us to understand the differences in research designs in the social sciences. But I am pre-empting the story.

Individuals

Individual human beings are probably the most common 'object' of research in the social sciences. Social scientists are of course interested in different 'categories' of individuals. Delimitation of these categories will vary with the research objectives of the study. These may include such 'categories' as adolescents, the aged, students, constituents, politicians, academics, factory workers or just the general public. It is important to realise that such categories of individuals are not 'given'. It is not as though there are natural kinds of human beings. Most of these categories are constructed. This means that how one defines a particular set of individuals is very important. Are 'students' defined as those who are enrolled full-time at a university or college or would part-time students also be included? Does the definition of 'employed' include only individuals who are employed on a full-time basis or in the formal sector, or what other individuals are included? The difficulties involved in distinguishing between 'economically active' people as a group and 'economically inactive' individuals, the 'political elite' and the 'masses', and so forth, are further examples of the problem of defining categories. A definition of the unit of analysis for a study is determined by what could be called the 'ontological complexity' of the category. Although gender distinctions do pose problems, they are still less problematic than racial distinctions. Age groups are usually more easily delineated than occupational classifications. When 'constructed units of analysis' or 'constructed cases', are being used, individual researchers will inevitably construct, define or interpret such distinctions differently.

Collectives

Another typical 'object' of study in social enquiry is 'groupings' or 'collections' of people who are members of larger geographical, political or cultural entities. As suggested, refer to such units of analysis as 'collectives' and include under this heading entities such as nations, cities, towns, communities and tribes.

Organisations (Formal and Informal)

An organisation is defined as any social unit that coordinates the activities of its members. It is common to distinguish between 'formal' and 'informal' organisations. In a formal organisation, rules and duties are officially prescribed and enforced. Corporations, banks, insurance companies, police departments and government bureaus are all examples of formal organisations. In an informal organisation, which is also referred to as a 'voluntary' organisation, members are expected to support the organisation, but rules are less formal and expectations more flexible. Examples are clubs, lodges, public service groups and groups serving special causes, such as Operation Hunger. The reason for sometimes having to study organisations rather than individuals can be attributed to the fact that organisations have characteristics that do not necessarily apply to the behaviour of individuals. Bhaskar and others have referred to these characteristics as 'emergent' properties.

Corporations for instance, have certain properties which could not be predicated of individuals. Such properties include phenomena like an ethos or corporate culture. Gangs, which are informal organisations, have a distinctive 'code of conduct'. For this reason it would simply be wrong to explain the 'behaviour' of organisations in terms of the characteristics and features of individual members.

Institutions

Peter Berger defines institutions as 'regulatory patterns'. People generally identify 'institutions' with organisations that somehow 'contain' people: hospitals and universities are examples. Berger common usage associates the term too closely with social entities that are recognised and codified by law. For Berger, institutions have the following features: externality, objectivity, coerciveness, moral authority and historicity.

He hence includes more 'common' types of institutions in his list, namely economic institutions like factories, companies and trade unions, political institutions like parliaments, senates and congresses, and religious institutions such as churches and educational institutions like schools, colleges and universities. He also includes language, which has all the features of an institution. It is clear that, in terms of Berger's interpretation of the word, 'science' can also be regarded as an institution. Here, as in the case of 'organisations', the focus is once more on the unique emergent properties of these social entities. Among these properties are institutional structure, lines of authority, promotional policy, the representativeness of minority groups on the payroll, labour relations practices and productivity.

Social Actions and Events

The 'object' of study is sometimes not an individual actor or group of actors performing certain actions and activities or holding certain beliefs, but the actions themselves. There is a fundamental ontological difference between human actions, which are dynamic and ongoing, and the outcomes of these actions. As suggested, discuss the latter under the section on 'cultural objects'. With regard to actions, there are various ways of classifying social activities.

Christopher Lloyd distinguishes between the following categories:

- Face-to-face interaction in small groups or social situations.
- Collective or group action in which individuals participate in more or less conscious collaboration to achieve their goals and perhaps also the collective goals of the group.
- Patterned social action in which individuals act in more or less unconscious collaboration with others to achieve individual goals. Traffic and speech patterns are examples of patterned social action.
- Political or structural action, which is more or less consciously aimed at maintaining or transforming the patterns and structures of a culture and society.

All social action is geared towards either maintaining or transforming pre-existing small- or large-scale structures. Examples of social actions or events would include marriage ceremonies, court hearings, traffic offences, divorces, race riots, acts of prostitution, and juvenile delinquency. Historical events would refer to 'mass actions' such as military battles, elections and revolutions.

Cultural Objects

In a general sense, the term 'cultural objects' is used to refer to all 'products' or outcomes of human behaviour. One would include here all the 'sediments' of human endeavour, that is, the achievements or outcomes of deliberate human decision making, for example, cultural and symbolic objects such as literary texts, paintings, sculptures and books.

Interventions

A special class of human actions consists of the continuous or sustained interventions in the social world such as programmes, for instance in education, health care and management training; policies, which include affirmative action and performance appraisal; and systems such as information systems. Such interventions constitute a different category or unit of analysis because they are more structured and patterned, but less permanent and stable than institutions and organisations. This concludes our discussion of typical units of analysis in the social sciences.

It should be obvious that more refined classifications of each of these categories will occur in the various disciplines. Such refinements usually take place within a particular theoretical paradigm, for example, two researchers who respectively adhere to a systems and a Marxist approach, might both study individuals and their actions, but would describe and interpret such actions differently. However, this stage was not intended as an attempt to analyse different theoretical approaches to the definition of the social world, but rather to present, in general terms, the main 'kinds' of units of analysis that social scientists typically encounter in their work.

CRITICAL REFLECTION AND ASSIGNMENT

Think of some typical 'objects' in the social world such as human beings, institutions and social events and in the natural world such as animals, plants and atoms and then list the similarities and differences between the two groups. How, in your opinion, do these differences influence the way we study them? Can you think of specific issues in the area of measurement and data collection that might be affected by these differences?

THE PROCESS OF SOCIAL RESEARCH

The epistemological dimension of research, namely that the ultimate aim of all science is to arrive at results that are as valid or truthful as possible. The second image focusses our attention on the equally important issue of resources and resource management.

We address a third image, namely research as a decisionmaking process. Our attention is now directed towards the researcher and the kind of decisions or judgement calls that he or she has to make during the research process.

Before discussing the kinds of decisions that have to be taken during research, we shall reflect briefly on the nature of the process itself.

What exactly happens in the research process? We have already made the point that it is in the World of Science that phenomena in World 1 are made objects of systematic and methodical enquiry. It is for this reason that the relationship between the scientist and the world has traditionally been referred to as the 'subject-object' relationship. This was taken to mean that, as the 'knower', the scientist is the subject or agent, and the phenomena that she is studying are the 'objects' of her enquiry. However, this has become a politically sensitive issue, especially for moral reasons.

The criticism is that such a description of the relationship between researchers and their human subjects opens up the possibility of reducing research subjects to mere instruments in the attainment of the larger research goal. It is argued that this results in the dehumanisation of the research subject and negation of the fact that the research subject is a free human agent with equal rights and freedoms to those of the researcher. Viewing this relationship in terms of subject and object disempowers those who participate in research projects. More recently, a number of scholars, including Reason and Rowan and Morgan have suggested using the notion of 'engagement' to describe the relationship between the scientist and the 'object' of enquiry.

The notion of 'engagement' suggests a kind of reciprocity and even mutual interdependence between the researcher and the research subject or participant. Despite these criticisms, this way of describing the relationship does establish an important principle, namely that, for the sake of research, the scientist 'objectifies' some aspect of the social world. The scientist transforms a certain phenomenon into a cognitive 'object' of study by abstracting certain features from the social world. Regardless of whether the relationship between the researcher and the social world is viewed primarily in terms of a 'subject-object' framework or in terms of an 'engagement' framework, the researcher still has to take certain decisions.

He or she has to make judgement calls based on the information that is available. What we refer to as the 'stages' in the research process or as the 'research cycle', are in fact 'clusters' of related decisions taken by the researcher. These stages are actually decisions to act in one specific way rather than in another. The following simple framework applies to all decision-making–also in research.

As rational agents we decide on a certain course of action against the background of the available information. A decision is deemed to be rational or reasonable when others, usually our peers, concur with our judgement. In other words, a decision is deemed to be a good one when there is consensus that, given the available information, it was the best decision. This implies that the most reasonable decision is the one that is judged to have the best chance of leading to whatever is defined as a successful outcome. We return to our analogy of the journey. The traveller who wishes to ensure that he reaches his destination as planned in terms of the time frame and the budget, will take the appropriate decisions regarding the route, schedules, resources and mode of transportation. Such decisions are taken against the background of the available information.

So, for instance, if the travel agent has informed the traveller that his plane leaves Johannesburg International at 19h00 on Thursday evening and he plans accordingly, one could say that he has acted rationally. If, in such a case, the traveller arrives at the airport and, owing to poor weather or a technical difficulty, the flight has been cancelled, no one would accuse him of having made a poor decision. Of course, if undertaking the journey is a matter of life and death, one would expect the person to have considered contingency plans.

If, on the other hand, our traveller simply arrives at the airport on the assumption that there will be a flight to his particular destination and that there are seats available, this would be seen as somewhat irrational behaviour. This example shows that what is accepted as 'reasonable behaviour' or 'rational decision making', depends on a number of factors such as the goal or destination of the particular action, the information available and the risk associated with the outcome. The notion of 'rational decision making' as it applies to research. But we must first identify the 'kinds' of decisions that a researcher has to make in a typical research project. The 'dynamics' of the process are illustrated in figure.

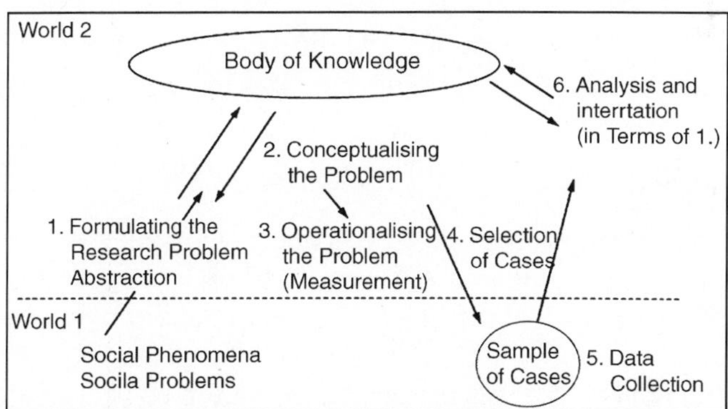

Fig. The Research Process

FORMULATING THE RESEARCH PROBLEM

All empirical scientific enquiry begins with a 'movement' from World 1 to World 2. Research commences at the point where someone, in this case the researcher, begins to reflect on some aspect of World 1. This reflection can be a very unstructured thought, a conjecture, a question or a hypothesis. Some phenomenon in the social world, like the nature of depth perception, the activities of drug addicts, the poverty of a large section of the population or the effectiveness of a new crime prevention programme, has prompted the researcher to ask a question that requires an answer. This 'phrasing of a question', this 'putting into words', involves a cognitive representation of some real world phenomena. Something concrete and socially real that has causes and effects, is cognitively or mentally represented in the form of concepts that are strung together to form coherent propositions in the form of research questions.

In simple terms, by formulating the problem, we are 'abstracting' from the 'concrete' social phenomenon.

CONCEPTUALISING THE PROBLEM

We distinguish between merely stating or formulating the problem and the next stage, which involves the conceptualisation of the problem. Conceptualisation involves at least two activities, namely the conceptual clarification or analysis of key concepts in the problem statement, and relating the problem to a broader conceptual framework or context. Conceptual clarification involves definition of the key concepts, usually those referring to the key features of the phenomenon to be studied.

If there are standard definitions in the field, these should be used. If not, the researcher has to ensure that the meanings of such concepts are clearly specified. But conceptualisation also means integrating or embedding the research problem within a larger body of knowledge. Obviously this only applies where such a body of evidence does exist. The reason for doing systematic literature searches is to determine whether previous empirical research or theoretical studies, which may guide one's own study, have already been conducted.

Operationalisation

Once the research problem has been conceptualised, we must specify how our conceptualisation, which is in the form of a hypothesis, theory or research problem, relates to the real world of things and events. We must establish linkages between our concepts and the phenomenon that we wish to investigate. This is done through the process of operationalisation or operational definitions. There is a clear connection between conceptualisation and operationalisation, based on the distinction between the sense and the reference of concepts. In the process of conceptualisation we analyse, inter alia, the meanings or connotations of concepts and their interrelationships. In the process of operationalisation, we define the references or denotations of these same concepts. The best way to operationalise is to list the measurement 'operations' or 'rules' in terms of which the classes of World 1 phenomena are uniquely determined.

Operationalisation consists of the construction of 'a set of operations' or 'measures' that link the research problem to the world. Such measures can be either highly structured, as in quantitative measurement procedures, or highly unstructured. But in any empirical social research, the formulation and conceptualisation of the research problem must be followed by a process of operationalisation.

It is important to note that the term 'measurement' is used in two senses in the literature. On the one hand, it refers to the construction of a measuring instrument such as a scale, a questionnaire, an interview schedule or an index. On the other hand, it involves the actual process of measuring some phenomenon such as the incidence of juvenile crimes in a specific geographical area or attitudes regarding specific issues. In the latter case, measurement is actually synonymous with data collection. In this book the use of the term 'operationalisation' is limited to the actual design and development of a measuring instrument.

Selection of Cases

When formulating the problem, we already identify the 'kind' of social phenomenon that we plan to investigate. We identified six kinds of 'units of analysis' in the social sciences.

However, this simply meant that a certain kind of social entity, namely individuals, groups, organisations, social objects, social actions, interventions and social events, was identified. This process does not identify the actual 'population' of entities in the real world that meet the definition of 'the unit of analysis'. The selection of subjects or cases refers to,

- Decisions regarding the population that we wish to study, and
- Decisions on whether, where practically possible, the whole population will be studied or whether as suggested,, in fact, select samples of elements from the population.

Data Collection

Data collection involves applying the measuring instrument to the sample or cases selected for the investigation. We must constantly remind ourselves that the human senses are our 'first-order' measuring instruments, even if they are qualitative.

On the basis of our visual, auditory and tactile observations and perceptions, we begin to classify responses, people, actions and events. However, because we aspire to truthful representations of the social world, we have to 'augment' our observations by more reliable and valid measuring instruments such as scales, questionnaires and observation schedules.

If properly constructed and validated over time, such instruments assist us in collecting data that are more likely to be reliable than they would be had we not used instruments.

DATA Analysis and Interpretation

Data collection produces new information or data about the world that requires further 'processing'. Data processing involves at least two kinds of operations, namely data reduction, during which the quantitative and qualitative data are summarised, and data analysis. Data analysis would include both qualitative analysis, which includes processes such as thematical and content analysis, and quantitative or statistical analysis. Data processing is followed by synthesis, which involves 'interpretation' or 'explanation' of the data. This concludes our discussion of the main stages in the research process. We argue that these are not merely consecutive steps in a chronological sequence of events, but that, underlying the process, there is a logic that is peculiar to scientific enquiry.

THE LOGIC OF RESEARCH

The logic of research is the logic of argumentation. Perhaps the best analogy is a legal one. What happens during for instance a murder trial? An attorney prosecutes someone by building a case on the evidence available. There may be different kinds of evidence such as eyewitness accounts, forensic evidence and ballistic evidence. The case is defended before a judge or jury, who have to make a judgement.

Their judgement is the outcome of a process of weighing, as impartially and objectively as possible, the evidence presented. The social scientist similarly argues for a specific point of view. She has also to adduce evidence in support of the particular point of view and 'defend' it before the 'jury' of peers–the research community. Many legal expressions, such as weight of evidence, burden of proof, arguing a case and beyond reasonable doubt, are just as applicable to scientific enquiry as they are to a court case! Making judgements on the basis of the evidence available is part and parcel of being human.

All our everyday decisions, for instance about what to wear or which route to take to work are judgements made on the basis of available evidence. Some judgements have further-reaching effects than others. Some examples are parents having to decide on a school for their child, a doctor who has to prescribe a specific course of antibiotics on the basis of a clinical diagnosis, or a politician deciding to implement a particular policy on the basis of the advice of policy analysts. But these are all examples of the general form of logical reasoning or argumentation. In all these cases, reasoning or argumentation consists of drawing certain conclusions or making certain judgements on the basis of some body of evidence. Scientific reasoning has a similar logical form: in a very basic sense, a scientific thesis or report is no more than an extended logical argument. We shall define argument, following Larry Wright as 'the dispassionate marshalling of support for some statement'. Just as, in everyday life, you might defend a certain point of view by citing evidence in its support, the social scientist attempts to muster scientific evidence in support of a specific point of view. If scientific reasoning can be correctly characterised as being like a logical argument, then it follows that any research study has to comply with the rules of logic, the rules of valid reasoning. This suggests that we need to have clarity about concepts such as 'argument' and 'logical reasoning'.

THE NATURE OF ARGUMENTATION

The following is the basic scheme of a typical argument:

S_1 S_2 S_3 S_4	Statements that are Offered as Support for or Evidence of the Conclusion Reached-also Known as the Premises of the argument
C Conclusion.	

Consider an everyday example:

- There is no doubt that Italian drivers are the worst in the world. Just note how they ignore red traffic lights and stop signs. And it is hardly necessary to refer to their lack of courtesy when they cut across traffic lanes without indicating their intention of doing so and the way they force their way into lanes without considering other drivers!

This 'loose' argument can be represented schematically as follows:

- S1: Italian drivers ignore red traffic lights.
- S2: Italian drivers ignore stop signs.
- S3: Italian drivers force their way into traffic lanes.
- S4: Italian drivers change lanes without giving the necessary signals.
- C: Italian drivers are the worst in Europe.

This particular example does not of course constitute a valid argument. Closer inspection reveals that the premises do not actually provide sufficient support for the conclusion. On the basis of S1 to S4 one would at best be able to claim that Italy has exceptionally poor drivers, but certainly not that they are the worst in Europe. Although they may well be the worst, this conclusion is not substantiated by the supporting evidence. This is a typical example of 'inductive reasoning'. The distinctive feature of inductive reasoning is that, even if the supporting evidence or premises are accepted as true, there is always the possibility that the conclusion may not be true.

The problem in such cases is usually that the conclusion is broader than the premises imply; the conclusion goes 'beyond' the data. Our example illustrates another important feature of logical reasoning, namely that 'inferential validity' does not refer to the truth or reliability of the premises but rather to the relationship between premises and conclusion. Drawing an inference refers to the 'logical jump' that one makes from the premises to the conclusions. The validity or acceptability of this 'jump' is determined, not by the validity of the premises, but by whether the premises provide support for the conclusions.

Empirical evidence that can provide support for the truth or likelihood of a conclusion must therefore be both 'true', or at least highly probable, and also relevant to the conclusion. But how does one assess 'relevance' of evidence?

Assume that we were to add the following premise to the preceding example:

- S5: Rome is the capital of Italy.

Although this statement happens to be true, it is clearly quite irrelevant to the conclusion. However, adding the following premise to the argument–'S6: The accident rate in Italy is the highest in Europe'–would constitute more supporting evidence. The reason why S5 is not relevant to our argument while S6 is, is obvious: the 'problem' that requires explanation or clarification, is the claim that 'Italian drivers are the worst in Europe'. S5 does not address this claim in any way, whereas S6 does. The notion of 'evidence' therefore presupposes a certain 'problem' or context. Relevance of evidence is determined by the problem or context. Thus: the statement in S6 is relevant to the conclusion and also increases the likelihood that our conclusion is true. Whether the addition of S6 constitutes 'sufficient' evidence is a matter for debate. Some people would regard the addition of S6 as adequate evidence, while others would want to investigate additional evidence such as the number of traffic violations per driver. The fact remains that S6 is not only relevant but also strengthens the conclusion and thereby increases its inferential validity–the second condition of sufficient support. To summarise then: there are three key 'elements' in any research project:

1. The problem or research question or issue that is being addressed.
2. The evidence required to address or solve the problem adequately.
3. The conclusions that will be drawn on the basis of the evidence collected and will resolve the problem either way.

In the remainder of the book I shall refer to this as the PEC-framework of scientific reasoning. The PEC-framework constitutes–albeit in an oversimplified way–the general form of all reasoning in science. The logic that characterises all sound research is illustrated in figure.

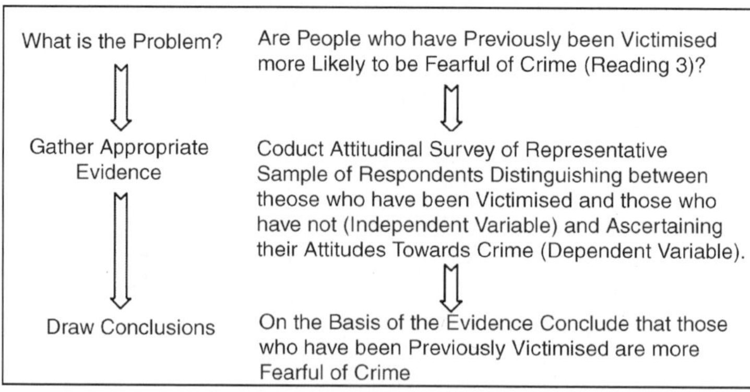

Fig. The Logic Used in Research

SOME COMMENTS

There are obviously many variations of P, E and C. Even a cursory perusal of journals in the social sciences will reveal the considerable variety of research problems in this field. In basic research, such as testing hypotheses or theories, the research issues differ fundamentally from applied research problems such as evaluating the effectiveness of a new social programme or intervention. There is a substantial difference between empirical problems, for instance, what are the causes of absenteeism? and theoretical or conceptual problems: for instance, how should we define alienation? This is an important point to emphasise because the kind of research problem ultimately determines the logic of the study. What do we mean by this? It means that the nature of the research problem determines what will constitute adequate evidence. The kind of design and logic required for a study that aims to develop a new explanation or hypothesis for a specific phenomenon will differ from the kind required for a study which aims to confirm an already well-established theory. A study that is breaking new ground differs substantially from a study that aims to evaluate a social programme.

INDUCTIVE AND DEDUCTIVE REASONING

We shall use an extended example to discuss the basic differences between deduction and induction. In the second half of the stage we shall discuss the difference between inductive generalisation, which is sometimes simply referred to as 'generalisation', and retroduction, which is also referred to as 'diagnostic induction' or 'abduction'. The following example taken from Larry Wright's excellent book entitled Better reasoning is a reconstruction of certain real events; and the reader must resist the temptation to allow any personal background knowledge–especially after JFK the movie!–to affect the reading of the example.

THE JFK EXAMPLE

Suppose we were considering various arguments in favour of the claim that President John F. Kennedy was in fact shot by Lee Harvey Oswald. A first formulation of an argument in support of C, could be the following:

- S1: Shortly after the assassination, Lee Harvey Oswald was noticed in the book depository from which the shots had been fired.
- C: Lee Harvey Oswald shot President Kennedy.

Although S1 does lend some support to C, it is obvious that this does not constitute a strong argument in favour of the conclusion. So we immediately proceed to strengthen our argument by the addition of S2:

- S1: Shortly after the assassination, Lee Harvey Oswald was noticed in the book depository from which the shots had been fired.
- S2: Oswald's palm print was found on a rifle left close to the window from which the shots had been fired.
- C: Lee Harvey Oswald shot President Kennedy.

There can be little doubt that the addition of S2 increases the likelihood of C being correct. However, if this evidence were to be presented before a jury, it is unlikely that it would convince the members. Let us assume, therefore–and remember that this is a creative reconstruction!–that we add two further pieces of evidence:

- S1: Shortly after the assassination, Lee Harvey Oswald was noticed in the book depository from which the shots had been fired.
- S2: Oswald's palm print was found on a rifle left close to the window from which the shots had been fired.
- S3: An eye witness identified Oswald as the assassin.
- S4: The ballistic tests, the fatal shots could have been fired from the rifle.
- C: Lee Harvey Oswald shot President Kennedy.

The support for C, offered by the arguments S1 to S4, now appears to be overwhelming. In most courts of law such evidence might even be judged sufficient. But let us continue and think of a somewhat more far-fetched possibility. Wright argues that the case against Oswald could have been made pretty much watertight had the following kind of evidence been available:

- Assume that the owner of the book depository from which the shots were fired had been concerned about the security of his store. As a precautionary measure he had had closed-circuit television installed, and the whole episode had been recorded on tape. The quality of the recording was such that there could not be the slightest trace of doubt that it had indeed been Oswald who had fired the shots.

What is clear is that each new piece of evidence increases the support for the conclusion. The addition of the final video-recorded evidence appears to have made the case watertight. On the basis of the evidence presented it is no longer possible to arrive at an alternative conclusion. One is virtually compelled to accept C! Or is one? Perhaps there is a possibility, however remote, that Oswald was not the assassin! Assume, says Wright, that the evidence just referred to was fabricated. Assume that an amazingly ingenious plot was hatched to frame Oswald for the murder of President Kennedy.

With this purpose in mind, an exact replica of the book depository was built elsewhere and equipped with similar video cameras; a similar motorcade was arranged, someone who bore an unusually close resemblance to Oswald did everything that the real Oswald was supposed to have done, everything was recorded, the actual video tapes were replaced with the forged tapes, and so on. Although this is perhaps not the type of evidence that anyone, and particularly not a jury, would regard seriously, it nonetheless remains a logically possible explanation of the existing evidence. In other words, the conclusion does not necessarily follow logically from the evidence because this conclusion, although seemingly outrageous, is at least conceivable. One could think up additional hypothetical examples, and even more outrageous ones but in the final instance, there is only one way to remove all possible doubt if C is to follow necessarily from the premises.

As Wright indicates, were that to happen, the nature of the argument would change radically. Up to this point we have been concerned with the issue of the weight of the evidence: in logical terms this is an inductive argument. However, when we modify the argument so that the conclusion necessarily follows from the premises, the argument loses its evidential character. When this happens, the supporting evidence is linked to the conclusion on the basis of semantic considerations rather than on any piece of empirical evidence. In such a case, either implicitly or explicitly, the conclusion is then already contained in the premises.

This type of argument is called a deductive argument and would include a statement such as S5.

- S1: Shortly after the assassination Lee Harvey Oswald was noticed in the book depository from which the shots had been fired.
- S2: Oswald's palm print was found on a rifle left close to the window from which the shots had been fired.
- S3: An eye witness identified Oswald as the assassin.
- S4: The ballistic tests.
- S5: Mary Oswald's husband shot President Kennedy.
- C: Lee Harvey Oswald shot President Kennedy.

The conclusion here is explicitly contained in the supporting premises. In fact, the inclusion of S5 immediately makes S1–S4 redundant. This is what is meant by the argument losing its 'evidentiary' nature. Of course, no-one would offer such an argument for any purpose other than to illustrate the difference between a deductive argument and an inductive argument. This example was used to illustrate the principle of degrees of inductive support and the notion of adequate support. It simultaneously shows that inductive and deductive arguments differ radically. This difference will now be explored more systematically.

SOME DEFINITIONS

It is important to reiterate that in our analysis of inferences–the inferential relationship between premises and conclusion–we are not questioning the epistemic status of the premises. For the sake of argument we accept the truth of all the premises, in other words, that the evidence is reliable. Having accepted the truth of the premises, we are interested in how much support they provide for the conclusion. In the Kennedy example, there were two possible answers to this question: inductive support, in which the premises provide gradual support for the conclusion, and deductive validity in which the truth of the conclusion is either implicitly or explicitly contained in the premises.

This example enables us to define induction and deduction formally:

- In an inductive argument, genuine supporting evidence can only lead to highly probable conclusions. In other words, in an inductive argument, supporting statements merely lend gradual support to the conclusion.
- In a deductive argument, true premises necessarily lead to true conclusions; the truth of the conclusion is already either implicitly or explicitly contained in the truth of the premises.

The following commonplace examples of deductive and inductive arguments illustrate the difference:

- *Deductive*:
  - All mammals have hearts.
  - All horses are mammals.
  - All horses have hearts.
- *Inductive*:
  - Horse 1 (was observed) to have a heart.
  - Horse 2 (was observed) to have a heart.
  - Horse 3 (was observed) to have a heart.
  - Horse n (was observed) to have a heart.
  - All horses have hearts.

The use of the same empirical evidence in both examples illustrates the important differences between inductive and deductive arguments. In both examples the truth of the premises is accepted. In the deductive argument, the conclusion is already contained in the premises, and the conclusion is no more than an explication of the premises. In the inductive argument, however, the conclusion is supported by the observations made and is hence supported by the premises. The conclusion is highly probable, but, however unlikely this may appear, there is still a possibility that a type of horse that does not have a heart may be discovered. Thus, in the inductive argument the conclusion does not follow of necessity. The differences between induction and deduction are summarised as follows by Salmon:

- *Deduction*:
  - If all the premises are true, then the conclusion must be true.
  - All of the information or factual content in the conclusion was already contained, at least implicitly, in the premises.
- *Induction*:
  - If all the premises are true then the conclusion is probably, but not necessarily, true.
  - The conclusion contains information not even implicitly present in the premises.

INDUCTIVE GENERALISATION AND RETRODUCTIVE INFERENCE

The two examples of non-deductive reasoning–the JFK example and the horse example–reveal an important difference between two kinds of inductive inference. In the first case, we drew a conclusion on the basis of various items of supporting evidence. Both the premises and the conclusion refer to a single case, namely the assassination of JFK, and the conclusion is offered as the 'best explanation' of why something happened.

In the second example, we drew a conclusion on the basis of a limited number of observations, but we generalised beyond the actual number of horses observed. In this particular case, the validity of our conclusion depends both on the accuracy of our observations and on whether the cases that we have observed are representative of the total population of horses. It has become common to refer to these two kinds of inductive inference as examples of retroduction and inductive generalisation. The common denominator in both examples is that our conclusions go beyond the premises in the sense that we add information that is not already contained in the premises.

The difference between retroduction and inductive generalisation lies in the fact that our conclusions 'go beyond' the premises. In the case of retroductive inference, our conclusion is an 'inference based on the best explanation' of the observed events. Our conclusion is offered as an explanation that provides an account of what has been observed. So, in the JFK case, the conclusion is offered as the 'most plausible' explanation of the events. In the second example, our conclusion goes beyond the data through the process of generalisation. The observed cases referred to by the premises refer are accepted as being sufficiently representative of a certain population of similar cases to enable us to formulate a generalisation that would apply to all such cases.

CONCLUDING REMARKS

These distinctions provide us with the following scheme of types of scientific reasoning:

- *Deduction*: An inference where the conclusion follows necessarily from the premises, that is, the conclusion is already contained in the premises.
- *Induction*: Inference where the conclusions–in different ways–go beyond the premises.
  - *Inductive generalisation*: An inference that generalises from the specific to the general.
  - *Retroduction*: An inference from the observed to the hidden or underlying mechanism that explains the workings of what is observed.

SOCIAL WORK AND ITS CONNECTION TO THE HISTORY OF VALUES

A further example of the power of the paradigm can be drawn from childcare policy. Lorraine Fox Harding has identified four paradigms or value positions in childcare policy. The first is the *laissez faire* and patriarchal approach applied up to the mid-nineteenth century that sought to preserve family privacy, and by which parents, particularly fathers, had power over children with minimal state intervention. The image of a disciplinarian Victorian patriarch held sway.

This is 'the view that power in the family should not be disturbed except in extreme circumstances, and the role of the state should be a minimal one'. Towards the end of the nineteenth century, state paternalism and child protection emerged. This saw the protection of children by an emerging group of professionals, and is associated with the growth of state intervention as the twentieth century progressed.

State intervention is often authoritarian, with the result that biological family bonds can be undervalued and good quality care substituted. Criticism of state paternalism in the post-Second World War period attempted to defend families from heavy-handed state intervention and offer greater levels of help and support. This saw 'kinship defenders or defence of the birth family' emerge as a dominant paradigm. The final paradigm in relation to child protection is the children's rights and child liberation perspective, in which children are seen as the bearers of rights and able to participate in decision-making processes.

Fox Harding's work shows the historic paradigmatic shifts of value positions in relation to childcare policy in social work theory and practice. Having examined the way in which ideas develop, we can turn our attention to the paradigm shifts that are evident in social work and social care values. We have provided a flavour of this process with Fox Harding, but will extend this argument. The following discussion examines the broad historical changes in values within social work, social care and human services. Further reading is provided at the end of the stage for those wanting to examine the philosophical basis of values, ethics and social work.

There is a multitude of varied value systems that could have been selected. For example, the Arab world, Africa and China, have all contributed philosophical discussion to questions of values. However, in terms on the impact and contribution made to social work, the selection for discussion is always going to be partial. This is not to do a disservice to the contribution made by a diverse range of thinkers or to devalue the knowledge they have produced, but to map out a digestible survey of the terrain of values that have a continuing legacy in the helping and social professions. Useful and wider ranging commentaries on this subject are Yelaja, Midgley and Osei-Hwedie.

SOCIAL WORK VALUES DEFINED

The profession's early concern with the value of charity has its roots in the Bible and religion. All the world's religions uphold ethics of duty, mutual responsibility, care, compassion and concern for others. Reamer argues that acts of charity were meant to fulfil God's commandments. The Elizabethan Poor Laws of 1598 and 1601 consolidated welfare legislation of the Tudor period and have their origins in the systems of relief provided to the poor by the parishes of the Church of England. The seventeenth century saw the emergence of what we could call 'modern values', with the intellectual, cultural and political movement that is collectively referred to as the Enlightenment.

This was characterized by an increased emphasis on the values of tolerance, freedom and reasonableness. Authoritarianism, particularly of a religious kind, was rejected in favour of respect for lay opinion, increased scepticism and a belief in progress, emancipation and scientific understanding. For some, social work stems from these roots. Modern values have been concerned with addressing the questions, 'What is the right thing to do?' or 'How should I act?' Early contributors to such questions were Jeremy Bentham and John Stuart Mill.

They developed an ethical system based on the consequences of action and hedonism, and the promotion of happiness as the basis of ethics. People should always act in ways that make the largest number of people happy. This form of utilitarianism had a significant impact on social, political and legal reform. Philosophically, the 1800s were significant in terms of Immanuel Kant's contribution. Kant's challenging philosophical system gives us an ethics based on duty, moral motivation and ultimately a respect for other people.

During the Georgian period, social welfare systems were most concerned with the threat to public order presented by those in poverty. The workhouse was the eighteenth-century response, with 2000 existing in Britain by 1776 as a result of the General Workhouses Act of the 1720s. *The Poor Law Report* leading to the Poor Law Amendment Act in 1834 saw the consolidation of workhouses across the country, acting as harsh and deterring institutions encouraging moral restraint. Foucault refers to this as the 'great confinement' that spread across Europe from the mid-seventeenth century and found its fullest expression in the 'institutional mania' of the Victorian era. 'Lunatics, idiots and imbeciles' were confined to institutions, away from the celebratory grandeur of Victorian public buildings. Horner suggests that this period threw up a range of middle-class reformers including Elizabeth Fry, Florence Nightingale, Mary Carpenter, Octavia Hill, Dr Barnardo, General Booth, Edwin Chadwick, Edward Foster, Dr Thomas Arnold and Lord Shaftesbury.

Although moral education was part of these reformers' programmes there was a growing awareness of other sources of difficulty for people. By 1900, the essentially religious base to charity gave way to secular ideas of social welfare. Reamer provides an insight into the historical emergence of the values base in social care. Values and ethics have been the cornerstone of social care's mission and have involved normative considerations of what should be done in terms of its ethical orientation. Reamer argues that the evolution of social work values and ethics has had four distinct stages: the morality period; the values period; the ethical theory and decision-making period; and the ethical standards and risk management period.

The morality period, when social work became a profession, was more concerned with the morality of the client than with the values of the practitioner. Responding to the 'curse of pauperism' and organizing relief was the principle mission. Reamer suggests that this led to paternalistic attempts to strengthen the moral rectitude of 'wayward' clients, and social reforms reflected this–for example, the 'settlement house' movements in the USA. The Society for Organizing Charitable Relief and Repressing Mendicity, later to become the Charity Organization Societies in the UK, aimed to raise the moral stature of individuals and society.

'The most important insight charity organizers left us was their view of society as a moral community ... a body of people held together primarily by intimate sentiments of responsibility, love and duty, caring and sharing'. These moral concerns laid the foundations for some of the primary values of social work, emphasizing the importance of individual worth and dignity, and service to humanity. The early part of the twentieth century saw a shift in concern from the morality of the client towards the structural problems of society such as housing, health care, sanitation, employment and poverty.

In a UK context this culminated in the *Beveridge Report* of 1942 that declared a 'War on Want' to address these structural problems. An emerging class of welfare professionals developed what we might call 'traditional social work'. 'Traditional' social work is seen as 'the technical management of personal problems and the maintenance of order' and has normally been composed of 'received ideas' relating to professional values and standards of practice. These have often taken a list-type approach. Biesteck, a Catholic priest, drew up one of the early and influential list-type approaches to practice that included: individualization; the purposeful expression of feelings; controlled emotional involvement; acceptance; non-judgemental attitude; client self-determination; and confidentiality.

In the USA in the 1950s, the National Association of Social Workers listed social work's basic values as: respect for 'individual uniqueness'; the right to 'the realization of the full potential of each individual'; and tolerance of 'the differences that exist between individuals'. The main opposition to this approach developed in the 1960s with radical social work, a broad church that drew from labelling theory, critical psychoanalysis, Marxism, feminism and discourse theory.

The criticism of traditional social work was that it held an ahistorical view of social work values and neglected the context in which social values emerge and change. A further criticism was that the structural forces which give rise to personal and social problems were being neglected.

THE RADICAL CHALLENGE EMERGES

Humanism and existentialism also exerted an influence as well as being established philosophical theories. Humanism argues that human beings have the capacity to reason, make choices and act freely, independent of religion. Payne argues that humanism gained favour as part of the secularization of welfare that separated it from the churches in the 1800s. Carl Rogers is the most influential writer on humanistic and person-centred ideas. He suggests three elements to relationships, stating that clients should perceive workers as genuine and congruent, that workers should have unconditional positive regard for clients, and that they should have empathy for clients.

Existentialism is built on the notion of humans as free, unique individuals whose 'existence precedes essence'. Sartre's imperious *Being and Nothingness* is focused on this notion of free will and the meaning that people create. Existentialism's contribution to social work came through the anti-psychiatry movement and the work of R.D. Laing. Its fullest recent application to social work is by Thompson. By the 1960s social work as a profession had become selfreflective and the 'values clarification' movement examined the value base of social work.

It drew on developments in related disciplines such as psychotherapy and social policy, and from social and political struggles such as the civil rights movements and women's liberation. Social workers became more reflective about their own value base and their relationship to the profession. Social work training examined a broad set of emancipatory issues such as social equality, welfare rights, discrimination and oppression. In a UK context, radical social work informed by Marxist social and political theory viewed received ideas of 'care' and 'concern' as part of social work's historical mission to aid capitalism by ensuring a compliant and healthy workforce and addressing the worst excesses of capitalism.

The ideological smokescreen of social work was to 'blame the victim' and locate social problems as instances of individual failing, not structurally defined problems. The central concern of the value base of radical social work was a focus on equality, understood in the Marxist sense of redistribution of income and wealth, and a notion of justice built on that redistribution. Bailey and Brake argue that radical practice is 'essentially understanding the position of the oppressed in the context of the social and economic structure they live in'.

Marxist-informed social work was criticized by feminists for focusing too heavily on class and for neglecting the family, gender, sexuality, patriarchy and domestic violence, as well as questions of culture and ethnicity. The 1970s saw a surge of interest in the broad subject of applied or professional ethics, that Reamer suggests also influenced social work ethics. High profile cases of social work failure consolidated this process. The 'ethical theory and decisionmaking' period characterized this boom in applied ethics and greater ethical consideration. In terms of social work ethics, Plant's *Social and Moral Theory in Casework* represents one of the first sustained attempts to examine the philosophical value base of social work. Previous attempts had been less philosophically informed and took the form of 'list approaches' to the types of values to which social workers should be committed. Hunt attempted a philosophically justified examination of the value base of social work and suggests that it is comprised of the uniqueness and worth of each individual human personality, the right to self-determination, the existence and value of freedom, the existence of obligations, plus a host of beliefs about the 'good life' and 'good society'.

In 1970s Britain, the British Association of Social Workers drew up a list in their code of ethics that included the principles of 'self-determination', 'non-judgementalism', 'compassion', 'professional responsibility' and 'confidentiality'. The end of this era was signalled, for Payne, by the general political developments in many western countries that gave rise to the 'New Right' of Conservative administrations. Conservative approaches to social values are built on the two tenets that the individual is paramount and that private activity should address social problems. Individual failures are to blame for a person's situation although there is a key role for the family and society's morality in socializing individuals into the correct forms of behaviour.

The 1980s was 'a watershed moment that dramatically changed social workers' understanding of and approach to ethical issues'. The Barclay Report into the future of social work argued that social workers should work in ways that recognize people have a need for 'respect', 'understanding', 'justice' and 'equality'. Respect, individualization, and confidentiality were central to the language of social work.

From the 1980s onwards there was a growing concern for social work to respond to ethnic and cultural dimensions by addressing anti-oppressive approaches and cultural and ethnic sensitivity. Developments in philosophy and social theory have also contributed to the paradigmatic change in social work values. Discourse analysis has displaced the idea that the language of social work is neutral or a formal and technical exercise of intervention into people's lives.

The notion of discourse suggests that power relations are inherent in language and help to shape the reality that individuals and groups inhabit. As such, language is central to the power of social work–for example, by defining people as 'abnormal', 'deviant', 'delinquent' or 'at risk'. The simplest example of this is to consider the terms 'man' and 'woman'. Woman is comprised of 'man' 'wo(man)', she always needs 'man' to be present to define herself, man comes first.

French poststructuralist philosophers who have informed discourse theory, such as Jacques Derrida, suggest that to clearly display the power relations inherent in social life, 'man' should be written as 'wo(man)'. Women are presented as passive, maternal, submissive, docile, virtuous and emotional whereas men are active, businesslike, decisive, rational and reasonable. Postmodernism, 'not so much a theoretical perspective as a style of theorizing' is the culmination of these developments.

THE CONTEMPORARY SITUATION IN THE HELPING PROFESSIONS

The 1990s saw the emergence of a further paradigmatic approach with anti-oppression, empowerment and advocacy emerging as themes. Anti-oppressive practice locates the worker and service user in a broader structural context, focusing on social difference, personal and political relationships, power, history and reflexivity. Empowerment involves supporting service users to identify the full range of possibilities, strengths and qualities required to meet their needs. Solomon, Lee and Gutiérrez *et al.* are representative of attempts to develop empowerment as a central approach as well as a fundamental value. Advocacy as a positive sense of self, knowledge, and strategies to gain goals is central to Rose and Black's argument, and Brandon *et al.* placed this value at the heart of modern social work and social care. Professional competences have also added to the present climate of social work values such as compassion, discernment, trustwor-thiness, integrity and conscientiousness. Compassion is a trait that combines an active regard for another's welfare with an awareness and emotional response of sympathy, tenderness and discomfort at another's misfortune.

Discernment is being able to bring 'sensitive insight, acute judgement, and understanding into action' without prejudice. Trustworthiness is the reliance on another person to act with the right motives and appropriate moral norms. Integrity refers to the soundness, wholeness and reliability of the moral character of an individual who has a coherent understanding of themselves in terms of their emotions, aspirations and knowledge, with a commitment to moral norms.

Being conscientious is to do what is right and exerting appropriate effort to do so. These are focal virtues that Beauchamp and Childress offer as critically important in work carried out by professionals. There are dangers in this type of list approach in that it leaves practitioners with little more than a set of fixed values that they should bring into complex situations. Beauchamp and Childress argue that such values are linked to four core moral principles.

Autonomy is self-direction and self-rule free from controlling interference. It is to become an author of your own destiny free from the control of others. *Non-maleficence* is the obligation to do no harm to others. *Beneficence* includes altruism, love and humanity and connotes acts of kindness, mercy and charity. *Justice* is a difficult term that refers to fairness, equity and appropriate treatment in the light of what is owed to a person. It is closely connected to equality and rights. This cluster of values includes professional competencies and core moral principles that cover Shardlow's expansive, midrange and restrictive values. The most recent stage of social work ethics is the maturation of ethical issues and the significant expansion of ethical standards to guide a practitioner's conduct and increased knowledge concerning professional negligence and liability. The risk management period has been consolidated by events such as the General Social Care Council's code of conduct for social care workers. This code contains six statements that should guide and inform social work's values and social workers' practice.

These are:

1. Protect the rights and promote the interests of service users and carers.
2. Strive to establish and maintain the trust and confidence of service users and carers.
3. Promote the independence of service users while protecting them as far as possible from danger or harm.
4. Respect the rights of service users while seeking to ensure that their behaviour does not harm themselves or other people.
5. Uphold public trust and confidence in social care services.
6. Be accountable for the quality of your work and take responsibility for maintaining and improving your knowledge and skills.

The changing nature of social care, human services and social professions has promoted two further contemporary developments in values. The first is the trend towards 'interprofessional' working. Collaborative working arrangements mean that problems or services are addressed or delivered by groups of professionals working together. Health visitors, social workers, educational psychologists, and the police would be one example of interprofessional working. Regeneration partnerships to tackle social problems within a community or neighbourhood often involve 'interagency' working between professionals. The 'modernization' or 'modern management agenda' of New Labour places a stress on 'joined up' policy and practice. This interprofessional working demands a focus on the values of each profession and the possibility of conflicting values between each profession. Similarly, more defensive ways of working have emerged. Banks argues that the 'new accountability' encapsulates a host of accountability measures that have developed with the growth of 'new managerialism' or 'new public management' from the end of the twentieth century.

Major changes in the delivery of welfare and the introduction of internal markets pose interesting challenges for the values base of professions working in social care. Working with first-year students there is a worrying trend towards what Reamer calls an 'amoralistic paradigm'. This is characterized by the absence of value-based or normative concepts or orientations and is evident in a technical, managerial or procedural approach to social work. The act of 'rule-following' or upholding a duty to the regulatory framework, uncritically and without question, would be an example of such amoralistic working.

The concern is that contemporary developments in the field of social care have returned us to the starting point of traditional social work as the technical management of personal problems and the maintenance of order. The challenge is to move beyond this paradigm and reinvigorate the value base of social care. The challenges of globalization, new technologies, regulation and government policy will set the agenda for new developments in how we define values.

To return to the notion of a paradigm shift in professional values, Banks argues that changes in values have 'not signalled a revolution' but a 'series of tremors, rocking the foundations, requiring some rebuilding and restructuring, but based on the solid traditions of the past, constantly evolving and changing'. It is this common but shifting ground that makes up the terrain of values. Our task is to map the route and enjoy the journey.

2

Social Work Research and Practice

INTRODUCTION

Research and social work practice with regard to families and parenting have traditionally focused on mothers, with fathers becoming increasingly recognized over the past three decades. The lack of attention to fathers is inconsistent with social work practice frameworks, *e.g.,* the ecological theory and family systems perspectives that are inclusive of all aspects of the family. Fatherhood became a topic of political focus with the Fatherhood Initiative in the 1990s and has recently become a widely recognized sub-specialty across a number of fields. Despite this recent growth in father-focused research, the very conceptualization of fathering as a sub-specialty reflects that fathers are still not considered as central to parenting as mothers.

There remains a great deal we do not know about fathers, particularly with respect to diversity and the effectiveness of father focused interventions. This is problematic for social workers, since it is difficult to engage and intervene with fathers without adequate knowledge. The inclusion of fathers in social work practice and research is of ethical relevance since just as to the National Association of Social Workers, "the primary mission of the social work profession is to enhance human well-being and help meet the basic human needs of all people....".

The NASW Code of Ethics was revised in 2008 to include several provisions facilitating the well-being of people without regard to sex or other aspects of cultural and social diversity. Specifically, "social workers should not practice, condone, facilitate, or collaborate with any form of discrimination on the basis of race, ethnicity, national origin, colour, sex, sexual orientation, gender identity or expression, age, marital status..." and "social workers should obtain education about and seek to understand the nature of social diversity and oppression with respect to race, ethnicity, national origin, colour, sex....". These ethical guidelines both prohibit discrimination against fathers simply on the basis that they are the male parent, and highlight the importance of research on fathers that informs both social work practice and policy.

The focus of the current document is not to provide a comprehensive review of the research on fathers, but rather to examine the recent inclusion of fathers in social work research, to review research evaluating social work practice with fathers, and to discuss barriers related to practice with fathers. It is in the spirit of recognizing the need for equitable representation of both mothers and fathers in research and practice as highlighted by social work's dominant practice frameworks and the NASW Code of Ethics that this document calls for the ethical consideration of the inclusion of fathers in familyfocused research and practice.

METHOD

The social work journals examined were: Social Work Research, Research on Social Work Practice, Children and Youth Services Review, Journal of Social Service Research, and Social Service Review. These journals were chosen due to their high citation ratings and clear relevance to social work. The one interdisciplinary journal examined, Family Relations, was selected due to its high social work citation rating and specific focus on family related issues. Titles and abstracts for each issue from 2004 through 2008 were first examined to identify the inclusion of family or parenting related variables. These substances were then further content analysed to identify whether mother variables, father variables, or both, were included.

If a study reportedly examined father variables whenever possible, for example in all dual-parent homes in a given sample, the substance was considered to include a father variable. When research was reported for "caregivers," "parents," or "families," the breakdown of mothers, fathers and other caretakers was examined and recorded when possible. If substance included fathers, the source of the data regarding the father was further recorded to reflect: father inclusion in the study and mother, caseworker, teacher or child report of father variables. Review substances were not considered in this examination. In addition to reporting descriptive statistics, t-tests were used to examine differences across groups.

SOCIAL WORK RESEARCH WITH MULTIRACIAL INDIVIDUALS

Growing diversity in the U.S. has prioritized social work's ethical obligation to develop specialized knowledge and understanding of culture and its function in human behaviour and society. This ethical requirement governs not only our practice, but recent initiatives to conduct and disseminate research with ethnic minority populations. This commitment evokes certain challenges for social work researchers since historically ethnic minority groups have been considerably more vulnerable to stigmatization, exploitation and harm in research. Ethical planning becomes a crucial component of research with ethnic minorities, and social work researchers must insure that investigations are not only ethically responsible, but flexible to the culture of its participants.

One ethnic minority group is receiving growing attention in social science research: multiracial persons or individuals who identify with more than one racial group. The U.S. census, approximately 7 million Americans or 2.4 per cent of the total population identify with more than one race. This population has steadily increased since the abolishment of antimiscegenation laws in 1967 and now represents one of the fastest growing minority groups in the United States.

Though racial mixing is far from a new phenomenon in the U.S., the increased visibility of multiracial persons in the media have inspired a growing number of people to claim membership in more than one racial group. Recent legislation allowing multiracial persons to check more than one race on federal race reporting forms have made the multiracial population a noteworthy demographic group in the United States. In fact some scholars propose that by the year 2050, one in five persons in the U.S. could claim a multiracial background. Due to the significant population growth and increased visibility of multiracial persons in the U.S., social workers are more than likely to see a rise in the number of clients and family systems who identify as multiracial. This heightens the need for social workers to understand how growing up in a complex society that continues to construct race based on historic ideals of distinct racial groups, may be challenging for multiracial persons.

For instance, there is limited yet mounting evidence that multiracial youth, in particular are at greater risk than their monoracial peers to use substances, engage in violent behaviours, and struggle with self-esteem. Researchers posit that this may be due to stressors associated with navigating a multifaceted identity in a mono-racial focused society. Unfortunately existing research is unable to capture the more dynamic and fluid processes influencing multiracial identity development, those which may or may not be linked to an individual's risk for developing mental or behavioural health problems. The growing presence and visibility of multiracial persons in the US demands that social work researchers critically examine and understand the complexity of identity as it applies to people who identify with more than one race. Such knowledge is critical to our field's development of culturally sensitive practice models with multiracial individuals and interracial families.

Unfortunately social work research efforts to understand the identity of this diverse group have been minimal. This is discerning since the profession is known, not only for its ethical obligation to understand culture and its function in human behaviour and society, but unlike other disciplines, social work has the potential to offer a unique, more inclusive understanding of multiracial identity by utilizing the professions ecological and strength-based perspectives. The dearth of multiracial research may be related to the political and definitional challenges associated with multiracial identification, which include the practice of compar-tmentalizing persons into separate monolithic racial groups. Due to this, multiracial research, like ethnic minority research in general, is confounded by certain methodological issues. This substance will discuss both past and present conceptualizations of multiracial identity, and the methodological challenges specific to investigations with multiracial participants.

This substance will conclude with recommended strategies for ensuring ethically responsible and culturally sensitive research with multiracial persons. The author recognizes that constructs of race and ethnicity are not static and are often conceptually confusing in social science research, therefore, for the purposes of this substance, the author defines the term multiracial as individuals who identify with 2 or more different racial heritages which is inclusive of derivative terms such as: biracial, mixed-race and mixed-heritage.

U.S. CONCEPTUALIZATION OF MULTIRACIAL IDENTITY: PAST AND PRESENT

The social identity of multiracial people is strongly influenced by the sociopolitical context of the U.S., including the stagnant societal belief in the biological existence of separate races. Certain national events have played a significant role in shaping social conceptualizations of multiracial identity and social science research with multiracial persons. These include: slavery, the legalization of interracial marriage, Census 2000, and the recent election of mixed-race President Barack Obama.

Slavery: Slavery in the U.S., particularly the raping of African female slaves by white males, led to the emergence of multiracial individuals.

In order to preserve the sanctity of the institution of slavery and protect White masters from having to provide patronage to their half-black offspring, legislation was developed in the 1600s to classify multiracial individuals with African American ancestry as black. This became known as the principal of hypo-descent or the "onedrop rule". Around the same time, biological and sociological arguments began to arise portraying multiracial individuals as maladjusted and dangerous degenerates due to their dual polarized heritage. This perspective was mostly shaped by false biological claims of the existence of a racial hierarch, placing whites above groups of colour, both on a genetic and societal level. For example, social scientists during the late 1800s and early 1900s considered mixed black/white persons less intelligent and capable than white due to possessing black blood. This transformed society's view of multiracial people and lead to the construction of the first multiracial identity theories which classified multiracial persons as "marginal".

Multiracial research at this time was often based on speculation and non-representative case histories that strongly emphasized the biased notion that interracial persons suffered from social and emotional problems. This prompted the rise of stereotypes popularizing the character notion of the genetically, mentally, and morally inferior "mulatto."

Legalization of interracial marriage: Following the legalization of interracial marriage in 1967, the U.S. saw a rise in interracial partnerships and a dramatic increase in multiracial children, also known as the "biracial baby boom". This prompted social scientists to again revisit the identity development of multiracial persons. An uprising of theories were proposed in the late 80s and early 90s, attempting to shed light on the racial identity options available to multiracial mainly Black/White children. Many of these emerging theories also followed the Eurocentric stage model frameworks of early identity development theorists.

These theories posited that multiracial identity development followed a similar linear path as other minority groups. Using this static approach many of these models pre-assigned and limited social identity options to a choice of either black or multiracial. In addition, most of these models were deficit-based, ignoring the contributing ecological factors impacting identity development, and consequently pathologizing the multiracial experience. Multiracial identity models developed during this time were either conceptual or based on research with small samples of biracial Black/White children. Despite relying on more pathological models of identity, research produced during this time introduced new conceptualizations of multiracial identity, namely that multiracial persons did not struggle psychologically. The changing sociopolitical climate of the 1990s and the growing percentage of persons who self-identify as multiracial prompted the formation of activist groups advocating the legal right of multiracial persons to claim the racial heritages of both parents. Their efforts elicited the ratification of the U.S. Federal Office of Management and Budget's categorizes of race, allowing multiracial persons to check more than one race on federal race reporting forms.]

The *2000 Census* marked the official end of the anonymity of multiracial persons in the U.S., making them visible in a country who for the most part had not acknowledged their existence. Prior to and following the 2000 Census, there was a notable increase in multiracial identity research, lead often by multiracial researchers themselves. One major priority that emerged from this research was the development of a complex theory of multiracial identity—one that was non-linear and reflective of the numerous contextual variables that may influence identity development. Using a more ecological lens, multiracial identity research has introduced new evidence that identities can change across contexts, differ within a family system, and shift over the life course. This has contributed to a more in-depth understanding of multiracial identity, which can include: experiencing prejudice, adopting multiple labels to describe one's racial identity, refusing to disown any part of their heritage, and feeling comfortable in multiple ethnic communities.

Age of Obama: Recently the U.S. has experienced yet another reputable and potentially influential shift in this country's conceptualization of multiracial identity. President Obama, who is multiracial has described his mixed-race background as the most important and powerful factor that has prepared him for his role as President of the United States. His presence has re-ignited nationwide debates on issues of race and multiracial identity, including earlier notions that multiracial individuals have the right to choose how they identify, and the right to claim membership in both multiracial and monoracial groups. This racial paradigm shift challenges social science researchers to contribute new advancements to conceptualizing multiracial identity. New research is beginning to emerge that utilizes more sophisticated methods to generate new insight into the complexities of multiracial identity. Throughout history the social identity of multiracial persons has challenged legislation on patronage, marriage, and racial classification.

There is a growing call for social scientists to examine, more constructively, how multiracial individuals experience and define their identity in a changing society, which up until recently was reluctant to acknowledge their existence. Therefore, ethical planning becomes a crucial factor in future research with multiracial persons, and social work researchers must become familiar with some of the noted challenges complicating multiracial investigations.

METHODOLOGICAL CHALLENGES IN MULTIRACIAL RESEARCH

The demand to include multiracial participants in research investigations evokes certain methodological challenges since long standing notions of racial categorization are still prolific in our social institutions. For instance despite recent changes in federal race reporting standards that allow multiracial persons to choose more than one race many schools and social service agencies continue to force multiracial participants to choose one racial category. This part will discuss the challenges that arise in research with multiracial participants.

These challenges fall into two major methodological categories: Sampling and data collection.

Sampling: Obtaining multiracial participants for research studies can be a difficult and complex venture due to the non-random distribution of multiracial people in the US. The U.S. census, the majority of people who identify as multiracial reside in Western states such as Hawaii, Alaska, California and Washington. This makes recruitment efforts in other areas of the country more complicated. For example, the majority of research involving multiracial subjects has taken place in Western states, such as California, and/or large cities, such as New York City, where there are greater percentages of multiracial persons, and others from diverse ethnic and racial groups. Researchers have also relied heavily on snowball sampling to recruit multiracial participants. This can substantially hinder the diversity of experiences and make samples more homogeneous. Similarly past multiracial identity research recruited convenience samples of college-age students, which represent a homogeneous age and developmental group.

Finally, advertisement can pose a substantial problem in multiracial research since some multiracial persons do not identify as multiracial and are unlikely to respond to ads that request persons who identify as mixed-race. Leaving out such individuals may constrain efforts to draw a more holistic picture of multiracial identity. Research describing the multiracial experience based on these constrained samples may be limited in their applicability to diverse multiracial persons who are more intermittently dispersed in homogeneous communities throughout the U.S., who do not necessarily identify as multiracial, and who are not college-age.

Data collection: Qualitative methods of enquiry are employed more frequently in multiracial research. This may be related to the methods ability to extract the complexities and intimate details of multiracial identity, in a way that conventional quantitative methods cannot. Despite this, means of collecting qualitative data with multiracial samples can introduce bias in research. Specifically, a researcher who relies on past conceptual frameworks of multiracial identity or one that is unaware of their own beliefs and values about race, interracial relationships and/or multiracial identity, can pose biased questions in interviews with multiracial persons. For example, asking a multiracial person questions that explicitly focus on any adjustment or psychological problems they have experienced due to being mixed-race. A second, less explored area of bias in qualitative studies is the influence of the ethnicity of the researcher and the potential bias this may introduce in interviews with multiracial persons. Specifically, the ethnicity of the interviewer could potentially influence a multiracial participant's response to interview questions about their ethnic identity. For example, some participants may feel restraint in sharing their true feelings about a certain ethnic group of people, or about their experiences with a certain community of colour, because of the interviewer's ethnicity. Traditional means of categorizing race continues to pose a problem in quantitative multiracial research.

In quantitative investigations this practice occurs both directly and indirectly. Both practices discriminate against a multiracial person's right to self-identify with more than one racial group. Recently there is evidence disputing this common practice in identity development research with multiracial persons. Specifically Townsend *et al*. found that forcing a multiracial participant to choose a race on measures introduces discrepancies between the outward identity multiracial persons report, and their desired or chosen identity. In addition, the same authors found that putting pressure on multiracial participants to choose a race subsequently caused decreases in self-esteem and motivation.

This directly contradicts earlier identity assumptions that multiracial persons who identify with only one racial group would have a stronger sense of self. Standard instrumentation poses an additional challenge in multiracial research. Researchers continue to utilize measures of racial and ethnic identity that have been criticized as inappropriate for understanding identity development among persons with mixed-heritage. Such measures are often based on monoracial samples and assume the necessity of a single choice. For instance, the Multi-Ethnic Identity Measure, though a highly reliable and useful instrument to measure ethnic identity, on the surface does not appear sensitive enough to gage a multiracial persons multiple ethnic and cultural associations. For example, specific items on the MEIM require the multiracial participant to reference one ethnic group which may pose a problem for those persons who simultaneously identify with more than one ethnic group.

Employing such instruments in investigations can draw biased conclusions about multiracial identity. The demand to include ethnic minority participants in research evokes certain challenges since they are considerably more vulnerable to stigmatization, exploitation and harm in research. Multiracial persons are no exception, and in order to expand our understanding of multiracial identity, social work researchers should become familiar with strategies to minimize these challenges in future multiracial investigations.

RECOMMENDED STRATEGIES FOR MULTIRACIAL RESEARCH

This part will present recommended strategies to design more ethically responsible and culturally sensitive research with multiracial participants.

These strategies include:

- Using recent theory to conceptually guide research methodology;
- Sampling more inclusively;
- Incorporating more culturally sensitive measures and instrumentation; and
- Including multiracial persons on research teams.

Strategy 1

Rely on more inclusive, ecological-based theories of multiracial identity to guide study methodology: Future studies should continue the pursuit to understand the complex individual, interpersonal, and contextual factors that interact to shape a multiracial individuals' identity. A number of ecological-based models have yet to be fully explored in multiracial literature. These models include, but are not limited to: Hall's Biracial Identity Development Across the Life Span Model; Rockquemore and Brunsma's Multidimensional Model of Biracial Identity; Root's Ecological Framework for Understanding Identity Development; and Wijeyesinghe's Factor Model of Multiracial Identity. Such models could be used as a guide to understand the interconnected effect individual, interpersonal, and environmental factors have on a multiracial person's identity experiences. For instance Renn applied Bronfenbrenner's Ecology Model of Identity Development to her examination of the identity of multiracial college students. By applying such a model, Renn was able to assess environmental factors influencing the racial identity of her multiracial participants, and offer suggestions of what areas institutions could do to enhance opportunities for supporting multiracial student development. Social work researchers are advantaged in the application of ecological-based theories due to our professions reliance on the ecological system's model to understand client problems and ascertain solutions.

These models can guide the methodology used in multiracial investigations. For instance, the idea that multiracial identity is fluid and changes over time is justification for longitudinal designs, which could take the form of narratives collected over time, or analyses of a national longitudinal data base. Also newer methodologies to emerge in social work, including the extended case method and participatory action research may serve useful for extricating some of the more complex contextual factors including the racial composition and attitudes of the community, which may be impacting a multiracial persons development.

Strategy 2

Sample more inclusively: Social work researchers should include more heterogeneous samples of multiracial persons, including persons from diverse ethnic backgrounds and persons from multiple generations. Specifically the voices of multiracial persons who identify with two or more ethnic minority groups and older adults are needed in multiracial literature. In order to offset challenges related to sampling multiracial populations, social work researchers can utilize recruitment strategies such as leverage sampling: when a multiracial participant recruits their sibling, who often identifies differently, in the study; or recruitment through multiracial friendly web sites on the internet.

Finally, in order to keep the sampling frame broad and avoid excluding those who do not identify as multiracial, social work researcher can leave identity verbiage out of recruitment material and instead ask for persons "from more than one racial group". Researchers should weigh the potential costs and benefits of utilizing the aforementioned sampling strategies prior to implementation. For instance, though recruiting siblings and persons from multiracial web sites could broaden the sampling frame, it may also limit the generalizability of study findings since such persons may be more demographically similar then different.

Strategy 3

Incorporate more culturally sensitive measures and instrumentation: Social work investigations of multiracial identity should allow participants to self-identify as multiracial or, at the very least, check more than one race on quantitative measures. For instance a study sponsored by the National Centre for Health Statistics found that multiracial respondents prefer a question format that allows them to self-identify as "multiracial". In addition, researchers interested in using standard measures of ethnic identity should make concerted effort to include measures that are sensitive to persons with multiple heritages, and inclusive of the numerous ways a multiracial person may express their identity. New measures have emerged that have been designed for, tested and proven reliable with multiracial samples. Such measures may prove useful in future multiracial identity research.

Strategy 4

Include multiracial persons on research teams: In order to make sure our research efforts are culturally sensitive to the ethnic minority groups being studied it is important to involve members of that group in the research process. In multiracial research, involvement of multiracial persons in both instrument development and data collection is crucial. First it is important to have several multiracial persons and/or experts on multiracial identity help develop and/or review constructed quantitative instruments or semi-structured qualitative interview guides, which have the potential to introduce bias in research designs. For example a recent study by Cheng and Lee assessing multiracial identity integration, used three experts in multiracial research to proofread and edit their newly constructed instrument.

Other researchers have used diverse focus groups, inclusive of multiracial persons, to construct identity measures. By allowing such careful review, social work researchers are less likely to develop insensitive surveys or questionnaires based on their own biases or past social scientific assumptions about multiracial individuals. Another culturally sensitive strategy is to use multiracial persons as interviewers to increase the comfort level of multiracial participants and allow them to share more personal and relevant information during the interview process. This strategy is frequently used in social work research to minimize miscommunication and power imbalances between interviewers and ethnic minority participants. Social work researchers are beginning to incorporate this strategy in qualitative investigations of multiracial identity by pairing it with efforts to enhance rigour and minimize potential biases associated with multiracial investigators collecting, analyzing, and/or interpreting data on the multiracial experience. These rigour enhancing strategies can include: reviewer triangulation, member checking, and using multiple data coders.

COMPARATIVE EFFECTIVENESS RESEARCH

On November 16, 2009 the Social Work Policy Institute will convene a think tank meeting, *Social Work Research and Comparative Effectiveness Research*: A Research Symposium to Strengthen the Connection. This symposium will examine how the social work profession might best contribute to the expanding attention to CER. The goal is to develop an agenda for action that addresses areas for further social work research, training of researchers, interdisciplinary collaborations, research/practice connections, and communication and outreach efforts.

SWPI created this briefing document to present background information on CER to stimulate issues for consideration for the upcoming symposium. It describes CER legislation through provisions of the American Recovery and Reinvestment Act of 2009 and the work of the Federal Coordinating Council on CER, and the Institute of Medicine's development of CER priorities. It also highlights the funding plans for the allocation of ARRA funds in the Office of the Secretary for the Department of Health and Human Services, the Agency for Health care Research and Quality, and the National Institutes of Health. Preliminary identification of potential CER issues for social work research and practice are identified. Resources on evidence based practice and research synthesis are included as well as comments provided by the Institute for the Advancement of Social Work Research to the Federal Coordinating Council on CER.

LEGISLATION TO FUND COMPARATIVE EFFECTIVENESS RESEARCH

The American Recovery and Reinvestment Act contained $1.1 billion for Comparative Effectiveness Research. These funds are designed to support research assessing the comparative effectiveness of health care treatments and strategies through efforts that:

- Conduct, support, or synthesize research that compares the clinical outcomes, effectiveness, and appropriateness of items, services, and procedures that are used to prevent, diagnose, or treat diseases, disorders, and other health conditions.
- Encourage the development and use of clinical registries, clinical data networks, and other forms of electronic health data that can be used to generate or obtain outcomes data.

ARRA provides:

- $400 million for the National Institutes of Health
- $400 million for the Office of the Secretary of the Department of Health and Human Services
- $300 million for the Agency for Health care Research and Quality

FEDERAL COORDINATING COUNCIL AND ITS REPORT TO THE PRESIDENT AND THE CONGRESS ON CER

To help develop a consistent understanding of CER and advise federal agencies receiving CER stimulus funding, the ARRA directed DHHS to create a 15 member Federal Coordinating Council. After conducting three public listening sessions and gathering input from a variety of stakeholders, the FCC for CER released its Report to the President and the Congress on June 30, 2009. This report includes a recommended definition, prioritization criteria, strategic framework, a long term outlook, and next steps.

FCC Definition

Comparative Effectiveness Research is the conduct and synthesis of research comparing the benefits and harms of different interventions and strategies to prevent, diagnose, treat, and monitor health care conditions in "real world" settings. The purpose of this research is to improve health outcomes by developing and disseminating evidence-based information to patients, clinicians, and other decision-makers, responding to their expressed needs, about which interventions are most effective for which patients under specific circumstances.

- To provide this information, comparative effectiveness research must assess a comprehensive array of health-related outcomes for diverse patient populations and sub-groups.
- Defined interventions compared may include medications, procedures, medical and assistive devices and technologies, diagnostic testing, behavioural change, and delivery system strategies.
- This research necessitates the development, expansion, and use of a variety of data sources and methods to assess comparative effectiveness and actively disseminate the results.

Prioritization Criteria

The report specifically suggests focusing on research that addresses the needs of underrepresented populations such as racial and ethnic minorities, persons with disabilities, children, veterans, the elderly, and patients with comorbidities.

Research Challenges

The report highlights several research challenges related to priority populations:

- Evaluating and identifying interventions that are tailored for priority populations
- Creating and enhancing potential databases looking at interventions for priority populations
- Increasing the number of community-based studies
- Increasing cultural competency
- Building workforce capacity
- Developing and implementing outreach strategies to various racial, ethnic, and health disparity populations for participation in research protocols

Strategic Framework

The report specifies four core categories for CER activities and investments:

- Research–Primary or meta-analysis
- Human and Scientific Capital–Enhance U.S.'s capacity for CER by strengthening relevant research skills or advancing CER approaches and methodologies
- CER Data Infrastructure–Creation of research data sets and repositories, aggregation of existing data sources, development of new tools to query and analyse existing data sets, or creation of standards for new data collection
- Dissemination and Translation of CER–improving processes for distribution and developing relevant practice guidelines

Themes for the research that cut across all core categories should focus on:

- Conditions–Focus on specific conditions highlighted in the IOM's 100 priorities
- Priority Populations–Focus on populations outlined in the prioritization criteria
- Types of interventions–Focus on medications, medical and assistive devices, procedures, behavioural change, diagnostic testing, and delivery system strategies.

Gaps in Current CER Landscape and Investment Opportunities

- Current CER and collection and organisation of data–there is no specific comprehensive picture of CER in the U.S.
- CER data infrastructure–need for patient-level databases to support researchers
- Need for formal mechanisms to disseminate and translate CER from research agencies to delivery systems.
- Training to conduct CER research
- Coordination across the CER framework
  - Limited coordination with private sector CER efforts
  - Unrealised benefits of stakeholder involvement–need to increase involvement to a wide array of stakeholders
- Research
  - "Practical" *vs.* "pragmatic" trials–"threats to internal validity of CER for causal effects of interventions on outcomes and external validity of CER to heterogeneous patient groups and routine health care settings."
  - Many research questions for important clinical health–care decisions remain unanswered.

INSTITUTE OF MEDICINE'S INITIAL NATIONAL PRIORITIES FOR CER

Congress, through the ARRA, also requested that the Institute of Medicine convene a study to identify the Initial National Priorities for CER, giving consideration to the FCC's report to the President and the Congress.

The IOM report defines CER as follows:

- "Comparative effectiveness research is the generation and synthesis of evidence that compares the benefits and harms of alternative methods to prevent, diagnose, treat, and monitor a clinical condition or to improve the delivery of care. The purpose of CER is to assist consumers, clinicians, purchasers, and policy–makers to make informed decisions that will improve health care at both the individual and population levels."

The distribution of research priorities was chosen based on criteria developed by the IOM. Criteria were divided into two parts, condition-level criteria and priority-topic level criteria. Condition-level criteria includes burden of disease, cost, variability, and appropriateness for CER; priority-topic level criteria includes gaps in existing knowledge and the likelihood that the results would improve health. The IOM committee went through three rounds of voting to establish the national priorities for CER. The IOM concluded in its report that the science of CER cannot be advanced without the creation of a supporting infrastructure and large-scale data networks. Capacity also needs to be built within the current CER workforce to ensure that the needs and provisions of CER as defined in ARRA are met. The IOM's top 100 priorities for CER are divided into four quartiles with the first quartile being the highest priority group and the fourth quartile being the lowest. The IOM report, the listed priorities are a starting point and will evolve as the research initiative progresses. The IOM priorities overwhelmingly focus on health care delivery, racial and ethnic disparities, and functional disabilities. All of these areas can involve social work interventions and CER methodologies could be utilized to determine best practices.

PRELIMINARY SOCIAL WORK—CER RELATED ISSUES

The FCC's Report to the President and to the Congress and the IOM's National Priorities for CER are the first steps in recommending development of the necessary infrastructure to advance CER methodologies in the United States. Social worker involvement in these developments is important as we work with many priority populations highlighted in the FCC and IOM reports and social work practice and research can contribute to CER. The following identifies a range of issues addressing scope of CER research, methodology, treatment and service delivery gaps, translational research and research synthesis.

- *Scope of CER*:
  - Social workers should advocate for CER to stress clinical and health outcomes. In addition to doctors and nurses, social workers are integral to providing the best possible outcomes for patients and their families.
  - The AHRQ CER Plan discusses barriers to implementation of CER and methods for incorporating key stakeholders through its Effective Health Care forum. A challenge for social work is to be a stakeholder, and to ensure mental health and psychosocial interventions are incorporated into research on medical interventions.
  - "Horizon scanning" and the identification of current and past research should include social work research. However, database search engines identified by AHRQ and NIH may be absent of substantial social work researchers' work. Systematic review databases, such as the Campbell Collaboration along with other psychosocial research databases must be included in horizon scanning efforts.
  - CER should not be used strictly for cost containment. There should be links between cost effectiveness, cost benefits, comparative effectiveness and the implementation and feasibility and adaptability of interventions. CER related to psychosocial interventions should cover these areas.
- *Challenges and gaps in methodology and validity for social work CER*:
  - Methodological aspects of psychosocial research look at complex variables of human behaviour as well as organisational, community and social contexts. These require use of multiple measures and methods. A viable CER framework for psychosocial researchers must be established and funded to advance CER that can evaluate behavioural change and delivery system strategies as identified in the FCC report.
- *Challenges and gaps in treatment/delivery systems*:
  - Social work researchers are part of interdisciplinary teams that can examine CER related to comprehensive treatment to fully address issues related to patients' daily living activities, quality of life, and impediments to treatment access. The IOM report stresses the importance of evaluating comprehensive treatment, behavioural elements of treatment, and adherence aspects of strictly medical interventions. Social workers and social work researchers can provide valuable input to these goals.
  - Is there sufficient infrastructure to address these critical issues and carry-out such research?

- *Translational research*:
  - All agencies stress the need for better dissemination of effective interventions into real world settings. Focus should be placed on how social work research on practice and outcomes can contribute to translational research and be disseminated within the social work practice community as well as to other disciplines. There needs to be an increased focus on comparative effectiveness of implementation of evidence-based practices into real world settings, considering different populations, cultures, age groups and co-morbid conditions.
  - *Effectiveness vs*. Efficacy *vs*. Implementation—The FCC and IOM reports stress the need for evaluating and comparing outcomes of interventions in routine conditions vs. controlled environment.
    (a) Efficacy is the determination of how well a treatment works in a controlled setting. Effectiveness is the determination of how well a treatment works in routine conditions. Effectiveness is a better indicator of how well a treatment will perform in the real world with the general population. For now, CER may be most relevant to implementation with diverse populations in situations where there are already numerous well-researched effective interventions.
    (b) It is difficult to compare effectiveness if there are few well-researched effective interventions. A challenge for researchers is to compare effective interventions that are implemented in real world settings.
    (c) Research design must focus on developing CER that most emulates real conditions of the diverse populations being studied.
    (d) Special attention should be placed on populations with comorbid illnesses and how individual treatments can be developed and tested effectively.
- *Research synthesis*:
  - It is important to ensure that social work interventions are included in the research synthesis carried out by AHRQ and by the Campbell and Cochrane Collaborations and other relevant CER synthesis efforts.

USING THEORY AND RESEARCH TO ENHANCE PRACTICE

In this stage, we begin by looking at the tension that exists within social work in the relationship between theory and practice. We analyse how different terms are defined and, drawing on these definitions, identify ten practice choices, using a case example to describe how these choices might be used in practice.

THE DIALOGUE BETWEEN THEORY AND PRACTICE

To be an effective practitioner requires that we have a sound theoretical base. This is not easy to achieve. In the past, there has been a reluctance among some practitioners to embrace theory and research. The stereotypical view is one where theory and research are considered to be irrelevant, obscure, abstract and untranslatable in terms of direct practice. Some practitioners feel that to refer to theory is to lose touch with the realities of social work practice, and likely to be deskilling experience if it leaves us questioning our 'innate' skills, particularly our ability to relate to others. From this perspective it is easy for the split between theory and practice to be reinforced because practitioners have not experienced the benefits and clarity that theory can bring to practice situations.

But take, for example, a practitioner working with a distressed child who is struggling to settle into a new placement. This practitioner may find a useful link between theory and practice in Bowlby's theory of attachment, particularly his concept of separation response (protest, despair and detachment). This may help to illuminate the practitioner's understanding of this child and, in turn, help foster carer(s) and parent(s) to understand and to tolerate certain behaviours. We can, no doubt, choose to look at different writers in this field or update our knowledge by referring to more recent research on attachment theory and relevant texts.

However, we would argue that our practice is impoverished without reference to those theories that attempt to bring together a range of explanations, including current research findings, because these have a bearing on the strategies or interventions that we might choose, or wish to learn about, in order to help children and parents overcome the dilemmas they face. Similarly, in direct work, we are more likely to recognize key issues or reactions if we have a knowledge base to draw on.

The concern that knowledge can 'be used to gain power over others' can be addressed in relation to service users by finding ways to share our knowledge with them, so that they have access to the same understanding – and the sense of confidence and resilience that knowledge can give. From this perspective, the value of a given theory and research lie in their usefulness in relation to practice and the degree to which they illuminate our understanding and future action.

If any theory can achieve this it has an important contribution to make, even if its value is limited or has to be adapted to fit different settings. Attachment theory provides a theoretical framework from which to hypothesize and analyse the behaviour of the child in question. References to present and past research findings attempt to test out those hypotheses —put flesh on the bone—by looking for evidence for and against the hypothesis put forward, and to develop new hypotheses or theories based on that evidence.

THE ANTI-INTELLECTUAL STANCE WITHIN SOCIAL WORK

This mistrust of theory has been described as an 'anti-theoretical or a theoretical stance' as an 'anti-intellectualism' or an 'intellectual purge'. It is seen when practitioners ignore or dismiss research findings as irrelevant, unrepresentative and too abstract, sometimes because research fails to confirm the unquestioned assumptions and 'common-sense' notions that some practitioners have learned to rely on. This antagonism, however, cannot be explained only in terms of how practitioners have reacted. Jordan suggests that at times academics and researchers have gone about the task of linking theory to practice quite insensitively, sometimes dictating to practitioners 'not only how they should work, but also what rationale they should follow'.

Also, a degree of wariness is understandable given the fact that some research findings have been critical of practice, and more positive accounts of social work successes tend to be ignored. Others suggest that practitioners fail to see the important part that theory can play because of a confusion about what constitutes a theory, which leads to the mistaken belief that they do not have or need to have theories when, in fact, we all use theory to inform practice:

> It is psychologically impossible not to have theories about things. It is impossible at a basic perceptual level, at a cognitive and at an emotional level. The search for meaning, as a basis for predicting behavioural success and avoiding danger, appears to have been 'wired' into our brains by evolution.

These theories or explanations of human behaviour or events may, however, be expressed in quite obscure ways. For example, some writers refer to 'practice wisdom': that is, skills based on personal experience of 'what works' in practice.

The difficulty here is that some of these 'wisdoms' are not always ordered in such a way that they can be identified or differentiated from more common-sense notions, described by Pinker as 'an anecdotal ragbag of folk remedies'. As a result we have no reliable way of knowing in what ways these 'practice wisdoms' contribute to our stock of knowledge nor how applicable or transferable these wisdoms are across different situations.

Instead, much of this knowledge remains beyond any evaluative process. One important reason why these practice wisdoms are difficult to identify is because they are sometimes on-the-spot responses to complex dilemmas for which practice is ahead of theory. For example, for some time there was little information for practitioners to draw on with regard to the impact of drug abuse, particularly solvent abuse, in relation to young people. A similar gap in our knowledge once existed in relation to the impact of sexual abuse. No doubt similar gaps will come to light as different social and emotional problems emerge and are acknowledged. On the other hand, there is no shortage of statistics or research in relation to the impact of poverty among people from more deprived sectors of the population, yet in recent years this knowledge has not influenced practice to any marked degree.

For example, although it is well documented that not all claimants receive their full benefit entitlement, we are still not at a point where all practitioners engage in benefit checks as a matter of course. This selective use of what we know has to be seen in a wider context than the practice orientation of particular social workers. For example, Jones locates this hostility to the 'peculiarities' of British social work education in a passage that is worth quoting at length:

> British social work education is also unique in its anti-intellectualism and its hostile stance to the social sciences. Since 1975 there has been an ongoing process of theoretical stripping out of the social work curriculum. In its place students are increasingly confronted with a mish-mash of methods, skills and values teaching, often lacking in any coherence. Values in particular have come to occupy a strangely central position, with CCETSW appearing to believe that they can be a substitute for knowledge and understanding. There is no comparable system of social work education in the world which is so nationally uniform, uninspired and tailored so closely to the requirements of major state employers.

These points are important and, given such obstacles, it is more than ever crucial that we remain intellectually and emotionally alive to the complexities that social work presents; that we keep hold of a critical faculty or an 'intellectual scrutiny and rigour': 'Good social work rests upon the process of criticism, a process of experience and understanding, of analysis and comparison. A critical faculty is integral to the very practice of social work, to enable the worker to evaluate his client's and his own communications'.

Certainly, one way that this aliveness could be inspired would be if social work texts and research findings could be presented in ways that are more visually appealing, relevant and interesting, so that they provide 'the possibility of a good read'.

Also, as practitioners we need to work in a learning culture where curiosity, enquiry and exploration are encouraged and where opportunity, encouragement, time and resources to update our knowledge are seen as priorities. This would, hopefully, encourage many more practitioners to write and to engage in research and this, in time, may provide the link that is needed in the theory–practice divide.

COMPETENCE BASED APPROACHES

Some of this tension between theory and practice, and the lack of clarity about what social workers' knowledge base should be, is exposed in the debate about the value, or otherwise, of a competence based approach to teaching and learning within social work. CCETSW categorizes the knowledge base that social workers are required to have in order to qualify for the Diploma in Social Work under the following six headings:

1. Communicate and engage
2. Promote and enable
3. Assess and plan
4. Intervene and provide services
5. Work in organizations
6. Develop professional competence

It is not possible to do justice to the wide ranging debate that has taken place since CCETSW first introduced competencies into the new Diploma in Social Work. What is striking is the degree of agreement among social work academics in their criticisms of the appropriateness of this approach within social work. These include the criticism that teaching the 'mechanics' or 'techniques' produces technicians rather than professionals and that this process misses all that is complicated in the interaction between social worker and service user.

Competencies are also described as constraining a reflective approach to practice and seen to ignore the central importance that process plays within a given interaction. Furthermore, competencies are accused of being inconsistent with the development of anti-oppressive practice and a more values based approach to social work.

Howe generalizes the concerns expressed: 'Such an outlook seeks to establish routines, standardized practices and predictable task environments. It is antithetical to depth explanations, professional integrity, creative practice, and tolerance of complexity and uncertainty.' The major advantage of a competence based approach lies in its emphasis on outcomes and on the importance of social workers being able to demonstrate the appropriate use and effectiveness of designated skills in relation to practice.

This includes a requirement that students and social workers are familiar with the law and how this relates in practice, and that students and practitioners should take 'responsibility for their continued learning and development' beyond the acquisition of a professional qualification. We believe that the emphasis on students being able to demonstrate that they have acquired certain knowledge is essential to good practice. For a helpful summary of the main advantages and disadvantages of a competence based approach.

TRANSFERABILITY OF SKILLS

The transferability of skills involves students and practitioners being 'able to explain in a coherent, comprehensive and convincing manner how their practice is informed by their knowledge base, and being able to apply their knowledge and learning to new situations through appraising what is general and what is particular in each situation'.

However, for skills to be reliable and enduring across different, often difficult, situations they have to be based on a sound theoretical understanding of human beings in their particular social contexts. This includes an understanding of theories in relation to human behaviour: 'The final factor for skill development which is reliable and transferable is an understanding of theories of human behaviour so that skills are related to individual clients and not just routine behaviour'. For example, if confronted with a situation where a service user is being aggressive or threatening, we would be very cautious before using interventions that are challenging or confrontational unless my purpose was to bring matters to a head. This kind of evaluative process requires that we have a body of knowledge to draw on in order to help us to explore what was happening and why. Establishing a relationship between theory and practice in this way means that both are constantly in dialogue, each informing the other in ways that illuminate different aspects of our work and that 'invigourate, fascinate and professionally uplift'.

KEY QUESTIONS

Much is asked of social workers, and the use of theory and research can be helpful markers when we find ourselves overwhelmed by the intractable nature of the problems presented. They can help us to address the key question posed throughout this text, namely 'what can we and others say or do to make a difference?' In addressing this question, theory can illuminate our understanding of people and their circumstances in five key areas:

(1) *Observation*: it tells us what we see and what to look out for;
(2) *Description*: it provides a conceptual vocabulary and framework within which observations can be arranged and organized;
(3) *Explanation*: it suggests how different observations might be linked and connected; it offers possible causal relationships between one event and another;
(4) *Prediction*: it indicates what might happen next;
(5) *Intervention*: it suggests what might be done to bring about change.

It is necessary to draw on theories or to 'borrow' knowledge from a range of other disciplines, particularly sociology and psychology, including social psychology. To this list Hardiker and Barker add organizational theory as a 'foundation knowledge'. However, borrowing from other disciplines in this way has given rise to considerable controversy about what constitutes a useful theory for social work. This controversy has been described by Payne as 'theory wars'. One of the best examples of this can be seen in the way that psychodynamic theory was misrepresented and discounted within social work in the 1970s and 1980s and, to some extent, continues to be attacked today.

Some of this controversy has been played out in relation to whether knowledge is primarily drawn from sociology or psychology, because these two disciplines look across at people and their social situations in different ways. In addition, different schools within these disciplines take up different emphases. The polarized way that psychology and social factors have been represented within social work denies that both are important. It should be clear that our interest in one discipline does not automatically cancel out our interest in the other. However, at different times, it may be necessary to focus on one more than the other. For example, a woman who asks for help in order to enable her to leave a violent relationship will need help and understanding from different sources. To have the courage to think through the emotional consequences involved in, say, leaving her home and moving to a new area, perhaps to a women's refuge, will require our focusing on feelings and the meaning given to experiences.

At the same time, in order to make it possible for this woman to leave, it may be essential to focus on her housing needs and on ensuring that she knows her legal rights and where to go for help. Or again, where poverty is likely to be an issue, we may focus our work on trying to ensure that she is in receipt of the right benefit and so forth. The list of possible tasks is endless but cannot be fully embraced unless we can bring social and psychological considerations into an intellectual climate where both can be recognized. Some of the tension between individual and social causation can be found in the current debate about the purpose of social work and the role of a social worker.

PRACTICE TERMINOLOGY: THE ABSENCE OF A COMMON LANGUAGE

The tension between theory and practice within social work is not helped by the different way that authors use terms such as theory, hypothesis, method, model, practice approach, perspective, intervention, and skills. Given this confusion, it is important to identify these differences and to define how these terms are used within this book.

THEORY

The knowledge base of social work derives from many sources. However, what constitutes a theory, particularly in relation to what constitutes a social theory, is subject to some debate. One way to define a theory would be as: 'A group of related hypotheses, concepts, and constructs, based on facts and observations, that attempts to explain a particular phenomenon'. Every attempt to try to make sense of the world or particular events constitutes a theory since one characteristic of a theory is that it goes beyond the descriptive to include explanations of why things happen.

This places theory and theorizing at one end of a spectrum as something accessible; something that we all do, whether intentionally or not. It is sometimes referred to as informal theorizing. At the other end of the spectrum, the validity of formal types of theory tend to be based on scientific criteria. Sheldon leans towards this more formal use of theory in his breakdown of the 'qualities possessed by theories', which should have built in:

- Potential refutability ('at greatest risk of potential refutation by stating clearly what ought not to occur')
- Riskiness of prediction
- Testability
- Logical consistency
- Clarity of expression
- Applicability
- Simplicity
- The potential to attempt to address 'important things not yet known' or those 'circumstances in which there is no convincing explanation available'.

The difficulty in relation to formal theories of this kind is that they run the risk of dismissing explanations that cannot easily be tested by more objective measures, which means it is possible to miss vital clues or to misread situations. Also, there is now growing agreement that all theories are influenced to varying degrees by the role, behaviour, values and assumptions of those involved in theorizing, including researchers. A final way theory has been categorized is through differentiating between grand and middle-range (micro-level) theories, with grand theories attempting to explain more or less everything in society (*e.g.* Marxism, psychoanalysis) and middle-range theories attempting to explain only a limited range of phenomena (*e.g.* inequalities, oppression).

Whether social work can lay claim to any distinct theories in its own right, independent of other disciplines, is debatable and if it can, it is not clear what a social work theory would consist of in terms of its distinct characteristics. My own view is that it is possible for social work to have its own unique theory base, built on knowledge-in-practice, which identifies how certain theories are applied and adapted to specific practice situations, and then to use the findings of practice as a basis for new hypotheses to be developed and further theory-building. In this process, the term theory is used within this text to include formal and informal, grand and middlerange concepts that attempt to explain phenomena.

Hypotheses

In between theory and practice lies the activity of formulating and testing working hypotheses. The dictionary definition of a hypothesis is 'a suggested explanation for a group of facts or phenomena, either accepted as a basis for further verification (working hypothesis) or accepted as likely to be true. An unproved theory'. Formulating hypotheses in this way marks an attempt to define, explain and predict certain events with a view to increasing our understanding in order to arrive at an agreed course of action. One way to see hypotheses is as a type of 'informal' theory-making, 'based on testable hypotheses'. For example, in a case of non-attendance at school, we might formulate a variety of hypotheses: that the child is absent from school because s/he is looking after a parent; s/he may be being bullied; s/he finds the teacher frightening; s/he finds the culture of school bewildering, and so forth.

Having formulated these hypotheses, which forms an important part of Schön's notion of reflection-in-action, the task is to 'test' against evidence that either confirms or refutes each hypothesis 'by showing that the conditions that would follow from each hypothesis are not the observed ones'. The importance of seeking verification has to be stressed and is consistent with an evidence based approach to practice. The use of unclarified or unconfirmed data based on intuition or common-sense notions alone is not enough.

Method or Practice Orientation

Again, confusion surrounds the use of the term method. One way that method is used, particularly in the USA, is to identify the four general forms of practice.

These are:

- Work with individuals (sometimes involving counselling)
- Groupwork (sometimes called social groupwork)
- Family work (including family counselling and family therapy)
- Community work (sometimes called community organization or community development).

Method is also used to describe specific types of interventions. For example, Pinker uses the term to include task-centred and problem-solving methods and also to describe what we would call practice approaches, namely 'crisis intervention and behaviour modification methods of intervention'. It describes a 'way of doing things, of working with facts and concepts in a systematic fashion'. Or again, sometimes method is used interchangeably with the term intervention, as a way of formulating an appropriate plan of action. Disagreement about the definition of social work methods, and how these should be categorized, particularly in relation to case work and community work, formed part of the argument of the Barclay Working Party and the Barclay Report. Since confusion still surrounds its use, within this text we use the term practice orientation to describe the four general types of practice (work with individuals, groups, families and communities) and practice methods to describe the application of specific practice interventions that form part of a particular practice approach.

For example, we would include unconditional positive regard as a specific practice intervention in a client-centred approach; modelling as an example in cognitive-behavioural approaches; impact as specific practice terminology used in crisis intervention; circular questioning as a specific practice intervention in family therapy (systems theory) and interpretation and insight for psychosocial approaches. Given the lack of consistency that exists among different authors about how they use the term social work methods, in this text we have avoided using this word except in a general sense or when quoting other authors.

Models

Howe, like Hardiker and Barker (1981), differentiates between a model and a theory, and does so by identifying a model as a description rather than an explanation of phenomena, acting not as a perfect representation but as an initial attempt to order, or simplify, information by illuminating the pattern of relationships or phenomena observed: 'Models, acting as analogies, can be used to order, define, describe phenomena.

They do not explain the things seen, but they do begin to impose some low level order on what is otherwise a jumble of information. Models act as bricks in theory building'. However, the word model is used differently within certain disciplines or by certain authors. For example, the medical model is closer to a grand theory. Others use the word model to describe what we would call a practice approach or perspective, or to describe both a theory and perspective, such as the social model of disability. Finally, England uses the word model to include client-centred, task-centred and unitary 'theory', which he differentiates from theories because they do not include explanations. Given the confusion that surrounds the use of the word, it is not my intention to use model within this text.

Practice Approach

The term practice approach, sometimes called theoretical approach, is used within the text to describe a systematic approach to practice, which draws on a distinct body of theory and, as a result, has its own specific practice terminology and interventions.

Although more could be listed, the main practice approaches used within social work include:

- Client-centred approaches (this often takes the form of counselling)
- Cognitive-behavioural approaches
- Task-centred work
- Crisis intervention
- Psychodynamic or psychosocial approaches
- Systemic family therapies.

Task-centred work, although important, is not included as a practice approach because it does not adhere to any distinct theory base. Instead, it describes a 'set of activities' rather than a 'theoretically-based approach from which a set of activities flows'. Thus, focusing on tasks could form part of other practice approaches.

An Eclectic Approach

Eclecticism can be seen as a response to the diversity and complex nature of many of the problems social work embodies and has important advantages: 'Eclecticism enables different ideas to be brought to bear, helps to amalgamate social work theories when they make similar proposals for action, deals better with complex circumstances and allows workers to compensate for inadequacies in particular theories'. Although many practitioners describe themselves as being 'eclectic', not all can identify the particular practice approach or specific practice terminology and interventions they actually use, and why they use them.

In fact, eclecticism can tend to confuse rather than clarify what is actually involved in practice because, in reality, few practitioners have the expertise to be able to dip into a range of practice approaches, which means that this 'pick-and-mix' approach may be less flexible or adaptable than is sometimes implied. Social work will always involve a degree of eclecticism, and some practitioners may indeed draw on a range of practice approaches and methods in the way this term describes.

However, we have not included it as a distinct approach because too often the term eclecticism is used too loosely and not in a way that denotes an approach to practice based on an identifiable knowledge base. Given the lack of vigour that surrounds the use of the word, it is not my intention to refer to eclecticism as a distinct practice approach within this text.

Perspective

The word perspective is often used but rarely defined in social work texts. One way to define it would be as a 'view of the world' but often a partial view. In this text, we use the term perspective to denote a partial but important way of thinking about, observing and ordering phenomena and how they relate to society as a whole.

In the framework we are describing, perspectives are differentiated from practice approaches because, although they order and make sense of experiences and events from the particular and partial viewpoint, they are not linked to a particular theory and practice method in the way that the five practice approaches identified are linked. For example, while consciousness raising may be a term associated with a feminist perspective, other perspectives may also lay claim to raising awareness in similar ways.

Again, others could be added to this list but the main perspectives relevant to social work include:

- An anti-discriminatory perspective
- An anti-oppressive perspective
- An anti-racist perspective
- A feminist perspective

- A user's or a survivor's perspective
- A radical social work perspective.

These perspectives are frequently called upon to do more than deepen our understanding because they influence practice in a more direct way. For example, some are, in fact, political perspectives such as an anti-oppressive perspective, which, for some authors, describes a specific type of practice (anti-oppressive practice), designed to deliver an anti-oppressive service. This terminology denotes Dominelli's desire to incorporate what we would define as a practice approach, practice method and perspective into one 'new practice paradigm', namely anti-oppressive practice.

Other perspectives described in social work texts explore how the world looks through the eyes of minority or disadvantaged groups: from a children's perspective, a disabled or older person's perspective or a lesbian/gay perspective.

Other perspectives look at the details and facts from a specific viewpoint or angle, such as an ethical, values, agency or economic perspective. Not enough is known about the ways in which particular perspectives influence practice and how effective this work is in bringing about desired change, but it seems to be the case that most practitioners undertake assessments from one perspective or another and that at times, different perspectives can clash. For example, a user perspective may clash with an agency perspective. Also, the partial nature of any perspective can mean that there is the risk that an individual's perception of events is 'blinkered' and prone to generalizations or bias.

Intervention

Intervention in social work 'is analogous to the physician's term treatment' and is defined as taking 'a decisive or intrusive role in order to modify or determine events or their outcome'. It is direct action, or a specific social work input, based on our understanding of the situation or problem presented, and can involve providing direct services or trying to effect change in the social environment, including organizations, in order to change 'the balance of forces in the social environment in the client's favour'.

This may involve acting as an advocate or a mediator on behalf of a service user. Whether, when and how to intervene is a complex issue. It requires that we are clear beforehand that we have a mandate to do so, particularly where the request for our intervention does not come from the person for whom the help is being sought. We also need to be sure that our involvement is justified at that time.

This should be based on how we, the service user and others judge the situation, based on a consideration of the following factors:

- The urgency of the problem;

- The consequences of not alleviating the problem;
- The chances of success in alleviating the problem;
- The ability of the worker and agency to help with the problem;
- The motivation of the client to work on the problem;
- The support which the client will receive from other people; and
- The specific nature of the problem.

3

Research Methods Used in Social Work

INTRODUCTION

Three research methods were used to gain enough information to carry out an accurate social audit of:

- Depth Interviews with residents at Wayside and Esther Community
- Participant Observation in Esther Community
- Interviews with hostel staff and managers and other officials working with the homeless in both Exeter and Reigate.

DEPTH INTERVIEWS

To gain a variety of good quality, detailed information unstructured and semi-structured interviews were carried out with residents at both Wayside and Esther community. Each interview lasted on average approximately 40 minutes. Information was gathered from both a retrospective and current perspectives, to gain an idea of how and why each person became homeless, what happened to them while they were homeless; and their hopes for the future.

This information gives a clear indication of the types of women KeyChange is working with, their problems and difficulties, and the type of help that they need. Ideally, interviews with current residents and past residents would have given a clearer picture of the extent to which women who had lived in KeyChange hostels had benefited from their time there.

However, neither hostel had a formal follow-up procedure of exresidents and therefore none could be contacted. The absence of followup was in part because most women already had social workers and keyworkers involved in their case, so extra contact from the hostel was not necessary for the residents well-being.

Some of these women, although housed, still remained vulnerable and in crisis and therefore it was inappropriate to add to their stress by interviewing them directly. Obtaining interviews with current residents was not without problems either.

Most women at both Wayside and Esther Community were wary about being interviewed, especially when they received no direct benefit, other women did not want to go over their problems and circumstances yet again. However, after assurances of confidentiality and assurances that they would not be pressed into to talking about issues that they could not or did not want to discuss, five people from each hostel were interviewed.

Esther Community, Exeter, was visited three times to gain the five interviews. At that hostel, there was open access, allowing time to be spent mingling with the women and getting to know them better in a relaxed atmosphere. The women were approached in the communal rooms for interview, the research was explained to them and they were invited to take part. Staff also tried to encourage some women to talk to me, or pointed out which women were most likely to consent to being interviewed.

Wayside hostel, Reigate, was visited twice to gain the five interviews. At that hostel, the women were far more suspicious of being interviewed after taking part in an educational video produced by KeyChange earlier in 1998. Etta Colville, the hostel manager, managed to persuade four women to be interviewed in a group, a fifth person was interviewed separately with Etta sitting in. Prior to the interview, Etta had discussed with that resident how much she could disclose on her behalf if she found it difficult to talk to me. The group interview meant that very personal information was not disclosed, but the general discussions round some of the topics proved very enlightening.

At the end of every interview, a wind-down session was initiated to allow the women to relax, to ask any questions about the research and the researcher and to discuss how they felt after the interview was over. The accuracy of these interviews was checked in two ways. Firstly, interviews previously conducted with other homeless women at different locations in London, acted as a guide to the plausibility of the information. Secondly, bearing in mind that confidentiality had been assured, some facts were checked with staff.

PARTICIPANT OBSERVATION

Participant observation was only possible at Esther Community, where open access was given. Time was spent chatting to the women as they prepared meals, joining them for meals and sitting with them to watch television. This offered insight into the dynamics of the community, the problems individuals were coping with, and the way the women supported and interacted with each other. Wayside residents attended the video launch, I was able to talk to some of the women who attended; although the conversations were brief, insight into the way they viewed and felt about their homelessness was gained.

INTERVIEWS

A number of interviews were carried out both with hostel staff and managers at Wayside and Esther Community, as well as other hostels in the areas. A spokesperson from each of: the police, the local housing authority and other key officials dealing with homelessness in their area were interviewed. Thus an overall picture of the extent, and type, of homelessness was gained for each area. In addition, to the facilities that were on offer; and the way that KeyChange fitted into the overall picture of provision for each area.

Most importantly, these interviews highlighted:

- The continuous shortfall between bed-spaces and demand;
- The types of people who were not catered for by anyone;
- *Gaps in Provision*: Where specialist help was needed but none existed in the area;
- The interdependence of each organisation on the others for referrals, specialist help and at times, moral support.

Representativeness of the Sample

Esther Community is a 9 bed hostel. Over the three visits approximately 15 women would have been resident. Therefore the five women that were interviewed would represent approximately a third of the residents. Wayside hostel is a 15 bed hostel, over the two visits that were made approximately 20 women would have been resident. Therefore the five women that were interviewed would represent approximately a quarter of the residents. It is impossible to do more than reflect the views of the sample interviewed, I believe they reflect the resident's views, life experiences and the value of the 'KeyChange' experience.

RESEARCH FINDINGS IN SOCIAL WORK

The ten interviews carried out for the social audit between November 1998 and February 1999 generated a number of useful and interesting findings. Most of the findings were not easily comparable across the two hostels.

This is due to four main factors:

1. The different record keeping methods used by each hostel. Exeter has a much more statistical quantitative record keeping method with easily quantifiable categories, whereas Reigate uses a more qualitative method of record keeping which offers rich detail about clients, but does not have easily accessible statistics on their clients. Both methods are adequate and have their own advantages and disadvantages. The main disadvantage is that there is no easy way of comparing the progress of both hostels equally.
2. The hostels are completely different, Exeter's Esther Community is a short stay direct access hostel, whereas Reigate's Wayside is a long stay hostel. This means that the type of intervention work done with the women along with the end results are vastly different, as

far more can be done to rehabilitate someone over a sustained period of time rather than three months.

3. The type of homeless people who apply for residence differs between the areas, as has already been discussed. Both types of homelessness require a slightly different management style, and the women on the whole, require different degrees of intervention and help.
4. Access for interviewing residents was different, due mainly to both the type of clients using the hostel and the fact that one hostel was short stay and the other long stay.

It is worth noting that throughout this section quotes from the interview transcripts have been used. To protect the women's identity, they have only been identified by their interview number and the hostels area. As a further means of protecting the interviewee's identity any names of people or places have been removed, where this has happened this is indicated in the text by square brackets, which are also used to indicate added words to help clarity.

WHAT CAN BE COMPARED

First Impressions of the Hostel

All the residents interviewed commented on the fact that when they first arrived at a KeyChange hostel they were surprised at the friendly atmosphere:

- "The staff were so friendly, they tried to make me feel at ease".
- "I like the fact that everyone seems to get on. The atmosphere's relaxed and friendly, the first night I was here, I had a good night's sleep, that's a good sign of how comfortable I felt".
- "Its not too bad here, it feels a bit like having a family. There is a really homely feel here; they even eat meals together".

Most residents had an impression of what a hostel would be like before they moved in. These were often negative impressions based on past experiences of hostel living or assumptions based on peer group talk or the media.

Most residents were pleasantly surprised by KeyChange's standards, often commenting about cleanliness and the standards of hygiene:

- "I had an impression in my head about what a hostel would look like before I moved into Wayside, the hostel is a lot better than that".
- "I thought the hostel would be a nasty place, with a lot of bitchy girls there. But it's not, the girls are friendly, you can have a laugh and a joke and they share their fags. The staff are friendly too, it feels like one big family, but I've only been here two weeks"
- "I lived in another hostel once before, it was a hostel with children in it. I had to sleep on a sofa because there was no spare bed. The kitchen was a mess, it was never clean, unlike this kitchen. I left that hostel to doss down with friends, I usually doss with friends now instead of using hostels".

- "It's warm and clean here and you are allowed to use the washing machine and dryer. The staff are OK too.

Demand for Hostel Beds

From the statistics of the number of people offered a bed, and the number of people either referred to the hostels or contacting the hostels for a place to stay; it was clear that only half or less of the applicants were actually offered residential accommodation within the hostel.

For example:

- Between August and December 1998 Esther Community received 88 referrals for accommodation. 46 of these had to be referred on to other organisations because Esther Community was full.

The over-riding reason for this was the fact that the hostel was full at the time of application. This meant that there was almost always a waiting list of some form for both hostels. This demonstrates the high demand for hostel beds in both areas. KeyChange hostels are always in demand because of the high standard of cleanliness, hygiene and the friendly atmosphere.

Although urgent referrals and enquirers are referred on to other hostels in the area, this does not mean that there are bed spaces available:

- "I heard about KeyChange hostel through St Petrock's Centre. I had to wait three weeks to get in here. I came for a meal and asked if I could stay. There aren't any other hostels, except the YWCA, and that has a waiting list".
- "There needs to be a system so if you're single and have nowhere to live you could find somewhere to stay immediately. When the housing would not help, I was sent to HAG [Housing Action Group]. At HAG, you have to go through all the rigmarole of an interview before you get a safe place, but you have to wait four days for an interview. I have no survival skills. I've never been in this situation before".

Exeter

In Exeter, despite the fact that a second YMCA foyer-style hostel is planned, there is and will continue to be a shortage of bed-spaces for women aged 16-25 who have drink, drug or behavioural problems. There is also a severe shortage of bed-spaces for women over the age of 25. There are no bed-spaces for women over the age of 35. There are no facilities in the area for women who have been through a drink or drug rehabilitation programme, and who need somewhere to live on leaving that establishment.

Often these women cannot get alternative accommodation or are not ready to take on a tenancy and live independently in the wider community. Esther Community is likely to continue to be full to capacity for some time to come. There will also be a tendency for them to take women with drink, drug or behavioural problems, and those who are over the age of 25 as these are the women that are not accepted by other hostels in the area.

Reigate

In Reigate there is a shortage of every type of hostel bed at the moment. According to the Director of Community Services, Tom Crowley, permission has been given for a YMCA hostel to be built in Redhill to alleviate the high rate of youth homelessness in the area. The YMCA hostel will not be in a position to receive residents for at least another 18 months.

Thus, there will continue to be a high demand for bed-spaces at Wayside hostel in Reigate throughout that period. Once the YMCA hostel is built, there is every indication that Wayside will continue to be in high demand. There will still be no other facilities in the area for women struggling with drink, drug or behavioural problems and no facilities for women over the age of 25.

In addition, because Wayside is a small hostel, it is ideal for women who are particularly vulnerable and who would not cope or would be bullied in a larger hostel setting. Both hostels have problems with 'silting-up'.

'Silting-up' is a phrase used by commentators on homelessness to refer to the way hostels become full to capacity, with some bed-spaces blocked by residents who have to stay either beyond the hostel time limit and/or after they are ready to leave; because there is no other suitable accommo-dation to move on to.

Suitable accommodation may be, for example, a drug rehabilitation unit or permanent rented accommodation. At the time of the research, both hostels had people staying over their time limit because there was nowhere else for them to live.

There are several points that can be made here:

- The nature of the housing market in both areas means that there is a shortage of suitable, affordable housing in the area. In particular, the high demand and high rents in the private rented sector, means that women who are ready to move back into the community and mainstream society cannot help themselves. They are dependent on Housing Association and local authority allocations.
- There is a need for Housing Associations and the local authority in both areas to consider the number of dwellings they offer to homeless people.
- There is scope for KeyChange to expand their work in both areas.
  - In Reigate, there is work in progress to build an extension to the existing premises, thereby increasing the number of bedspaces, but this will make little impact on demand. There is every indication that there will be room for a second KeyChange hostel in addition to the YMCA hostel once it is built.

- In Exeter, there is room to expand the work in two directions:
  (a) A second stage hostel akin to Wayside that could work with women with long-term problems over a much broader time scale. Thereby allowing them time to be rehabilitated and to recover fully from homelessness and/or alcohol, drug, behavioural or mental health problems.
  (b) There is a need for a direct access night shelter style hostel for women who are not ready to leave the streets but periodically want a break from the streets. This hostel could feed people into the existing Esther Community hostel.

The Amount of Help Received

Practical Support

Residents commented on the fact that the staff were prepared to "go the extra mile" to help them sort things out, especially practical issues, like collecting belongings, sorting out DSS or housing benefit claims. The residents seemed surprised both at the level of practical help and the sensitive and caring way in which it was often carried out.

Even the residents who had lived at Wayside for a number of years, still commented on the level of practical support they received:

- "The staff are wonderful and helpful, they even leant me the bus fare for an important visit–I paid them back later when my giro came".
- "When I first moved in, Andy took me back to my old flat to collect some things. Most of the furniture was sold for drugs, but I managed to get some photographs. The landlord was closing the place down"
- "When there is a problem, Etta helps and she keeps on helping until the problem is sorted out. She just won't give up".
- "Etta is very understanding and caring, it's the extra little things that really count and mean a lot. At Christmas, I got a present and card, today it's my birthday, and she remembered it and bought me another present and card".

Keyworker Support

Both hostels use a keyworker system. This is much more overt at Esther Community, where regular sessions are actively pursued by keyworkers. The difference between the two approaches to keyworking is due to the difference in the length of stay at each hostel. Wayside has time to let residents settle in and work with residents over sustained period of time, at the resident's own pace.

Whereas Esther Community has to make an impact on the women's lives within three months, during this time they need to find out what the woman's needs are and help them to find the most appropriate form of accommodation to move on to. Most women did not talk about their keyworker, as this was their private space, where one-to-one advice and counsel is received. Those who commented liked their keyworker and found the sessions useful.

However, it is sometimes hard for the keyworker to arrange sessions as residents can forget about appointments, stay in bed or go off the premises to avoid meeting and keeping previously arranged appointments. It seems to be that when women are in crisis and in need of the most help, they have a tendency to either cancel or not arrive for the appointment. This makes it very hard to support them.

Keyworker sessions can be harrowing for the keyworker as they listen to residents pain, absorb their anger and frustration, try to support them through difficult times, depression or suicidal feelings. Meanwhile they still have to remain objective, guide individual women along the best paths to resolve their problems and empower the women to take control of their own lives.

This will never be an easy task. Many people when reaching difficult times in their lives prefer a quick fix solution, homeless women are no different. The keyworker has to work with their client to help them realise that there are often no quick answers to complicated problems, that often they will make mistakes and fail, but failure is part of life and part of recovery.

The research showed that some of the newer residents at Esther Community, did not realise that they could have keyworker support, that there was a time limit to their stay, and what type of help was available to them. The amount of information they had received seemed to depend on who had booked them into the hostel, and what time of day or night they had arrived.

The assistant hostel manager, explained that often residents were given a lot of information on induction, which was easily forgotten as there was so much to take in. To compensate for this, another meeting was usually held with the resident at the end of their first week, to go through some of the details again and to assign them to a suitable keyworker.

Support Workers from other Agencies

Both hostels liase with and use specialist support workers for women with specific problems.

The most commonly used by both hostels are the following:

- *Social Worker:* For residents either because of their age, mental health or disability, and if they have children.
- *CPN—Community Psychiatric Nurse*: For residents with mental health problems and in need of counselling and psychiatric support.
- *Probation Officer:* For residents who have been in prison or have been taken to court and placed on a probation order.
- *Drug or Alcohol Support Worker:* For alcoholic or drug addicted residents.

- *Sexual or Needle Transmitted Diseases Specialist:* For residents in need of support for diseases like Hepatitis, Aids and other illnesses or diseases associated with drugs. They monitor the illness/disease, give health advice and in some cases counsel clients.

A by-product of using other agencies and support workers is that the number of keyworkers assigned to individuals rises and this can cause confusion. Each keyworker discusses the woman's life history and the problems they are going through at that time and the type of help that is needed.

- "I've a keyworker with counselling as well as here [Esther Community]. I'll have three key workers eventually. I like my keyworker here."

Residents wanting to find work or who were house hunting found that multiple keyworker sessions ate into their spare time. Those with compulsory sessions, sometimes resented these, viewing them as an invasions of privacy, or as "bureaucratic red-tape that gets you nowhere". There is a need within both hostels to keep formal records of the number of keyworkers and professionals assigned to each individual and the nature of the support they offer. This would not only allow KeyChange to fill in any gaps in provision, but also to support the women in seeking help and talking through issues with the most qualified person to help.

After Care

- Neither hostel has any formal aftercare set up for residents after they leave the hostel. However, residents do know that if they want to stay in touch, need a chat or advice they can contact hostel staff or visit the hostel after they have left.
- Four out of the ten residents interviewed felt that they may need support after they left the hostel. Of those that would have preferred follow-on support, two were anxious about their ability to cope on their own if they had a "big problem" with anything from bills and DSS forms to ill health.
- Other organisations or officials, *e.g.* social workers, probation officers, housing association keyworkers do carry out a lot of aftercare with residents. However, there does not appear to be any formal agreements between the hostel and these organisations regarding the nature and extent of aftercare, or even any guarantees that aftercare is available. There is a need for KeyChange hostels to formalise aftercare arrangements, making proper agreements with providers with regard to the extent and nature of the support being offered. It may be necessary for KeyChange to consider filling any gaps in provision to help homeless people back into mainstream society.

After care is an important issue in the long-term success of the resettlement of homeless people. Recent research has shown that homeless people who are resettled into the community need follow-up support for a minimum of 6-12 months, which is 2-3 times that recommended by the Rough Sleepers Initiative. Too many keyworkers can cause confusion, and lead to inadequate and fragmented support.

Most resettled people trust their hostel keyworker or hostel staff more than any other keyworker or professional. This is mainly because the hostel keyworker has been there through some of the most difficult transitions in their life, they have not let them down or rejected them and thus earned their trust. Especially in the smaller hostels, staff are viewed as good friends rather than workers.

In the case of Wayside in Reigate, the hostel manager is often viewed more as a mother figure than a hostel manager. This level of after support is not easy to maintain as it is time consuming and exists over and above hostel staffs regular duties. Although Esther Community in Exeter is a short-stay hostel, some women do move directly into accommodation.

The longer a person has been homeless, especially if this has included street homelessness, the more long-term sustained support they are likely to need if they are to remain housed and cope with a tenancy and all the responsibilities that go with that tenancy.

This suggests that despite the fact that Esther Community "is not designed to be a therapeutic hostel", some consider-ation as to after care ought to be given to those women moving into their own accommodation directly from the hostel. After Care for Wayside residents, on the whole, does not need to be as intensive as the type of after care needed for long term rough sleepers.

The three year maximum stay means that most women do not leave the hostel until they are capable of coping. However, they still remain vulnerable to homelessness, loneliness and the fears of living alone. The relationship that Wayside residents have with the hostel and hostel staff is far more intense than that at Esther community, by virtue of the length of stay.

Thus links with the hostel and hostel staff become very important. At Wayside, there have been attempts made to keep in contact with women once they have left the hostel, this is predominantly carried out on an informal basis, *i.e.* they telephone Etta, the hostel manager, to update her on their progress.

Etta also organised regular, shared meals on Monday evenings at the hostel for ex-residents to come back and visit. This has been met with varying degrees of success, often no one actually turns up. More formal after care is needed, some of this is absorbed by other professionals, but on the whole it is difficult to offer such help with existing staff levels and time commitments.

Benefits and Income in General

Money is always a contentious issue and this is no different with homeless people. Common myths are that they either have no money and that is why they are destitute or that they have lots of money and get a good income from begging, but drink all their money or spend it on drugs.

The truth lies somewhere between these two extremes. Homeless people over the age of 18 have access to DSS benefits whilst on the streets. Once in a hostel they can claim housing benefit and Income support or Job Seekers Allowance. Although they have an income, this does not mean that it is easy to make ends meet, the need to 'eat out' most of the time is a big drain on finances, without the added burden of cigarette, drink or drug addiction.

For the women interviewed at both Wayside and Esther Community, money was at issue on several fronts:

- Why should we have to pay rent for a hostel room?
- Why should we have to pay for food?
- It is difficult to survive on a benefits cheque.

Why should we have to Pay Rent for a Hostel Room

Women questioning why they should have to pay rent for a hostel room, were predominantly found at Esther Community. None of the women interviewed commented, but the women who chatted to me in the kitchen or TV lounge during the observation times, commented on the fact that they had to pay rent for their room.

They argued that as they were homeless, housing benefit ought to cover the whole cost of rent. This attitude was confirmed by staff, who noted that a minority of women simply did not pay their rent, and after being warned several times had to be evicted. Other women also managed to play the system very well, they knew the upper limit of arrears permitted before eviction so always paid enough money to keep themselves from being evicted, but never fully cleared their debts and often left still owing money.

Although at first sight it may seem harsh that women are evicted for not paying rent, which means there is a strong chance of them having to sleep on the streets or in squats, it is still a necessary part of resettlement. Women who truly want to leave homelessness behind them need to start taking responsibility for themselves and their actions.

They know before accepting a place in a hostel that they have to register for housing benefit and contribute towards their rent, still there are some who push the rules to see how much they can get away with. There are others who either have such chronic drink or drug problems that they would rather run the risk of having to sleep rough than pay £10 per week rent.

Some women just want a room for a while so they can get a few good nights sleep, hot baths and clean clothes or escape some of the coldest nights. They are happy to be evicted and see no reason why they should waste money on rent. Here again, there is an argument for having a night shelter type hostel arrangement for these women.

A place where women who need somewhere to stay, but are not ready for rehabilitation and assessment, can stay on a first come first served, ad hoc basis until they are ready to commit to rehabilitation.

Why should we have to Pay for Food

Comments were made by interviewees at both hostels with regard to paying for food, although this was for very different reasons.

Esther Community

On my first visit to Esther Community in November, many women complained that they had to pay a contribution of £20 per week towards their food. They argued that they would never normally spend that much money on food and that they could provide for themselves more economically. The hostel manager had already taken action on this matter and after that month meals were no longer to be provided.

Cheap meals could be bought at the homeless drop-in day centre at St Petrock's, or women could buy in and prepare their own food. At my next visit, most women seemed happy with this arrangement, but some newer residents felt that they should still be able to get some food items free at the hostel. One interviewee objected to having to use St Petrock's day centre for food, feeling that she did not want to mix with the "sort of people that use St Petrock's".

Another interviewee was happy to use St Petrock's for food and a warm dry place to meet up with street friends and make new friends in the area.

- "I go off down St Petrock's on a morning and stay there all day. I get food there its only 25p a meal, extra if you want pudding. It's a good place to go, I am meeting up with some of the friends that I made, the men all look out for me, they look after me. You can have a good laugh, depending on who's there".

Two residents thought that food really ought to be free and local shops, churches or businesses should provide it:

1. "...now we are going to have to buy our own food as well, so that will make it even more expensive. It's a shame that the hostel cannot get food donated to make it cheaper"
2. "They ought to have food given for free, they should ask the shops and businesses to give them food and the churches".

Wayside

Wayside residents took a slightly different angle when talking about paying for food.

Two of the residents in the group interview discussed the way they went without food if they wanted to buy something in particular.

1. "I don't have a lot of money. Sometimes I starve myself so that I can

buy something that I want. Don't get me wrong, I don't starve myself for luxuries, I starve myself for things like a dress that I want. If I starve myself for a couple of weeks, then I can save enough money for what I want".

2. "They reckon that you can live on £18 a week but you've £10 rent to pay before you buy any food or toiletries...I have to starve myself sometimes too. It's not for luxuries either, its stuff that you need. You know deodorant, shampoo, that sort of stuff."

Although both girls referred to starving themselves, it is most likely that this was an exaggeration. However, there is every reason to believe that they did cut down considerably on the amount and quality of food they bought, to save money. This demonstrates the problems experienced with the level of income from state benefits, especially for 16-25 year olds especially those under 18.

It is Ddifficult to Survive on a Benefits Cheque

The level of benefits is a contentious issue for both the homeless and people living in poverty, there is no doubt that it is difficult to make ends meet when on benefits for a sustained period of time.

Thus interviewees had plenty to say about benefit levels:

- "The future's not going to be easy. I'm going to need a deposit for a flat and I'll need to get badged up for the Big Issue, if I'm going to be able to afford to keep me and my kids. You can't live on the social".
- "It's not my fault that I'm short of money, I've got a job, but you don't get that much, it goes in tax and then rent. It's no wonder some people start stealing. They don't steal to make money, they steal because they haven't got enough money"
- "The professionals should try it, they should live like this, before they work in those kinds of jobs, then they would understand what it is like and how hard it is. Instead professionals just talk down to you, they think you should just get a job, but getting a job is easier said than done."

More importantly, there are often delays with benefit offices sorting out peoples claims, so women have to wait some time before getting any money. This can cause acute stress and anxiety as they worry about paying for food etc. Benefits can also be cut or stopped without warning, if someone spends anytime in hospital or a rehabilitation centre. The women often do not know that this will happen or do not understand why it has happened.

Once they have left the hospital or rehab centre, it takes time for their claim to be reassessed and their full entitlement reinstated. This often involves more form filling and interviews, all of which is time consuming and adds to the stress levels of already vulnerable women.

The long delays in processing housing benefit is one of the main reasons for private landlords disinterest in taking on homeless tenants or people on income support, in both Reigate and Exeter. This effectively excludes them from the rented housing market, which is already over burdened.

Hostels also experience funding problems as a result of delays in housing benefit claims, especially short stay hostels like Esther Community. Delays in payments of housing benefit to cover the cost of hostel rooms can deprive them of much needed cash. Similarly, if claims take up to three months to be assessed, accepted and paid, residents can leave during that space of time, making it more difficult for the hostel to claim the full amount of rent that they are due.

THE HOUSING SITUATION IN BOTH AREAS

Residents at both Wayside and Esther Community were shocked to find that they were advised to take Bed and Breakfast accommodation or directed to hostels. However, without money, these were inaccessible.

Even with money, there was no guarantee that a hostel would have vacancies:

- "I'm 23 and I've no kids, I think the council expected me to go away and have a kid so that I could get emergency housing. I went to the council the day I had to leave my fiancé's house. I sat there all day, trying to get a room and then trying to get a crisis loan for Bed and Breakfast. At the end of the day I was thrown out of the offices with no help and I had to stay the night in a squat. I can tell you that was a big shock".
- "Social Services don't give you much help. When I became homeless, I went to Social Services and reported myself as homeless they told me they couldn't pick me up. I was told the nearest places for me to go to for help were Guildford or Leatherhead, but I'd no money for the train fare so that wasn't a great deal of help. When I got into Wayside I found out Social Services did have a duty to pick me up and do something. I feel cheated...they lied to me and because I didn't know any different they got away with it".

These examples are common occurrences, a significant number of people have slept rough or in squats, because they did not receive adequate help from local authority departments. It would appear that some local authorities regularly breach or bend the law laid out in the Housing Act 1996 and Children Act 1989.

They either refuse to house people who clearly meet the legislation criteria, or they exercise their duty to offer advice and assistance, but offer advice that is rendered useless, because housing and DSS departments do not work together. For example, advising some one to take Bed and Breakfast accommodation or travel to the nearest town or city for a hostel place without dealing with the fact that they have no money is of no help or assistance.

This places hostels and charities working with the homeless in an awkward position, as amongst other skills required, they are now increasingly in need of a good knowledge of the law and access to legal services to enforce the law on behalf of their clients. These are not services currently offered by Wayside or Esther Community.

Residents ready to leave the hostels and move into rented accommodation also find great difficulty gaining access to accommodation in the private rented sector:

- "It doesn't matter how many times you try ringing landlords that advertise their flats in the papers, landlords in the private rented [sector] will not rent to people on housing benefit"
- "In the [private] rented [sector], no one takes people on housing benefits. When you ring up and tell them that you are on benefits they tell you that they don't rent to people on the DSS".

Several of the interviewees were also frustrated with the way that housing waiting lists appeared to work. They felt that they were often being bypassed in favour of people who they felt did not need accommodation as much as they did.

- "It's unfair to everyone when you have to wait on the waiting list, only to find that someone else can jump the cue and get moved into accommodation before you".
- "What's really needed is more help for people of my age. Students get help, so do those on probation. You've got to break the law to get a flat–the system stinks".

There was also a strong recognition amongst the women that if they had children, they would be able to find accommodation much more easily and quickly.

- "The housing system is unfair, some people on the waiting list are not desperate for somewhere to live, but they get housed. I'm desperate for somewhere to live and can't get housed; I have to live in a hostel. The length of the council waiting list is disgusting; you can get a flat if you have a baby".
- "I still need help finding somewhere to live. I'm on the council waiting list, but they say I've to wait three years before I can be housed. Because I've been sensible and not had a baby, I can't get a flat, I'm being penalised for being good."

WHAT DO THE RESIDENTS HAVE IN COMMON

Last Place of Residence

It is interesting to look at where each interviewee last lived before they became homeless. There is every indication to suggest that these ten people are representative of the rest of their respective hostel residents.

Table. The Last Place of Residence

ID No.	Age	Hostel	Last Place of Residence	Ever Slept Rough?
Int.02	16	Wayside	Boyfriend's home	No
Int.03	18	Wayside	Foster care then a hostel	No
Int.05	19	Wayside	Boyfriend's house then an auntie	No
Int.01	34	Wayside	Fiancé's house	No
Int.04	36	Wayside	Lived with her partner	No
Int.10	18	Esther Community	Father's home them mothers house	No
Int.07	20	Esther Community	Boyfriend's house, then slept rough in the bus station	Yes
Int.06	23	Esther Community	With fiancé, then in a squat	Yes
Int.09	27	Esther Community	In boyfriend's house, then slept rough	Yes
Int.08	28	Esther Community	Lived with partner, then slept Rough	Yes

Table shows a marked divide between Wayside and Esther Community hostels in terms of the number of residents who have slept rough. This demonstrates the different types of homelessness in each area and the different types of people the hostels are dealing with.

With regard to the last place of residence, eight out of the ten women last lived with a boyfriend or partner, often the property they lived in belonged to the man, so that once the relationship broke down the woman became homeless.

- "I left my parent's home to move in with my new boyfriend, he's older than I am. But once I moved in I found that we did not get on very well, I stayed there for a little while but things got worse and worse. I left of my own accord. I had no relationship with my mum so I could not ask for help, so I was on my own".
- "I've been homeless now on and off for a year, this is the latest episode. This time I became homeless when I left my boyfriend. He'd a drink problem and was heavy into debt. He did cruel things like water down my methadone. I tried leaving him several times, but he kept wanting me back. I felt trapped because the flat was in his name, he kept reminding me of that. He kept saying he could throw me out whenever he wanted to.

Victims of Domestic Violence

Domestic violence featured strongly among the inter-viewees as one of the main contributory factors that lead to them becoming homeless. In some cases, it was a direct cause of their homelessness.

Table. Victims of Domestic Violence

ID No.	Age	Hostel	Victim of Domestic Violence?
Int.02	16	Wayside	No
Int.03	18	Wayside	No
Int.05	19	Wayside	Yes
Int.01	34	Wayside	Yes
Int.04	36	Wayside	Yes
Int.10	18	Esther Community	No
Int.07	20	Esther Community	Yes
Int.06	23	Esther Community	Yes
Int.09	27	Esther Community	Yes
Int.08	28	Esther Community	Yes

Table shows that seven out of the ten women interviewed had experienced domestic violence at some point in their lives.

- "I became homeless through domestic violence. I kept calling the police but they would come round and then leave me without any help. Eventually I ran away to a hostel in [area she used to live in]. Etta was the hostel manager there, I moved to Reigate when Etta took over the hostel here".
- "I used to live with my fiancé in [area she used to live in], he was violent towards me, he's hit me several times in the past. When I mean violent, I mean being kicked and punched, thrown across the room and things like that. One time he pushed me so hard that I hurt my back quite badly".
- "I had a bad relationship, I lived with a man who battered me. I left him and tried to hide from him, but he kept finding me. So I left [the area she used to live in] and moved to Exeter because I thought I had friends here, but I ended up sleeping in a bus station".
- "I was engaged and working, my life seemed normal. My relationship with my fiancé ended violently, when he drank he became very violent. I moved out to get away from him, I stayed with friends to hide from him. I ended up in a squat living with people I knew from the streets".

Many women find it difficult to break free of these kinds of relationships, it can take several attempts. Once free, many women find themselves attracted to similar men and so break free from one violent relationship only to enter another and another.

- "I'll tell you why women become homeless, its because of violent men. They live with men that become violent and then they have to leave, but they've no where to go so they end up on the streets.

Take me I had four good men but the relationships were trashed because of drink. Drink turns the man bad, he goes violent. One of my ex's got done for dealing, another for burgling, they were all bad."

Often leaving a violent partner in a hurry results in a woman loosing all or most of her possessions. This not only means that she has to replace these, but this can affect her sense of self-identity and selfworth as well. Women have to start again from scratch and rebuild their wardrobe, possessions, etc.

- "In [name of town] I lived with a man for a while, but he was violent–in the end I had to leave. But when I left, I left all my clothes behind and couldn't go back for them. This meant that I had to start all over again."

In the autumn of 1999, new rules for housing benefit are due to take effect, these will affect homeless women and women fleeing from violent relationships, as well as the hostels they apply to. In future, they will need their National Insurance number to be able to apply for housing benefits, women who leave home in a hurry are most likely to have no proof of identity and no National Insurance number. This may increase their vulnerability to street homelessness.

Family Breakdown

Family breakdown is a term used to describe the breakdown of relationships between the parent and child, rather than divorce or separation. For interviewees at both hostels, a breakdown in the relationship between their parents and themselves contributed to their initial homelessness.

There was some evidence that, in some cases, this had contributed to repeated episodes of homelessness. Table shows that seven out of ten interviewees discussed the breakdown in their family relationships and associated that with, either the cause of their homelessness, or as a factor that exacerbated their homelessness.

Table. Evidence of Family Breakdown

ID No.	Age	Hostel	Family Breakdown?
Int.02	16	Wayside	Yes
Int.03	18	Wayside	Yes
Int.05	19	Wayside	Yes
Int.01	34	Wayside	No
Int.04	36	Wayside	No
Int.10	18	Esther Community	Yes
Int.07	20	Esther Community	No
Int.06	23	Esther Community	Yes
Int.09	27	Esther Community	Yes
Int.08	28	Esther Community	Yes

Once homeless, or on the brink of homelessness, these women felt that they could not contact their parents for help.

This was not simply because they were ashamed of what had become of them, but because they felt that there was:

- Breakdown in communication;
- Abuse or abusive behaviour during childhood;
- A lack of interest in them or in bridging the gap on the parents part.

All two factors made it either impossible for the women to re-establish contact, or made them reluctant to make contact:

- "I don't want to talk about my family background, it upsets me too much. All I can say is I had problems with my mum, she went on too much and was very strict, she pushed me about a bit. As a kid I was always threatening to leave home, but she told me there was no point because the police would bring me back. She kicked me out when I was 16, then rang the police for them to fetch me back... my sister told me that the police couldn't do anything now I was 16. So I was free to go, to stay away for good. That's when I started dossing down on friends floors".
- "My dad is a very violent man, he often booted me around the house. I haven't spoken to him since I left home.

Some of the women interviewed moved in with their boyfriend because they were not happy at home. When this relationship broke down, or when the boyfriend became violent they became homeless, because often there was no one else to turn to for help.

- "Her mum died when she was only 8 years old. Soon after her dad got a new partner and she fell apart. She met an older man and lived with him for four and a half years. She used to be beaten regularly. She became depressed and began drinking. When she came to Wayside she had a serious drink problem, and was in such a state that she took four overdoses"–
- "There was no one that I could turn to, to prevent me from becoming homeless. I had no relationship with my mum, so I couldn't ask her for help, I was on my own. Other than winning the lottery nothing could've stopped me from becoming homeless".

People who have been in care at some point in their lives are far more vulnerable to becoming homeless and, in particular, becoming rough sleepers, than the rest of the general population. One of the women interviewed, who had been in care for most of her life, spoke about the lack of support and help they received from their social services departments, and the lack of facilities that had meant that they had to move from foster care into hostels.

- "At the end of the day Social Services is basically cruel, they don't support you or help you. You go to the council for help and they send you back to Social Services. Social Services send you back to the council... I lived with foster parents just before I became homeless, but the relationship with them broke down. I've lived with 6 foster parents, none of the placements lasted. I didn't get a choice about where I came to this time. I was simply sent to Wayside whether I liked it or not".

A woman at Esther Community, who did not want to be interviewed, but wanted it 'on record'; told me she had been in care, and that

- "If you want to know why I am homeless you should ask Exeter social services because they put me here, and they know all about how it feels to have been in care and have no one to turn to".

People are in care because the relationship between them and their parents has broken down, for whatever reason. Often they have no recourse, no opportunity to mend bridges and return to their family. Social services are legally their parent until they are aged 18, and have a duty to offer assistance and advice until they are aged 21.

However, if a young person drops out of a foster care placement, or has to leave home between the ages of 16 and 18, they are often found hostel places not foster placements. In addition, young people under the age of 18 are not legally able to hold a tenancy agreement, so they cannot gain access to accommodation.

Even when accommodation is found and offered, under the age of 25 they can only draw reduced housing benefit and income support, this means that even the lowest priced accommodation is often too expensive.

- "I am on the job seekers at the moment, they are helping me. I have to work to get benefit. My age is against me, I can't get proper money because of my age and I can't get enough housing benefit because of my age. I think this is unfair. I worked it out, the number of hours I work and the amount of job seekers I get, it means I am earning 50p an hour. Talk about minimum wage, no one should be expected to work for that, it is slave labour".

Young people who find themselves homeless after relationships with their parents breakdown or who have been in care, are vulnerable financially to becoming homeless. They are excluded from attempting to take responsibility for themselves and live independently by a benefit system that expects their housing, food and clothing costs to be cheaper than those for adults over 25.

There are occasions when a case for some form of family mediation can be made. It would be dangerous for some young people to return home, for others it is the breakdown in communication between child and parent that needs resolving. This can still be very traumatic for all concerned.

However, after listening to the young person carefully and establishing that home is a safe place and that there is no abuse happening there, family mediation could be offered to some people. This would be time consuming, and the young woman may need to live in a place of safety while family problems are being sorted out. A family mediator could either be employed by KeyChange, or alternatively there may be adequate facilities already in the area that could be utilised. The following is an example of why this could be an alternative to a hostel place, and in this particular case, being offered any bed. The young woman speaking in the quote below said she was 18. She arrived at Esther Community the evening before this interview took place. She only stayed at the hostel approximately two weeks before being found a place in the local YMCA hostel.

- "I did not get on with my dad, he always said I was rubbish at things. We had a row and I left home and stayed with a friend for a few days, but they said I could not stay there indefinitely. I had to leave [the area she used to live in] and come to Exeter because my mum was here. I can't get a place in [the area she used to live in] because my dad has to write a letter saying he kicked me out. He won't do that because he hasn't kicked me out, he loves me and he wants me to come home so that we can try again. But I can't go back now, not once I have made the break. So the only thing to do was to move away and declare myself homeless. What I really wanted was a place in the YMCA but they were full so my mum got me in here"

From the interview, it was possible to ascertain that there had been no abuse, she loved her dad and he loved her and wanted her back. They had been having a few arguments over who should help with the housework and the fact that her little sister was annoying her, after one row she walked out.

The father's occupation, as well as her appearance, leisure pursuits and vocabulary all suggested that she was from a middle class family. She did not use drugs and only drank socially. To a certain extent, she was quite naive about street culture, and the drug scene. Having arrived at her mothers' house, her mother allowed her to stay there until she could find her a hostel place.

Thus she moved from her fathers home, to her mothers home and then into a hostel, that she shared with women some of whom had been smack addicts for years. Others were on Methadone and trying to come off drugs. One of the women interviewed, had a boyfriend who is a drug dealer and she visited him daily.

Another had been a drug dealer in the past. There were also women with serious drink problems and psychological problems living there. Most of the other women that I chatted to in the evenings or in the kitchen as part of the participant observations had spent some time on the streets and/or had smaller drink or drug problems.

If a YMCA hostel place had not come up so quickly, this young girl could have been in danger of learning new life skills that would take a lifetime to overcome. There are two points to make here; firstly, this is clearly a situation where communi-cation had broken down within the family. Ideally, attempts at reconciliation between father and daughter ought to have been made in the first place. No accommodation would have been necessary, and could have remained so until more appropriate accommo-dation could be found. Secondly, KeyChange, need to seriously think about exactly who they are trying to help in each hostel and whether some people would be in more danger in the hostel than, for example, sleeping on a parent's floor.

The YMCA in Exeter has very good facilities and are well equipped and better suited to deal with homeless young people who do not have any current drink or drug problems. However, they do have a waiting list of up to three months. The girl and her mother knew that she could move up the queue for the YMCA if she managed to get into Esther Community.

Children

In both hostels, there are a number of women who have children. Many of these women are in contact with social services and fighting not only to find accommodation but also to be allowed to have their children back. Often, the women have supervised access visits with their children, as Social Services try to keep the family together while the woman gets her own problems sorted out.

Staff at both hostels have to deal with the roller-coaster of emotions that these women go through. This is both in relation to access visits with their children and as they go through the various social work and legal channels. Esther Community and Wayside differ in the type of women they receive and therefore problems relating specifically to women and their children are slightly different.

Wayside

Wayside often deals with Asian women, some of whom belong to a culture where their partner and in-laws take custody of the child, while the mother is thrown out or has to flee and seek alternative accommodation.

Although social workers and legal experts deal with custody claims, Wayside staff have to help such women both practically and emotionally, to deal with the loss of their home, relationship and children in the first instance, and then to support them as they piece their life back together and fight for their children.

Esther Community

The Esther Community takes in far more women with serious alcohol and drug related problems than Wayside, some of these women do have children. For obvious reasons, when the mother is found to have a drink or drug problem, the children are taken into care, the drink or drug problem is often the cause or a strong contributory factor in them becoming homeless.

Overcoming their addiction is often one of the prerequisites for getting their children back. These women often still have supervised visits with their children. They suffer the same grief and pain that any other woman would when they are separated from their children.

These visits can cause anger and severe distress:

- I saw my kids and their foster mother, the youngest, my little boy, hardly recognised me. My kids are not supposed to be in care, they were just supposed to be in care for two weeks while I went through detox and got my head together. I wanted me and [partners name] to go into detox together with the kids as a family, but Social Services said no. While I was in there the DSS didn't pay my rent, I was in so much arrears when I came out that we got thrown out of the place. Now me and [partners name] are both homeless and they won't let me have my kids back. Now they are talking about having them adopted. I love my kids".

This dialogue was shouted at the on-duty evening staff member while I was observing. Hostel staff regularly have to contain and defuse this kind of anger and distress safely, by listening to outbursts and talking calmly through issues.

The woman's loss of her children can cause a number of reactions, it can spur her into recovering from her addiction and regaining control of her life, or it can make her withdrawn and depressed and cause her to give up on life. Some women attempt to recover from drink or drug problems for their children's sake rather than their own.

The following example is of a woman battling with a serious heroine addiction:

- "They say plan A is not working, plan A's for me to go into [name of drug rehabilitation centre] and get sorted out. I said I'd do it, but they can't get me a place.
- I was supposed to go before Christmas, then after Christmas, then sometime last month but they can't get me a place. Now they say we have to go on to plan B and my kids will be adopted, if they're adopted they're gone forever.
- I tell you, if [partners name] finds out, he will check himself out of 'dry-out' [alcoholic rehabilitation centre] and kill himself. If my kids go into adoption there is no way I am coming off smack, that's all I'll have left and I'll need it then to go on living.
- If they get adopted, I will be out of here and I don't care where I go".

KeyChange have a difficult task in situations like these, they offer such women a place to stay and through specialist help from outside agencies; motivate, encourage and work with women to overcome their drink/drug problems. They also sort out other personal and emotional problems and support the women to comply with social services wishes.

In cases of acute alcohol or drug problems, women are found places at specialist rehabilitation centres, where women can safely 'detox'. However, there is often a three month waiting list or more for residential facilities in areas outside London, making it very difficult for women needing help straight away to keep motivated to change.

RESEARCH FINDINGS FROM ESTHER COMMUNITY HOSTEL–EXETER

The interviews and observations conducted at Esther Community were far more qualitative than those at Wayside and therefore have much richer detail that have generated more findings.

FIRST EPISODE OF HOMELESSNESS

It is significant that all the interviewees at Esther Community first became homeless whilst in their teens. For the youngest two interviewees, this was their first episode of homelessness. This is a critical point for their future, in terms of what happens to them next, as the right help now could prevent them from becoming repeatedly homeless in the future.

Interviewee.06 is slightly different, she began the interview by claiming that she had never been homeless before, but later in the interview went on to describe a period when she was in a different hostel and went through a three stage programme of resettlement.

This may have been part of a drug rehabilitation programme, but either way the programme ended with the provision of housing. They are so accustomed to surviving on the streets, that it is often easier and cheaper for them to return to the streets for a while, in the sure knowledge that when they are ready they will find a place in a hostel and then find somewhere to live. They are no longer afraid of sleeping rough and soon make friends on the streets.

This makes it difficult to find a resettlement programme that will have a lasting affect. Both women have drug problems, both stay off heroine and cocaine for a while but then go back onto drugs and repeat the cycle of drugs, debts and homelessness. Esther Community is not in a position at present to help these women long term. It can only act as a holding place, giving them a secure safe place to stay until they can be found an appropriate rehabilitation programme or long stay hostel place.

The age of the resident's first episode of homelessness has two main implications for Esther Community's work:

1. There is a need to ensure teenagers find a swift long-term solution to their homelessness, which not only provides them with accommodation; but also equips them with the necessary life skills to maintain a settled life.
2. Teenagers are encouraged to develop friendship networks with people

in the housed population in the area they are going to live in–as opposed to making friends with mainly homeless or exhomeless people. In this way, the amount of street culture that they absorb will be reduced, they will feel that they fit into and belong in mainstream society.

Currently, the YMCA has the best youth programme for resettlement, so liaison with them or hostel transfers to the YMCA is probably the best action. Esther Community already works closely with the YMCA, so this needs to be continued and encouraged.

In addition, residents who have had recurring phases of homelessness throughout their life; need long-term resettle-ment programmes, that incorporate not only life-skill training, but counselling and a realistic after care support programme, that supports them as they integrate back into the community. The provisional plans for a second longer stay hostel for Exeter would be the ideal vehicle to help such women and could incorporate such facilities. At present, there are no facilities for women who need intensive longer term help in Exeter. There is another aspect to resettlement that needs addressing, although this is not easy.

Many homeless people see the answer to their drink, drug and homeless problems as finding a partner or being in a relationship. This is part of their search for love and understanding, and in some senses, is no different from the yearnings of the housed population. However, as has already been shown, many women enter violent and abusive relationships, many women become homeless after leaving the partner's home.

- "I met a guy yesterday, he took me back to his place for sex and wants me to meet him again today. Life must be more than sex though, mustn't it? I want to see him again, but I need to get my head straight. I want to see him, but I don't want to get to know him and I don't particularly want him to know me, it would just be for sex. But it never works out like that. Anyway, sex is not all that it is cracked up to be. What is sex anyway? "

The women interviewed at Esther Community would still leave any accommodation provided for them to move in with a man. This leaves them vulnerable to becoming homeless if things do not work out. Women on the streets are also in danger of being encouraged/dragged into prostitution. One interviewee had become a stripper and then a maid in a sauna where she took bookings for prostitutes in order to get a place to live. The only reason that she did not become a prostitute herself was because by this time she had Hepatitis C.

The Experience of Sleeping Rough

Most of the women at Esther Community had slept rough at some point, even if that was only for one or two nights. Table Shows that four out of the five residents interviewed had slept rough at some stage in their life.

Table. Residents that Slept Rough at Some Stage in their Lives

ID No.	Age	Hostel	Ever Slept Rough?
Int.10	18	Esther Community	No
Int.07	20	Esther Community	Yes
Int.06	23	Esther Community	Yes
Int.09	27	Esther Community	Yes
Int.08	28	Esther Community	Yes

This way of life is not an easy option even though some women repeatedly returned to the streets to live. They simply became used to this way of life, regardless of how hard, cold or dangerous that was. One woman had been raped three times when living on the streets, but no longer had any fear of sleeping rough. She treated it almost as an 'occupational hazard'.

In some senses, this was indicative of the way she felt about and viewed herself. In her understanding, the worst thing had happened to her and she had survived, nothing would ever be that bad again.

After the first period of homelessness, those women who repeatedly become homeless know what to expect, how to cope and how to get by, they also know that they can make good friends on the streets, which makes the hardships tolerable. In street culture there is a strange inverted logic where they see a street homeless person that becomes housed actually being weak.

Being housed becomes the sign that they can not handle the street life:

- "I enjoyed living with them because they were friendly and you could have a lot of friends. You could move round the country and were always welcome on a traveller's site, even if you had not known them before. It can be dangerous too, I remember [name] beating the...out of someone with a shovel for breaking an ambulance window [they slept in an old ambulance at the time]. Site politics I suppose."

Some of the residents tried to explain what it is like to sleep rough, what can happen and how it made them feel:

- "I ran away from [boyfriend's name] but [friend's name] would not let me in so I had to sleep rough that night. I remember waking up with my hair and hand frozen on the pavement. It hurt a lot. Can you imagine that?
- [*The following is a different episode of homelessness for the same interviewee*] I left [boyfriend's name] and just got on the bus from [name of area] to Exeter. Our friend [friend's name] attacked us with an axe and smashed the flat up, so I had to get away. I was raped the day after I arrived in Exeter in a graveyard. It was another tramp; he would not leave me alone. He was very violent and threatened me with a dog chain and scissors."

- "...That's when everything started. I started dossing down at friend's places, sleeping on floors, settees, bed-bases, even in bathrooms–but never in a proper bed. Living like that does not make you feel good about yourself, you feel dirty and horrible. It's not good for your health either. I've slept rough all over the place, on the street, in train stations, sheds, derelict buildings."
- "So I left [the area she used to live in] and moved to Exeter because I thought I had friends here, but I ended up sleeping in a bus station. I met a man there who knew a girl in here, he asked if there was a place. There was and I'm glad because I was really frightened on the streets".

In addition to the dangers of sleeping rough, there are problems of personal hygiene and where to get food. Some areas have good drop-in day centre facilities like St Petrock's in Exeter, where cheap food can be obtained. However, in other areas rough sleepers have to be creative, they have to beg for money or food, steal it or look in dustbins.

- "When I was on the streets in [name of city] we looked through the bins and skips at the back of shops, restaurants and hotels. But then they used to put bleach on the food they threw out in skips to stop homeless people from taking it. They prefer homeless people to die in [name of city] than to feed them."

Drink or Drug Addiction

- A number of residents at Esther Community did have drink and/or drug problems, of the five interviewees three had drug problems and two had serious alcohol problems.

Table. Residents with Drink or Drug Addiction

ID No.	Age	Hostel	Drink Problem	Drug Addict
Int.10	18	Esther Community	No	No
Int.07	20	Esther Community	No	No
Int.06	23	Esther Community	No	Yes
Int.09	27	Esther Community	Yes	Yes
Int.08	28	Esther Community	Yes	Yes

Alcohol

- Many people who sleep rough have serious drink problems, those who do not have a drink problem when they begin to sleep rough usually develop one soon after. The first stage is caused by social factors and boredom. This is followed by drink becoming a useful way of getting to sleep especially when it is cold. After a period, drinking until you pass out on a regular basis, soon develops into an addiction.

- "When you're on the streets you drink yourself into a stupor just to get to sleep–especially if you're on your own. When you're on your own it's very scary. Most alcoholics have a bad record for violence to women, there are a lot of alcoholics on the streets because their wife kicked them out because they're violent."

Alcoholics often take time out periodically to get their drinking more under control. Thus they often enter rehabilitation programmes but to curb the strength of the addiction, rather than to give up drinking forever. Similarly hostels, especially the hostels where they can stay on the premises all day if they choose are a good place to go when they want to slow down on drinking and get it under more control.

- "In the next three months [while at Esther Community] I'm hoping to clear my head a bit and stop panicking. I want to get some peace. When I'm stronger I'll be able to do more things. I want to get my determination back...I've slowed down on the booze. The good thing about that is that I actually got a bit of money now, so I can buy clothes and things. I bought some clothes the other day, it made me feel good".

Drugs

Drug addiction is a major cause of homelessness; two of the interviewees became involved with hard core drugs in their late teens. They have entered the cycle of drug addiction, methadone substitute, back on drugs etc.

When addicted, the acquisition of drugs becomes the sole aim, nothing else matters and rational decision making ceases, the drug addict will do anything for their next fix. It is common that drug taking leads addicts to loose not only their possessions but also their accommodation.

- "We did anything for drugs. We swapped the telly for drugs, we sold the furniture for drugs. We sold or swapped anything we had for drugs... "
- [*Some years later and during a different episode of homelessness*] "When I first moved in [to Esther Community], Andy took me back to my old flat to collect some things. Most of the furniture was sold for drugs, but I managed to get some photographs."
- [*A different episode of homelessness*] "I went back to stay with [name] after I'd lost the baby. And I stayed there until I was kicked out of the flat 'cos I was dealing drugs to students underneath. When I was kicked out of the flat, I lost my deposit, so I couldn't find anywhere else to live".

As far as the drug addicts at Esther Community were concerned, becoming a drug addict does not happen overnight. It is a long slow process as the addiction begins to take hold, gradually more and more heroin is needed to induce the same effects.

- "Getting a drug habit is hard, it takes three years to get a heroin habit, but just one year to get a methadone habit. It takes a long time to earn enough money to develop a real habit".

Methadone is used as substitute for heroine and cocaine, but this can be just as addictive and equally as difficult to wean yourself from it. Even the prescriptions of methadone are abused by the addicts, some use methadone along side hard drugs to make their drugs last longer and their money go further. Others experiment with different ways of taking methadone for maximum impact.

- I'm on sugar free methadone, because the stuff is really bad for your teeth. I've seen people who've rotten teeth because they've been on methadone. Someone told me the other day that you can inject the sugar free stuff straight into your veins. I'm not doing that, that's not why I asked to be put on the sugar free. I don't shoot up, I don't want to get into shooting up".

There was very definite evidence of a pecking order of drug addiction and addicts at Esther Community. The bigger the habit, the better drug addict you were, and the longer you had spent living on the streets the greater authority you were on all aspects of homelessness. Residents who had been homeless or addicted to drugs for longer took great pride in this, and classed themselves as a cut above the rest of the residents.

- "The smack and coke in this area is weak, so I've to get hold of a lot more to feed my habit. I've never lived anywhere where the drugs are so poor, not even the E's are good. When I tested the coke, you know by rubbing it on my gums, it didn't even make my gums go numb. That proves just how weak it is... normally when I inject coke I get a rush up my arm, but with this stuff I didn't, that's how I know it's weak... People in this area and in here [Esther Community] say they are going over on the coke they think they're drug addicts, but they're not. They wouldn't be able to take the real stuff that I've taken in the past. They aren't heavy users like I used to be. Some people here [Esther Community] wish they'd a drug habit, but all they really want is to belong to people, they're sad."

However, there is mutual respect amongst addicts and homeless people who feel that they are the 'same grade'. There is often a comradeship and friendship between them that can be both comforting and supportive.

The common bond means that they are not on their own, someone else knows and appreciates what they are going through, they know just how big an achievement every seemingly small success is. There is also an appreciation that they are not in a drug rehabilitation centre, where people can feed off each others problems or flout rules.

- "I get on best with [name of resident], she's on the same medication

> and going through the same kind of things... It's nice to have someone who knows what you are going through... I like it here because there are no users. There are ex-users having counselling, but that is different, they are in the same boat and don't drag you back into using."

Medical Problems

A number of residents had long term medical problems ranging from Asthma to Hepatitis. There was some evidence that residents regularly shared their medications, during the periods of observation residents on more than one occasion shared their inhalers. There are obvious dangers with sharing medications that could have serious consequences.

At the time of the research, one member of staff commented that there were no official records as to whether residents were on any medication and if so which type. This was something that she was concerned about and was hoping that management were going to look into. The connection between hepatitis and drug abuse was clear.

One resident had Hepatitis C another Hepatitis B; both were receiving counselling, medical advice and drug treatment from specialists at the St Petrock's day centre. Both types of hepatitis are contagious, Hepatitis is usually only passed on through bodily fluids, but Hepatitis B is highly infectious and hygiene of plates and cutlery needs to be observed closely.

Hepatitis B is both easier to catch than Aids and is also a bigger killer than Aids. The presence of hepatitis and the ever-present threat of Aids means that hygiene and health and safety, needs to be observed. At the time of the research, there was no obvious evidence of precautions being taken surrou-nding the hygiene of communal plates and cutlery in the kitchen.

Although the Hepatitis B infection can easily be cleaned away using hot water, on one of my visits there was no hot water or heating, the residents informed me that this had been the case over the previous weekend, this was confirmed by the staff member on duty. After repair the boiler system had broken down again that day, meaning that they would be without hot water for at least another night and morning.

The Homeless Community

There is a strong homeless community in Exeter, most of the homeless people know everyone else or at least several other homeless people and newcomers are easily spotted. This has both advantages and disadvantages. New comers to the area and people living on the streets for the first time are often helped by other homeless people. However, they are also in danger of being raped, beaten or having their possessions or money stolen from them.

This young woman was fortunate:

- "...but I ended up sleeping in a bus station. I met a man there who knew a girl in here, he asked if there was a place. There was and I'm glad, because I was really frightened on the streets".

There are often conflicts within the homeless community that can be transferred into the hostel and cause serious problems within the hostel. These are usually connected with squabbles or problems with the male members of the homeless community.

- "I'm worried about meeting him again for another reason, though. He knows where Esther Community is; he is someone else who lives at Esther Community's ex. That might make things complicated. Meeting him might cause me problems, some of the other women might mind."
- "I know [resident's name], she was baby sitting for a friend of mine while I couldn't work. She was baby sitting for free, she says, but she wasn't. He is one of the biggest drug dealers in the area. She was doing it for drugs. I don't know what possessed him to choose her, I mean you've seen her, the way she dresses compared to me. He's taken me back now, [resident's name] doesn't like it, but he has a standard to keep up. Anyway his little girl has now got nits and she must have got them from [resident's name] because there's no where else for her to catch them. [resident's name] is gunning for me now, because she thinks I told him that she has scabies and that is why she can't baby sit anymore."
- "I am stopping in the hostel at the moment a lot, it isn't safe out there at the moment. [resident's name] has been telling everyone that I grassed up [man's name] for raping me, when I first arrived. But I tell you I haven't grassed him. I haven't told no one and there's no way I've spoken to the Bill."

There is little that staff can do about such squabbles and quarrels, they have to listen when appropriate but remain impartial and neutral at all times when residents are in conflict. Such problems can make the streets a very dangerous place to live and increase tension and anxiety amongst the homeless population and hostel residents.

There was evidence that Esther Community had a hierarchy among residents. Those residents who had slept rough the longest, had the most episodes of homelessness and/or had the most serious drug addictions, classed themselves as a 'cut above' those residents with fewer problems that were of shorter duration.

This meant that some older residents were intolerant of younger hostel residents that had never slept rough or had small or no drink/drug habits.

- "I hate 16 year olds in the hostel showing off about their homelessness, when they can't know what it's like to be really homeless because they haven't been homeless for long enough".

The common bond between residents who saw themselves as 'the same grade' served a useful purpose as it allowed the residents to form informal support networks with people could appreciate what they were going through.

Religion

Three out of five interviewees discussed the fact that Esther Community is a Christian hostel. They expressed their observations and fears about the way staff communicated their beliefs. It would appear that most residents were very wary when they first arrived at the hostel, in case there would be heavy preaching or attempts at indoctrination. However, once they had been there for a week or so they realised that there would be no 'hard sell' of religious beliefs.

- "They sometimes have community meetings, everyone here is invited, but we don't go because they just want to tell us about God and stuff and we're just not interested. I won't listen to any of the religious bits. This place isn't bad though, they have their posters and things on the walls, but this place doesn't force religion down your neck like some of the places I've been to. Some of the drug rehab places do that you know, force religion down your neck".
- "This place has a lot of Christianity in it, but it's not bad, there's a good balance, they don't force it on you, it's not like the God squad or anything. When you first arrive you're scared that you're going to be preached at, and you can't hack that, but it's not forced on you, you're not pressurised into having their beliefs. It's just that there are morals and respect there if you want it."
- Residents also appreciated the fact that they are free to ask staff questions about their beliefs and that they will be given an honest answer, but no one will go into the 'hard sell' mode and try to preach at them.
- "I was talking to Andy [hostel manager] about this place and the God posters and telling him what happened to me. He gave me a New Testament Bible. But he did it in a nice way, no strings attached, no preach, he just said that I might like to read it if I wanted to. I don't mind that, it's not in your face, there's no heavy sell, it's just there if I want it. Another time I was talking to Cindy [night staff] in the night and she invited me to church with her sometime. I don't know if I'll go, but I might. The good thing is I don't have to."
- "The staff are good here and friendly, you can chat with them any time day or night. I was chatting to Cindy, she invited me to go to church with her. I did, it was all right. She says I can go again with her some time, if I want to".

Residents did not seem to be offended by invitations to church or when they were given literature and to a certain extent found it comforting and a sign that staff cared and wanted to be friends.

RESEARCH FINDINGS FROM WAYSIDE HOSTEL–REIGATE

THE STIGMA OF LIVING IN A HOSTEL

Short conversations with some of the hostel residents at the video launch, pointed to a lot of feeling about the way hostel residents are viewed in the wider community.

The dramas at the video launch presented the homeless as the dishevelled beggar on the streets approaching people for money, and the cause of homelessness as simple misunder-standings between mother and daughter, where the daughter stormed out because she was unhappy and did not feel that her mother was listening to her.

This upset Wayside residents, because although those two scenarios represent some homeless women, they felt that it trivialised what they had been through or were going through. The women wanted people to understand that at Wayside most women have never slept rough. They regard themselves as middle class, and most have had a decent education.

They are at Wayside for a variety of reasons that led to them becoming homeless and in need of somewhere to stay:

- "You know most of us aren't anything like that. We are decent middle class girls, we've never been on the streets and we've never begged.
- Most of us have a good education and a lot of us have jobs. We are just homeless, that's all."

There are several stigmas that have to be faced by residents, including:

- That they are seen as dirty and smelly or young people out of control.
- They are disadvantaged in the labour and further education markets.
- A perceived lack of freedom due to curfew rules.

Seen as Dirty and Smelly or Young People Out of Control

The group interview at Wayside revealed that friends and other people in the community viewed them as dirty and smelly or young people out of control. They felt that they were struggling enough with being homeless and its associated problems of low self-esteem and low selfworth as a result.

The need to constantly prove themselves in the wider community was felt to be an additional and unnecessary burden.

- "When you are in a hostel people stereotype you. As soon as you say you live in a hostel they make a judgement about you. They think that if you live in a hostel you must be dirty and smelly."
- "They think all youngsters are trouble. This is how they stereotype people like me. They just think that we are poor."

- "I think all hostels have a stigma attached to them. Most people think that if you have to live in a hostel, then you must be a psycho or mental patient. This is insulting."

Disadvantaged in the Labour and Further Education Market

Residents found that the stigma of living in a hostel is a stumbling block when trying to find work, settle into a new job or get onto a college course. They felt ashamed of their circumstances and where they have to live. Also, when someone leaves home in a hurry, they rarely take with them all their paperwork, the last thing on their mind is picking up certificates that prove to potential employers their educational achievements.

- "Living in a hostel makes it hard for you to get a job. So instead of having a permanent job, a proper job, now I have to do voluntary work to get Job Seekers Allowance. They don't believe you have qualifications if you live in a hostel either. They just assume that you lie about your qualifications, because they think that all people that live in a hostel are thick, stupid and poor."
- "Look I had a very rough life, ok. I have really messed up, and that hurts. I had hopes and dreams of a career, but when I became homeless in the way that I did, all those hopes and dreams just go down the drain."

The women interviewed do not actually tell potential employers or friends and work colleagues exactly where they live, for fear of either not getting work, losing work or what other people may think of them. Instead, it is common practice in the hostel, to use the house number and street address only, rather than the title Wayside.

A Perceived Lack of Freedom Due to Curfew Rules

Stigma is not just confined to access to work or the way they feel about themselves. They find it difficult to conduct what they call 'normal lives' from the hostel setting. Simple things like having to be in by 11.30pm or finding a friend's floor to sleep on for the night, means that they feel different, they complain that they cannot go out to the night-clubs like the rest of their friends.

- "My mum is very strict so I prefer it at Wayside, but I don't like having to be in by 11.30pm at night or find somewhere else to stay overnight. And you're only allowed to stay out three nights a week and no more. I think there should be more lea-way and that we should have a key to get in or night staff to let us in especially at weekends".

They say they are embarrassed about having to tell them that they can't stay out late. This provoked a lot of discussion in the group interview, as two out of the four interviewees wanted the rules relaxing and the other two women felt safer if the rules were kept as they were.

Here age had a big impact on the interviewees point of view, with the 16 and 18 year old wanting the curfew lifted and rules relaxed and the 34 and 36 year olds wanting the security of knowing that the building was safe and no one could wander in and out.

- "There are very good reasons for the hostel rules being what they are, the hostel rules used to let you have a key and come back late, but the rules were broken. These rules make it safer now"

This issue of curfews and keys was later discussed with the hostel manager, who confirmed the rules and explained them in more detail. In the past, some women tried to sneak boyfriends into their rooms. Also, the partners and ex-boyfriends of some women fleeing from domestic violence had tried to gain entry to the building making those and other women feel unsafe.

In addition, some women were involved with drugs and they have had times when drug dealers have been at the door trying to find one of the women. However, to a 16 year old just free of strict parents and dreaming of adult freedoms, no set of rules seem sensible if they prevent you from doing what you want.

Part of the hostels' role is to provide a safe and secure home for all their residents and to protect vulnerable residents. The hostels' role is also to encourage residents to become responsible citizens. The residents are interviewed before they are accepted for a place, the rules are explained to them so that they can choose whether or not to accept that place.

Part of being a resident and preparing to live in mainstream society, is learning to accept a given set of rules. Whilst these stigmas are entirely understandable, the residents' reactions to them must be born in mind as they play a key part in the success of their rehabilitation.

Learning to Accept the Rules

All aspects of society have a set of rules in some form or another, most are so implicit or second nature to the majority of us that we follow them without thinking. People who have been homeless for some time, or perhaps in care do not always remember, understand or know these rules. This leads to problems, for example, when a homeless person has to do things such as, start paying contributions towards rent or food.

An unrealistic understanding of the cost of living causes many tenancies to fail. Newly housed people not only do not budget properly, but are surprised by the cost of living, or defer payments until they can afford them. A part of rehabilitation within the hostel is teaching homeless people about what is acceptable in society and how to handle their money and budget wisely.

These are not easy lessons to learn. One 18 year old at Wayside discussed the fact that she thought she was being cheated out of some of her money, but did not know who she could trust to find out the truth. When she first arrived at Wayside, she filled out various forms and could claim housing benefit and Job Seekers Allowance. After some time she found a job, she stopped receiving Job Seekers Allowance, which seemed perfectly fair to her, as she was no longer looking for work. However, despite social workers and several different members of staff at the hostel explaining that her housing benefit would either stop or be reduced. She saw this as unfair, mainly because she knew other residents were still only paying the £10 contribution towards rent after full housing benefit.

- "Because I have a job now, I am expected to pay £260 a month rent. I don't think that's fair, because when I had no job I only had to pay £10 a month. What I really want is for someone to come and sit down with me and tell me what to do and how to get help. I don't know who to trust I can't tell whether or not I am being ripped off. Most people have parents that help them sort their bills out and things, they explain everything. This sort of thing is an adult thing and I am expected to just suddenly be able to cope with it. It is very frightening"–*Interviewee aged 18*

Unrealistic expectations caused this young woman to doubt the level of rent that she needs to pay. She knows that rent costs a lot of money, but there appears to be a difference between what seems a lot to her and the amount that she is being charged.

- "To get a flat in the [private] rented [sector], you really need to have a job first, because it costs a lot of money"

It is sometimes very difficult for people who have been let down by most of the adults in their lives, to trust people again. They don't know who to trust, and therefore trust becomes a very frightening issue. The young woman in this example is battling with trust more than anything else. She desperately wants the help and warmth of friendship that Etta and the other hostel staff and volunteers offer her daily, but cannot bring herself to trust them, despite having been at the hostel for nearly two years.

This is a good example of how long it can take to really help some women, to turn them around and help them to live a more productive life, where they feel physically, mentally and emotionally secure. This is the strong advantage of having a three year time limit for staying at Wayside, it gives residents time to really sort themselves out. The limit also spurs them into action, rather than drifting on aimlessly for many years in the hostel system.

Fear

All five interviewees at Wayside spoke of their fear.

Their fears came into three main categories:

1. Fear of violence
2. Fear of trusting other people especially officials
3. Fear of failure once they left Wayside

Fear of Violence

Three out of the five women had lived in violent domestic relationships before living at Wayside. The level of fear of violence varies from woman to woman, but one past resident was in so much fear of being found by her ex-partner that she ran away and eventually had to be found an alternative safe hostel in another area.

Although none of the women would speak specifically of their childhood, there were some indications that violence had featured strongly in their childhood, and this had affected their relationships and confidence as adults. It can take a long time for women to overcome their fear of people being violent towards them.

Some do gain enough confidence in themselves to feel safe again, however, other women never fully recover and the best that Wayside can hope to achieve, is that they learn how to cope and make themselves feel safe in their own homes when they leave.

Fear of Trusting other People Especially Officials

Trust is a very big issue for several wayside residents, it not only affects the way residents arrive and settle into wayside, *e.g.*

- "When I first arrived at Wayside I was petrified. I was terrified because I did not know who I could trust and who I couldn't trust. I did not know if people at Wayside were trustworthy. When I first arrived I used to cry myself to sleep. At first I would not come downstairs to be with the other girls in the lounge or kitchen because I was so afraid".

Trust also affects the type and level of help that staff can give to them. Often help is rejected through fear of trusting, this means that staff have to spend a lot of time building up trust and waiting until a woman is ready to be helped. When one interviewee arrived at Wayside she had a serious drink problem, it took months of patience and hard work before the hostel manager could earn her trust.

- "When she came to Wayside she had a serious drink problem, and was in such a state that she took four overdoses...She didn't trust anyone. Now she trusts some people, she will now talk to me."

Now that same resident is waiting on the council waiting list for a place to live, has a job and generally has more self-respect. As part of learning how to budget her money, she has started to buy items of things that she will need for her new place.

She already has everything she will need for the Kitchen and has begun collecting things for the bathroom. This was only possible once she learnt to trust Etta and herself. A different resident spoke about her fears, but she has not learned to trust yet, thus there is a stark difference in attitude and outcome.

- "I feel really frightened at the moment, everyone I've ever trusted in the past let me down. Now I'm afraid to trust anyone...When I leave, I am going to need help with getting my own things together, ready for when I move into a new place. I need some kind of social worker who will help. Someone who visits the hostel say once a week to advise me about what to do and how to do it".

The type of help this woman is asking for already exists both within Wayside and via her own social worker. All the help and assistance that she will need is there, but she does not feel it or see it, because she is too afraid to trust the people offering her help.

As she trusts no one at the moment, it is impossible to give her the help and feelings of security that she so desperately wants. It can take a long time before women regain their trust, hostel staff can only be patient and wait until such women realise that there is help and that they can trust some people.

Fear of Failure once they Left Wayside

The interviewees who were preparing for leaving viewed their leaving with a mixture of fear and optimism. They were excited about the prospect of getting their own place and moving on, but were afraid that things might go wrong once they left Wayside or that leaving Wayside might be emotionally difficult.

- "I want to feel secure and safe in my new place, I don't want to live in fear of being evicted or loosing the place once I have it."
- "I'm looking for a place to live with the council. I want to go; I'm ready to go. I don't want to hang on because it'll be harder to go then. I don't know what help I will need when I leave, but I'll stay in touch with Etta".

Work

Four out of the five residents at Wayside were either in fulltime employment, training schemes or in education. The interviewee that was neither in work or education has learning difficulties and so finds it more difficult to gain employment. In spite of this, she was hoping that her disability worker was going to be able to find her employment. This is in stark contrast with Esther Community, where none of the interviewees were in work, training or education.

Table. Residents in Employment or Education

ID No.	Age	Hostel	In Employment	In Education
Int.02	16	Wayside	No	Yes
Int.03	18	Wayside	Yes	No
Int.05	19	Wayside	Yes	No
Int.01	34	Wayside	No	No
Int.04	36	Wayside	Yes	No

However, residents at Wayside were limited with the type of work they could find in the Reigate area. Most of the jobs in the area were for secretarial or office jobs that required a high degree of technical and communication skills. The interviewees were either too young to have gained the level of skill required, or too vulnerable to cope with a job that was so demanding.

Thus all the interviewees that were in employment, worked in the caring sector, typically as care assistants or working with the elderly or children. This means that they were not working in the types of jobs that would pay average or high salaries and thus are neither able to pay the rents required in the private sector nor pay the bond that is required by landlords.

Unrealistic Expectations

Throughout the group interview, the interviewees demonstrated the fact that they held unrealistic expectations on a wide variety of issues. These issues varied from the trivial to important issues for the residents future ability to cope and function in wider society.

For example:

- *Housing:* Residents felt that they should not have to wait on local authority housing waiting lists, and that they should have priority over other people because they were living in a hostel. One exception to this was the resident who had lived in the same hostel for three years and then was told that she would have to wait a further three years on the housing waiting list. Whilst she should have applied for housing sooner, this clearly was not an unrealistic expectation. However, some residents who had been at the hostel for only a matter of months expected to find a fast and easy route into housing and were disappointed to find that there were no short cuts.
- *Ex-partners and Accommodation:* For some residents there were unrealistic expectations concerning the breakdown of relationships, this was mainly due to age or intellectual ability. For example, two residents complained that after moving into their respective partners own home and then leaving when the relationship broke down, they felt that it was unfair that they had become homeless and not the partner. There was no recognition that the partner owned the property, paid all the bills and that they had no entitlements as they had not lived there for very long. Neither woman seemed to think they should have any financial settlement or that they should keep the property, but felt that someone should have ensured that the partner was made homeless too.
- *Cost of Living:* The younger residents were surprised at the level of rent they had to pay both before and after housing benefit. They felt that it was unfair that they should pay so much, but were unsure

whether this was unfair or 'normal'. Younger residents understood that they needed to learn to budget and learn to control their spending, so that they could make their money last and save up for when they moved into their own place. However, they were shocked by the cost of living compared to the level of benefits they received. One resident also felt that housing benefit should not be reduced or stopped when she managed to get a job. There appeared to be a basic belief that, all bills were paid for and any money they had was all theirs.

- *Storage:* One resident had stored her things in a garage after leaving her fiancé, however, she felt that social services or the local authority should either pay the garage rent or pay for her things to be moved and stored elsewhere. There was no appreciation that these were her things and her responsibility, the rent was cheap and easily affordable on benefits.
- *Pets:* A minority of residents felt that hostels should allow you to take your pets in with you as the hostel is your home and at home you would be allowed to keep your pets. At times, some residents failed to realise that hostels are not home from home and that rules had to be applied that respected all residents.

SOCIAL WORK ETHICS

The Association of Social Work Boards (ASWB) Guide to Social Work Ethics Course Development is the first attempt by a national organization of social work regulatory boards to develop a set of guidelines for the content of social work ethics courses, workshops and seminars. This guide is the result of two years of work by members of the ASWB Approved Continuing Education (ACE) Committee, guided by input solicited from social work regulatory boards, social work practitioners, and social work educators. The purpose of this resource is to provide a social work ethics course structure for continuing education (CE) providers that is informed by the perspective of social work regulators.

The Guide to Social Work Ethics Course Development establishes standards for common course goals and objectives and core content as well as acceptable teaching methods, resource macial Work Boards believes that social work boards can better protect the public when they have access to resources, such as the Guide to Social Work Ethics Course Development, that reflect the most current thinking on issues relevant to professional regulation and discipline.

Over the past few years an increasing number of social work regulatory bodies have begun requiring specific continuing education in social work ethics for licensure renewal.

In some ways, this trend has created a new set of challenges for continuing education providers, regulatory boards, and social workers: providers are eager to provide social work ethics CE but unsure of board expectations, boards are clear about the need for ethics CE but unsure of how directive they should be as to actual course content and delivery, and social workers are willing to comply with the requirements but unsure of whether the courses they take will satisfy board requirements and provide relevant CE on social work ethics. One of the most important goals of the Guide to Social Work Ethics Course Development is to facilitate greater standardization of ethics courses among jurisdictions both nationally and internationally.

Use of this guide will make it possible for boards to develop common course goals and objectives while allowing jurisdictions to modify content to reflect the practice of social work in their particular area. Providers—many of which deliver CE in multiple jurisdictions, or over the internet—will have access to more standardized information on appropriate content and delivery methods. Finally, through the ASWB Approved Continuing Education programme, social workers will be able to connect with providers whose courses meet certain standards for social work ethics content.

DEVELOPMENT OF THE MANUAL

Members of the ACE Committee who drafted the social work ethics course guide reflected diversity among the profession and the regulatory community. Three members had faculty positions in a school of social work teaching a range of students from the baccalaureate to doctoral level, one member was a clinical social worker working in a community mental health agency in a rural community, two were in full or part time private practice, and one member was a doctoral student specializing in indirect practice. The committee met four times in person over two years and numerous times by teleconference in addition to attending to ongoing ACE programme work.

The ACE Committee considered several domains of social work professional ethics related to continuing education, and examined connections to the licensure and renewal processes and discipline. Data were collected from a range of sources beginning with a survey of boards. Published materials focusing on practice competence, malpractice, risk management, and the social work profession's evolution in the field of ethics were reviewed. Data from educational sources, both colleges and universities, and continuing education materials were investigated. The committee queried the National Association of Social Workers (NASW) Insurance Trust and the ASWB Disciplinary Action Reporting System (DARS) report.

Input was solicited from professionals with expertise in ethics during the development of earlier drafts of the model course guide. In the May 2003 Spring Meeting in Buffalo, NY, the final draft of the Guide to Social Work Ethics Course

Development was distributed to all participants for comments. Finally, the ACE Programme Committee members met in July 2003 to make any final changes to the model course outline and decided upon plans to present the ASWB Guide to Social Work Ethics Course Development to the ASWB Board of Directors. The Board of Directors approved the dissemination of this guide as an association resource document in November 2003.

BASIC FRAMEWORK

The guide establishes three levels of course work; basic, intermediate, and advanced as well as an emphasis on either direct or indirect practice. Common course goals and objectives are established and course content is identified. Course goals cover a range of topics from understanding the history of social work ethics to critical thinking skills.

Course content reflecting these goals and objectives includes the history and evolution of values and ethics in social work, ethics theories, professional standards of practice, legal requirements, self-awareness about ethical professional behaviour, and an examination of ethical decision-making processes. The guide goes on to provide examples of course objectives at the basic, intermediate, and advanced levels. Acceptable teaching methods, resource materials, and instructor qualifications are outlined. A listing of key definitions is included. The Guide to Social Work Ethics Course Development is the beginning of efforts to standardize ethics education in the regulatory community. The profession is changing and many forces are at play making the practice of social work more complex. As practitioners look at ethics and ethical practices, this curriculum outline can be used a resource guide for upgrading and adopting a standard for the ethics courses in their jurisdictions.

COURSE GOALS SHOULD BE CLEARLY STATED, AND MUST BE RELATED TO SOCIAL WORK PRACTICE

The overall purpose of this model course is to encourage and help participants develop a better understanding of and manage the ethical issues and dilemmas they encounter in practice.

The goals are:

- To enable participants to increase their appreciation and understanding of the history and evolution of values and ethics in the social work profession
- To enable participants to develop skills in applying relevant ethics concepts and theories of ethics to social work practice
- To provide opportunities for participants to acquire knowledge about professional, legal (state, jurisdictional and federal) and ethical standards of practice, their role in competent, ethical social work, and times at which legal and professional standards may conflict
- To provide opportunities for participants to increase self-awareness

and develop an awareness of the interplay of personal values and professional behaviour

- To enable participants to increase their ability to recognize ethical issues and to apply ethical decision-making frameworks and protocols through enhanced use of critical thinking skills
- To enable participants to increasingly recognize and embrace the role of diversity and social justice in understanding and addressing ethical dilemmas.

CORE CONTENT

The core content areas are:

- History and evolution of values and ethics in social work
- Ethics theories (*e.g.* Abramson, Gilligan, Levy, Keith-Lucas, Loewenberg, Reamer, etc.)
- Professional standards of social work practice, such as exhibited in the ethical codes of the National Association of Social Workers, the Association of Canadian Social Workers, the Clinical Social Work Federation and the Council on Social Work Education.
- Legal requirements and other considerations for each jurisdiction that registers, certifies or licenses social workers
- Professional values and self-awareness about ethical professional behaviour
- Ethical decision making processes and dilemma examples

APPLICABLE AREAS OF PRACTICE

Social work ethics applies to all aspects of social work practice, and is not limited to clinical direct practice. Providers should understand that social workers may come to an ethics training from a wide range of professional backgrounds, and should be aware of whether the content provided is applicable to direct practice, indirect practice, or both practice areas.

DIRECT PRACTICE

Direct practice can be defined as the range of professional social work activities with or on behalf of clients in which goals are established, worked towards and reached through personal contact and immediate influence with those seeking social services. Potential ethical issues include but are not limited to sexual misconduct, boundary issues, dual and multiple relationships, conflicts of interest, confidentiality, informed consent, service delivery, professional competency, fraud, client rights, professional impairment, mandatory reporting, discrimination, diversity, billing practices, social justice, supervision and consultation.

INDIRECT PRACTICE

Indirect practice can be defined as those professional social work activities such as administration, supervision, research, publication, policy development, education (classroom and field instruction) which may not involve immediate or personal contact with clients being served.

Potential ethical issues include but are not limited to use of authority, representation to the public, sexual misconduct, boundary issues and dual relationships, fiduciary responsibilities, research and human subjects protocols, impaired professionals, mandatory reporting, discrimination, personnel and administrative decisions, supervision and consultation, diversity, billing practices and social justice.

OBJECTIVES

Providers should have a clear idea of what a participant who takes an educational course will be able to do at the end of the course presentation, and should clearly communicate these objectives to participants. Both providers and participants should be able to measure the degree to which these objectives were met through the course. Objectives for a course will vary depending on the purpose of the course, the skill level and experience level of the social worker, and the educational preferences of the person and/or organization designing the course.

The first step in designing course objectives is to develop a clear idea of the target audience for the course. Just as social workers are employed in a wide variety of clinical and non-clinical settings, they bring a range of knowledge and skill levels to any continuing education course. Courses in ethics could be designed to meet the needs of practitioners of three general skill levels: basic, intermediate and advanced. These skill levels may be conceptualized by using a variety of factors.

The following are a few examples of these factors:

- Level of competency in assessment, knowledge and skills of the social worker
- Level of education; level of licensure; years of practice experience
- Use of specialized methods or ability to use more complex methods
- Focus on a particular population, problem or area of practice

DEVELOPING OBJECTIVES–AN EXAMPLE

The following part contains examples of possible course outcomes or objectives for a core content area entitled "Ethical decision-making processes" for three skill levels. These sample objectives contain references to a "social work practice situation"—in the basic level this is referred to as an "uncomplicated social work practice situation, " while in the intermediate level there is a reference to a "moderately complex social work practice dilemma." The differences in these practice situations would lie in the factors that may complicate an ethical dilemma: for example, the relationship between the severity of the problem and a client's strengths, or the experience level of the social worker, the number of people involved and/or degree of magnitude of the problem (*e.g.* life or death situation). Suggested action verbs are given for each level as a guide to help potential course developers write objectives or outcomes that are measurable and action-oriented.

SUGGESTED TEACHING METHODS AND RESOURCE MATERIALS

A variety of teaching methods should be used during each course whenever possible to accommodate the different learning styles of participants. Similarly, providers should consider using a broad range of resource materials to support their presentations.

Because interaction in the form of discussion, roleplay, and/or debate is an important part of the learning process in an ethics course, it is recommended that one of these three teaching methods be used.

Following is a list of a variety of teaching methods, which address the various learning styles of students:

- Case studies
- Mini-lecture
- Group discussion
- Role play
- Debate
- Presentations
- Professional audio/video
- Appropriate audio/video from popular media
- Pre and post tests
- Web enhanced instruction—may be interactive or web-based
- Multi-media presentations
- Assigned readings

Resource materials can include:

- Readings
- Web sites
- Professional audio and video
- Case scenarios
- Appropriate readings/videos from popular media

INSTRUCTOR QUALIFICATIONS

While there are elements of ethical practice that apply to many health and mental health care professions, the relationship of these ethical principles to the practice of social work, and the integration of ethics into the core values of the profession, demands that presenters be members of the social work profession, and that they have extensive knowledge in broad ethical principles and theory, values and ethics within social work, and the practical application of these concepts.

At a minimum, presenters should have the following qualifications:

- Degree in social work
- Certified, registered or licensed as a social worker
- Knowledge of social work values and ethics
- Knowledge of ethical theory
- Knowledge of high risk areas of practice
- Practice competence in course content

CO-PRESENTER

There may be instances when it is desirable to include a co-presenter from another professional discipline. In these situations it is important that the other professional is licensed, registered or certified in his or her field, if applicable. Individual regulatory boards may require specific instructor requirements or qualifications. Providers should check with the individual boards to determine specific requirements.

PRACTICE OF CLINICAL SOCIAL WORK

A specialty within the practice of Master's Social Work requiring the application of social work theory, knowledge, methods, ethics, and the professional use of self to restore or enhance social, psychosocial, or bio-psychosocial functioning of individuals, couples, families, groups, organizations and communities. The practice of Clinical Social Work requires the application of specialized clinical knowledge and advance clinical skills in the areas of assessment, diagnosis and treatment of mental, emotional, and behavioural disorders, conditions and addictions. Treatment methods include the provision of individual, marital, couple, family and group counseling and psychotherapy. The practice of Clinical Social Work may include private practice and the provision of clinical supervision.

CLIENT

The individual, couple, family, group, organization or community that seeks or receives social work services.

CODE OF CONDUCT/PRACTICE STANDARDS

ASWB. 2002. Standards of Practice/Code of Conduct, Model Social Work Practice Act, contained in Social Work Laws and Regulations, a comparison guide.

CODE OF ETHICS

An explicit statement of the values, principles and rules of a profession, regulating the conduct of its members.

CONTINUING EDUCATION

Education and training oriented to maintain, improve or enhance social work practice.

COUNSELING

A method used by social workers to assist individual, couples, families and groups in learning how to solve problems and make decisions about personal, health, social, educational, vocation, financial and other interpersonal concerns.

CULTURAL COMPETENCE

Cultural competence in social work continuing education implies a heightened consciousness of how individuals experience their uniqueness and deal with their differences and similarities within a larger social context.

Courses should reflect:

- Understanding of diversity between and within cultures
- Consciousness of the dynamics inherent when cultures interact
- Understanding of how personal and professional values may conflict with or accommodate the needs of diverse clients
- Understanding of history, traditions, values, family systems and artistic expressions of diverse cultural groups
- Methodological approaches, skills and techniques reflecting understanding of the role of culture in CE course content
- Information in language appropriate to participants

DIVERSITY

Differences in and among societal groups based on race and/or ethnicity, gender, age, physical/mental abilities, sexual orientation, religion, size and other distinguishing characteristics.

In social organizations the term usually refers to the range of people who more accurately represent minority populations and people from varied backgrounds, cultures, ethnicities and viewpoints.

ETHICAL DECISION MAKING

The process through which practitioners make ethical decisions and attempt to resolve ethical dilemmas. Most protocols include an outline of steps that practitioners can follow to help them approach ethical dilemmas systematically, drawing especially on ethical theory, relevant professional literature, statutes, regulations, codes of ethics, and policies, and consultation.

ETHICAL DILEMMA

A situation that occurs when two or more moral values seem to be equally valid but contradictory and the individual is required to make the best possible choice from among them.

ETHICS

A system of moral principles and perceptions about right versus wrong and the resulting philosophy of conduct that is practiced by an individual, group, profession or culture. Emerging from value conflicts, expressions or guidelines distinguishing right from wrong and describing a community's positive moral standards.

GENERALIST PRACTICE

In social work, a practitioner who has knowledge and skills which encompass a broad spectrum and who assesses problems and solutions comprehensively.

Generalist practice typically includes three dimensions:

- Multiple interventions which involve "the use of 'thoughtful and planned efforts to bring about a specific change'" with individuals, families, groups, organizations and communities; "
- "A knowledge base carefully chosen from a range of theories; "
- "A focus 'both on private issues and social justice concerns'".

INDEPENDENT SOCIAL WORK PRACTICE

The practice of social work outside the auspices of traditional social agencies or government organizations, after completion of all applicable supervision requirements in which the social worker assumes responsibility and accountability for services provided.

In addition to private practitioners, those engaged in such social work include self-employed proprietary social workers who have autonomous consulting firms or who organize and manage private, for-profit institutional facilities or educational institutions.

MACRO PRACTICE

Social work practice aimed at bringing about improvements and changes in the general society. Such activities include some types of political action, community organization, publication, education, campaigning, and the administration of broad-based social services agencies or public welfare departments.

NASW CODE OF ETHICS

The explication of the values, rules and principles of ethical conduct that apply to all social workers who are members of the National Association of Social Workers (NASW). The original Code of Ethics was implicit in the 1951 Standards for Professional Practice of the American Association of Social Workers (AASW). NASW developed a formal code in 1960 and has made subsequent revisions; the most recent in 1999.

PSYCHOTHERAPY

The use of treatment methods utilizing a specialized, formal interaction between a clinical social worker and an individual, couple, family or group in which a therapeutic relationship is established, maintained and sustained to understand unconscious processes, intrapersonal, interpersonal and psychosocial dynamics, and the diagnosis and treatment of mental, emotional, and behavioural disorders, conditions and addictions.

VALUES

The customs, standards of conduct and principles considered desirable by a culture, a group of people, or an individual. The mission of the social work profession is rooted in a set of core values, comprising service, social justice, dignity and worth of the person, importance of human relationships, integrity, competence, ethical conduct.

4

Principles and Practice in Social Research

INTRODUCTION

Social research refers to research conducted by social scientists.

Social research methods may be divided into two broad categories:

1. Quantitative designs approach social phenomena through quantifiable evidence, and often rely on statistical analysis of many cases to create valid and reliable general claims
2. Qualitative designs emphasie understanding of social phenomena through direct observation, communication with participants, or analysis of texts, and may stress contextual and subjective accuracy over generality

Social scientists employ a range of methods in order to analyse a vast breadth of social phenomena; from census survey data derived from millions of individuals, to the in-depth analysis of a single agents' social experiences; from monitoring what is happening on contemporary streets, to the investigation of ancient historical documents. The methods rooted in classical sociology and statistics have formed the basis for research in further social sciences, such as political science, education, and market research.

Social research is a practical activity aimed at answering a research question by means of a research strategy, a research design and a method of data collection and analysis. Any research strategy has implications for research design and the use of methods of data collection and analysis.

As suggested, be very much concerned with the three components of social research:

1. Strategy
2. Design
3. Method.

As suggested, be examining two major research strategies: quantitative and qualitative. When we talk of quantitative research strategies, we mean counting the numbers of people in defined categories. For example, Durkheim used counts of the number of people in a community who had committed suicide. Qualitative research strategies record and analyse talk and actions, or analyse text that someone has written. This distinction between quantitative and qualitative social research serves as a vehicle to learn how to describe strategy, design and method in social research. Social research is a technical subject and has a precise language. Although not every term used has been defined in the literature in exactly the same way, it is important for the purposes of this part that you are both clear and consistent in the use of technical language.

This stage includes a large number of definitions that you will need to:

- Remember
- Understand
- Spply

To understand what social research is about you must clearly understand what is meant by each of the following:

- A research strategy
- A research design
- A research method.

As suggested, now examine each of these in turn.

CONCEPTS IN SOCIAL RESEARCH

We deal with the basic building blocks of social research: concepts Concepts are crucial to social research because they are the key to description and explanation:

- Concepts are linked 'empirically' in various ways to data and these linkages aim to provide descriptions or 'accounts' of the social world.
- Concepts are linked 'theoretically' to form sequences of defined stages in a social process, or to classify descriptions or typical forms, or linked to form explanations.

As in the case of research strategies, approaches to concept formation reflect contrasting ontological and epistemological themes in the philosophy of social sciences.

First, as suggested, be looking at what concepts are and how they function in everyday life, and in sociology and social research. This will involve considering how sociological concepts are formed, defined and changed over time. The process of concept formation is rather different in quantitative and qualitative social research and this difference is summed up in comparing the use of two terms:

1. Operational definitions
2. Sensitising concepts.

Of particular importance is the relationship between abstract concepts used in theoretical thinking and empirical data. This relationship between concepts and data is further explored by examining one of the most basic functions of social research: the process of coding data in quantitative and qualitative social research.

WHAT IS A CONCEPT?

Concepts are so fundamental to our way of thinking about the world that it is all too easy to take them for granted.

Here are two different ways of describing concepts:

1. *Labels*: concepts allow us to label experience by applying the concept to an experienced event, observation and meaning.
2. *Categories*: concepts divide the social world into fragments that are differentiated.

The concept of 'crime' labels a wide range of events that have been observed and have a 'shared' meaning, albeit one that can be contested and refined or expanded. The concept of 'father' is a category that separately defines a person as different from non-fathers; again the concept of father, and what it might involve, are not precisely defined and may change over time. We inherit a vast range of concepts embodied in our language and we use these to participate in the social world. In everyday life, we do not have to use precisely defined concepts.

For example, when young people use the word 'cool' to describe actions, it has only a very vague definition or perhaps it is simply a way of affirming that actions are 'approved' to some degree. In social research, we must go beyond everyday concepts and be more systematic in the way in which we define concepts, relate them to empirical materials and deploy them in interpretations of the social world.

This does not mean that at all times, in social research, concepts are precisely defined. As we shall see, sometimes it is important to have only working definitions of concepts that are refined in relation to data and only precisely defined at the conclusion of the research process.

ABSTRACTION

An abstract concept can be defined with reference to the specific instances that it labels or categorises. In practice, using empirical referents as examples will help to clarify and convey the meaning of a concept.

It may be hard to define 'sport' as an abstract concept other than by using examples such as netball, basketball, soccer, cricket and rugby to convey the meaning. However, my copy of the Pocket Oxford Dictionary offers a formal, more precise definition:

- 'Outdoor competitive activity usually involving physical exertion'

The concept of sport specifies an abstract content that can be seen in all the various sporting activities. Even so, it is often possible to think of exceptions to such definitions such as, in this case, indoor athletics. On the other hand, we may quibble as to whether a sport can avoid physical exertion, in which case archery might be excluded from our definition. The abstract version of the concept of sport may be precisely defined as a construct.

The concepts of everyday life are directly linked to the empirical 'things' they describe, the constructs of social science require a specification of how they can be measured. For example, the abstract concept of 'institutionalised racism' must have a set of specified measures before it can be recognised and analysed in social research. Concepts transcend, but are related to the world of experience. Dictionaries are continually revised to refine definitions as well as to include new concepts, and the same is true in social research.

THEORY, CONCEPTS AND CONCEPT FORMATION

We learned that conceptualisation involves two discrete elements:

- An abstract label or category
- A set of empirical referents described by the abstraction.

In social research, when we define a concept as an abstraction, and then link this abstraction to a set of empirical referents, we are thinking deductively, working from theory or applying theory to data. We can think up a theoretical definition of a religion in which something is a religion if it meets the following criteria:

- Belief in superhuman power
- Belief in an afterlife
- Belief that obedience to superhuman power will lead to afterlife.

We can then analyse all belief systems and decide which are religions and which are not religions. On the other hand, when we use a set of empirical referents to generate and define an abstract concept, we are thinking inductively, working from data to theory. Here we might start by finding out about all belief systems and then try to see what they have in common.

This may lead to different subtypes of religion. Concept formation in sociology and social research can be a largely theoretical activity. In the case of social class, for example, attempts to define the concept of social class as 'a relation to the means of production', or 'a labour market position' came prior to the development of a classification scheme designed to measure social class in social research. Historically, the Registrar General's classification was not based on such theorisations, it was designed as a practical way of categorising people who did similar sorts of work in order that deaths in these occupations might be recorded, data collected and death rates across different occupational groups compared. This 'practical' classification scheme lasted from its inception in 1911 until 2001 when it was replaced by the National Statistics Socio-Economic Classification.

CONCEPT FORMATION IN SOCIOLOGY

The concept of social exclusion is a useful one to examine since it has quantitative and qualitative aspects and is fundamentally concerned with social relationships.

Following the review by Burchardt *et al.*, the concept of social exclusion can refer to each of the following social groups:

- 'Those whose circumstances have led them to be separated from the bureaucratic forms of the state that would otherwise include them in systems of income support, the educational system, gaining access to employment, and health services'
- Those groups that 'are unlikely to experience regular secure employment and [whose] economic insecurity excludes [them from] participation in otherwise "normal" aspects of social life'.
- 'Those who live in well defined, but separate areas of cities and urban conglomerations [that are] spatially and socially marginal, like ghettos or no-go areas for those not socially excluded.'

RESEARCH STRATEGIES

A research strategy is a collection of philosophical and theoretical commitments that may influence decisions made about the research design and the choice of specific methods of data collection and analysis. Strategy also relates closely to the questions the research can address and determines the type of findings that can result from the research. As suggested, be using the distinction between qualitative and quantitative research strategies to introduce you to the defining characteristics of social research.

Qualitative research strategies are meaning-centred and informed by the interpretivist tradition in social theory. In this tradition, the description and explanation of the social world must refer to subjective meanings. Interpretivist research aims to reveal the meaningful aspects of cultures as in the case of social anthropology and Chicago School of sociology. This tradition has used ethnographic methods to reveal the meaning of 'other' cultures, including sub-cultures in urban and rural areas.

Ethnography involves observing communities, interviewing individuals, reading the text found in documents, and collecting this data directly in the natural context shared by those being studied. This use of the natural context is essential if the researcher is to learn to see the social world as it is seen by those being studied.

The aim of ethnographic methods is learning to see the social world as it is seen by those being studied. Qualitative research often aims to explain social action in terms of the subjective meanings of the actor and the constructions placed upon their actions by themselves and other actors. Ethnography is a way of accessing those meanings.

Thus if we attempt to understand the reason why some young women decide to have children, we must refer to the 'frame of reference' that informs such decisions. Although constructed as 'a problem' by policy makers, teenage pregnancy may represent an attractive change of lifestyle for young women since it can lead to greater autonomy and status. An interpretivist sociological explanation provides a meaningful account of the action concerned.

For quantitative social research, the social world consists of contingent relationships between well-defined concepts. Quantitative research strategies emphasise the measurement of concepts and can be described as variablecentred in contrast to meaning-centred. Examples of variables include the annual income of a household or the number of children in a household. A sample of data collected for these variables will tell us what the averages are and how typical they are.

If we are using systematic randomly sampled data, we can estimate the accuracy of our descriptions for the population as a whole. There may be contingent relations between variables, for example, income may influence the number of children in a household. There is no certainty or determinism, only defined 'odds', that an income level will be associated with the number of children. These contingencies are often relatively stable, but may vary between regions and may change over time.

In sophisticated data analysis, we would want to assess:

- The explanatory power of each variable
- How much confidence we can have in the estimates of explanatory power.

Subjective meanings are not necessary for these contingencies to operate effectively. After all, the consequences of smoking were experienced by those who died of lung cancer whether or not they subjectively attached that risk to their smoking behaviour.

So far, we have seen that qualitative and quantitative social research have very different core themes: one is meaning-centred, and one is variable centered. These distinctions are not mutually exclusive in research practice, but here they are used to help us identify the differing aims of each of the two major research strategies. Qualitative research seeks to reveal subjective meanings in cultures and sub-cultures, while quantitative social research seeks to establish contingent relationships between variables.

EPISTEMOLOGY AND RESEARCH STRATEGIES

All aspects of social research tend to imply a specific intellectual stance in relation to epistemology. Epistemology concerns the theory of knowledge and is the study of how we can come to accept that a research finding is 'true'. Qualitative social research seeks to establish knowledge of the social world by the study of people's own interpretations of the social world.

Those who practice quantitative social research use a version of the natural science method for establishing knowledge and are often called positivists. Positivism is not the only way of describing those who favour a scientific approach and those that argue that quantitative data analysis provides important insights into the social world. I prefer the term 'realism' since this conveys a commitment to a scientific approach, but has a much more sophisticated view of the process of scientific research than that conveyed by the term positivism.

ONTOLOGY AND RESEARCH STRATEGIES

Ontology refers to the nature of the social: 'social constructs' for interpretivists and 'social objects' for positivists. The contrasting epistemologies of positivism and interpretivism are linked to contrasting versions of ontology namely objectivism and constructionism. In Durkheim's classic study Suicide, he aimed to establish sociology as a discipline in the French academy by arguing and demonstrating that 'social facts', such as the suicide rates of a community, were social objects, that they were 'things' that were:

- External to the people in that community
- Constrained a number of them to commit suicide.

His research sought to establish that the measured variation in the objective conditions of social integration, prevailing in different regions and nations, determined the suicide rate in those regions and nations. He did this using the classical techniques of multivariate analysis. In the interpretivist tradition, Douglas displays the rival ontology used in qualitative strategies.

He shows that suicide is a social construct by describing:

- How the label 'suicide' was attached to an action as a result of a process of negotiation that constructed the meaning of the action
- How even in the classic, discipline-defining study of Suicide Durkheim was unable to explain variations in suicide rates without some references of the social meanings of the social facts of suicide.

It is widely accepted in contemporary sociology that the social involves both meaningful construction and objectification and that these two processes are continuous and inseparable. However, quantitative research is predominantly concerned with the influence of 'object-like' institutionalised constructions on social action, while qualitative research is concerned with the process of constructing and negotiating 'fluid-like' social constructs. The difference between the two approaches can be made clear by examining the case of attitudes, such as political attitudes. In quantitative attitude research, it is assumed that people have varying attitudes to political parties and that these can be recorded using standardised measuring instruments such as questionnaires.

Thus 'attitude' is presumed to be a reasonably coherent and stable set of values and beliefs that can be measured by asking people a series of questions about political issues. What is called 'multi-dimensional attitude scaling' measures subject's attitudes and then correlates these summary scales with other social variables such as gender, income, social status, etc. that explain variations in attitudes to political parties. Attitudes are assumed stable social objects that can be used to explain why people support and vote for political parties. For interpretivists, multi-dimensional attitude scaling imposes the researcher's construction of meaning on the subject's own perspective.

Surveys pre-structure the subjective in order to develop standardised measures. Using the qualitative research strategy one could first explore the assumed coherence stability of 'attitudes' by analysing their expression in specific contexts such as a focus group. As suggested, be exploring the validity of attitude measurement in a subsequent stage, but it is worth considering why most political parties now use focus groups rather that relying solely on survey methods to establish public opinion on political issues. Focus group methods collect data on the expression of attitudes in a more natural setting of a group discussion.

The attitudes expressed to a survey interviewer may be influenced by the specific context of the interview. In survey research, the attitude is expressed in the researcher's words as defined in the questionnaire, and the research cannot measure how stable or sincerely held the attitude or opinion is. Focus group methods access attitudes largely in the form of the subject's own words, and the method allows for the possibility that attitudes can be measured by the developed position on an issue taken by a group after some discussion. The more natural the research situation, the more valid the respondent's measured attitudes are likely to be.

Table. The Components of Social Research Strategies

	Qualitative Research Strategy	**Quantitative Research Strategy**
Defining characteristics	Meaning-centred	Variable-centred
Descriptive aims	Detailed descriptions of core meanings of a culture. Interpretation of the meaning of action. confidence in these	Summary descrip- tions (averages and variation) of social variables and the degree of estimates.
Relationship between theory and research	Theory generation by means of revealing or reporting the constructions of reality in talk and text including official documents. theoretical	Theory testing via the establishment within a specified context of contingent relationships between variables taken as representing constructs.
Epistemology	Interpretivism. The human nature of social objects requires reference to the subjective meaning when	Positivist or post- positivistic. Theoretical models are developed by deduction and

	explaining social action. Theory is generated by analysis of the subjective. criteria of causal	tested by measurement of concepts and applying inference.
Ontology	The 'social world' is constructed in our attempts to understand it and act upon it.	There is a knowable social world independent of our constructions of it.
Theoretical perspectives	Symbolic Interactionism to postmodernism. Social structure is formed by institutionalised meanings and constructs.	Structural behaviourism. Meanings and action derive from occupancy of structured social locations.

It is possible that survey methods can measure some well-defined attitudes. For example, people's attitudes to the British monarchy may be regarded as unproblematic to measure. However, survey methods may be less suited to establish attitudes to topics that are more remote from everyday experience and less well defined, such as the use of stem cell research in medicine.

This example flags up the possibility that relevance of ontological commitments to research practice is itself an empirical question. In their study of alcoholic liver disease, Law and Singleton describe how the patient experience and organisational processes that are supposed to structure pathways through diagnosis, treatment and outcome are in fact ill-defined with unstable and problematic connections between activity and outcomes. In these circumstances, they argue, orthodox approaches to social research may not capture what they call 'a mess'. However, it is incorrect to assert that 'mess' characterises every social context.

Some social contexts are highly structured with well-defined social processes that secure a fairly stable and regular set of outcomes. For these contexts what he terms 'standard research methods' remain important. We can think of gender socialisation and education as involving relatively well-defined institutionalised social processes that are productive of stable and regular outcomes.

Goldthorpe, for example, has used a case of social mobility research, to react against the abandonment of traditional research strategies. Some ontological assumptions suit some but not all research topics. We have established that the two major strategies of social research have contrasting stances on both epistemology and ontology. The third component of the research strategy concerns the relationship between theory and research.

THEORY AND RESEARCH STRATEGIES

Qualitative research is often described as inductive. Induction describes the process of constructing and validating theory using data analysis. Data analysis precedes theory construction. One methodology for qualitative and inductive theory construction is 'grounded theory'. Grounded theory involves working as closely as possible with the constructs used by the people who are being studied and building up from these to abstract concepts that may be linked together in qualitative models of processes or meaning systems. Quantitative social research is usually organised around the aim of testing theory.

A common practice in quantitative social research is to review both theoretical and research literature with the aim of summarising previous research in the form of a causal model. This model of the contingent relationships between theoretical concepts is then translated into a model of variables or indicators of concepts that informs a research design. The data analysis is then conducted to evaluate the relative importance of each causal variable in the model or to determine whether the most important causal mechanisms are operating to determine outcomes.

It is important to see how these three components of research strategy tend to 'hang together': an interpretivist epistemology, constructivist ontology and an inductive view of the relationship between theory and research, positivistic epistemology, objectivist ontology and a deductive view of the research process. This synergy between elements of research strategy facilitates learning about social research, but you must expect to come across quantitative research that uses inductive 'data dredging' or qualitative research that aims to test theories using a realist ontology and deductive logic.

RESEARCH METHODOLOGY

Social scientists are divided into camps of support for particular research techniques. These disputes relate to the historical core of social theory. While very different in many aspects, both qualitative and quantitative approaches involve a systematic interaction between theory and data. The choice of method often depends largely on what the researcher intends to investigate. For example, a researcher concerned with drawing a statistical generaliation across an entire population may administer a survey questionnaire to a representitive sample population.

By contrast, a researcher who seeks full contextual understanding of an individuals' social actions may choose ethnographic participant observation or open-ended interviews. Studies will commonly combine, or'triangulate', quantitative and qualitative methods as part of a'multi-strategy' design. For instance, a quantitative study may be performed to gain statistical patterns or a target sample, and then combined with a qualitative interview to determine the play of agency.

SAMPLING

Typically a population is very large, making a census or a complete enumeration of all the values in that population infeasible. A'sample' thus forms a manageable subset of a population. In positivist research, statistics derived from a sample are analysed in order to draw inferences regarding the population as a whole. The process of collecting information from a sample is referred to as'sampling'. Sampling methods may be either'random' or non-random/ nonprobability. The most common reason for sampling is to obtain information about a population. Sampling is quicker and cheaper than a complete census of a population.

Ethics

The primary assumptions of the ethics in social research are:

- Voluntary participation
- No physical or psychological harm to subjects
- Integrity
- *PAC*: Privacy, anonymity and confidentiality

Types of Method

The following list of research methods is neither exclusive nor exhaustive:

- *Quantitative methods*:
  - Chi-square test
  - Cluster analysis
  - Regression analysis
  - Spearman's rank correlation coefficient
  - Structured interview
  - Statistical surveys and questionnaires
  - Student's t-test
  - Quantitative marketing research
- *Qualitative methods*:
  - Analytic induction
  - Archival research
  - Content analysis
  - Ethnography
  - Focus group
  - Historical method
  - Life history
  - Longitudinal study
  - Morphological analysis
  - Participant observation
  - Semi-structured interview
  - Survey research
  - Textual analysis
  - Unstructured interview

FOUNDATIONS OF SOCIAL RESEARCH

Social research is based on logic and empirical observations. Charles C. Ragin writes in his Constructing Social Research book that"Social research involved the interaction between ideas and evidence. Ideas help social researchers make sense of evidence, and researchers use evidence to extend, revise and test ideas". Social research thus attempts to create or validate theories through data collection and data analysis, and its goal is exploration, description and explanation. It should never lead or be mistaken with philosophy or belief.

Social research aims to find social patterns of regularity in social life and usually deals with social groups, not individuals themselves. Research can also be divided into pure research and applied research. Pure research has no application on real life, whereas applied research attempts to influence the real world. There are no laws in social science that parallel the laws in the natural science. A law in social science is a universal generaliation about a class of facts. A fact is an observed phenomenon, and observation means it has been seen, heard or otherwise experienced by researcher. A theory is a systematic explanation for the observations that relate to a particular aspect of social life. Concepts are the basic building blocks of theory and are abstract elements representing classes of phenomena. Axioms or postulates are basic assertions assumed to be true. Propositions are conclusions drawn about the relationships among concepts, based on analysis of axioms.

Hypotheses are specified expectations about empirical reality which are derived from propositions. Social research involves testing these hypotheses to see if they are true. Social research involves creating a theory, operationaliation and observation. Social theories are written in the language of variables, in other words, theories describe logical relationships between variables. Variables are logical sets of attributes, with people being the'carriers' of those variables. Variables are also divided into independent variables that influences the dependent variables. For example, in a study of how different dosages of a drug are related to the severity of symptoms of a disease, a measure of the severity of the symptoms of the disease is a dependent variable and the administration of the drug in specified doses is the independent variable. Researchers will compare the different values of the dependent variable and attempt to draw conclusions.

RULES FOR SOCIAL RESEARCH

Although there are no laws in social science that parallel laws in the natural sciences, there is general consensus about fundamental rules or principles about how to do social research. When social scientists speak of"good research" the focus is on how the research is done-whether the research is methodologically sound-rather than on whether the results of the research are consistent with personal biases or preconceptions. Glenn Firebaugh summaries the principles for good research in his book Seven Rules for Social Research. The first rule is that"There should be the possibility of surprise in social research. " As Firebaugh elaborates: "Rule 1 is intended to warn that you don't want to be blinded by preconceived ideas so that you fail to look for contrary evidence, or you fail to recognie contrary evidence when you do encounter it, or you recognie contrary evidence but suppress it and refuse to accept your findings for what they appear to say. "

In addition, good research will "look for differences that make a difference" and "build in reality checks". Rule 4 advises researchers to replicate, that is, "to see if identical analyses yield similar results for different samples of people". The next two rules urge researchers to "compare like with like" and to "study change"; these two rules are especially important when researchers want to estimate the effect of one variable on another. The final rule, "Let method be the servant, not the master, " reminds researchers that methods are the means, not the end, of social research; it is critical from the outset to fit the research design to the research issue, rather than the other way around.

Types of Explanations

Explanations in social theories can be idiographic or nomothetic. An idiographic approach to an explanation is one where the scientists seek to exhaust the idiosyncratic causes of a particular condition or event, *i.e.* by trying to provide all possible explanations of a particular case. Nomothetic explanations tend to be more general with scientists trying to identify a few causal factors that impact a wide class of conditions or events. For example, when dealing with the problem of how people choose a job, idiographic explanation would be to list all possible reasons why a given person chooses a given job, while nomothetic explanation would try to find factors that determine why job applicants in general choose a given job.

QUANTITATIVE/QUALITATIVE DEBATE

There is usually a trade off between the number of cases and the number of their variables that social research can study. Qualitative research usually involves few cases with many variables, while quantitative involves many phenomena with few variables.

There is some debate over whether "quantitative research" and "qualitative research" methods can be complementary: some researchers argue that combining the two approaches is beneficial and helps build a more complete picture of the social world, while other researchers believe that the epistemologies that underpin each of the approaches are so divergent that they cannot be reconciled within a research project. While quantitative methods are based on a natural science, positivist model of testing theory, qualitative methods are based on interpretivism and are more focused around generating theories and accounts. Positivists treat the social world as something that is 'out there', external to the social scientist and waiting to be researched. Interpretivists, on the other hand believe that the social world is constructed by social agency and therefore any intervention by a researcher will affect social reality.

Herein lies the supposed conflict between quantitative and qualitative approaches-quantitative approaches traditionally seek to minimise intervention in order to produce valid and reliable statistics, whereas qualitative approaches traditionally treat intervention as something that is necessary. However, it is increasingly recognised that the significance of these differences should not be exaggerated and that quantitative and qualitative approaches can be complementary.

They can be combined in a number of ways, for example:

- Qualitative methods can be used in order to develop quantitative research tools. For example, focus groups could be used to explore an issue with a small number of people and the data gathered using this method could then be used to develop a quantitative survey that could be administered to a far greater number of people allowing results to be generalised.
- Qualitative methods can be used to explore and facilitate the interpretation of relationships between variables. For example researchers may inductively hypothesie that there would be a positive relationship between positive attitudes of sales staff and the amount of sales of a store. However, quantitative, deductive, structured observation of 576 convenience stores could reveal that this was not the case, and in order to understand why the relationship between the variables was negative the researchers may undertake qualitative case studies of four stores including participant observation. This might abductively confirm that the relationship was negative, but that it was not the positive attitude of sales staff that led to low sales, but rather that high sales led to busy staff who were less likely to be express positive emotions at work!

Quantitative methods are useful for describing social phenomena, especially on a larger scale. Qualitative methods allow social scientists to provide richer explanations of social phenomena, frequently on a smaller scale. By using two or more approaches researchers may be able to 'triangulate' their findings and provide a more valid representation of the social world.

PROCESS OF SOCIAL DEVELOPMENT

Social development is a process which results in the transformation of social structures in a manner which improves the capacity of the society to fulfill its aspirations. Society develops by consciousness and social consciousness develops by organiation. The process that is subconscious in the society emerges as conscious knowledge in pioneering individuals. Development is a process, not a programme. Its power issues more from its subtle aspects than from material objects.

Not all social change constitutes development. It consists of four well-marked stages—survival, growth, development and evolution, each of which contains the other three within it. The quantitative expansion of existing activities generates growth or horiontal expansion. Development implies a qualitative change in the way the society carries out its activities, such as through more progressive attitudes and behaviour by the population, the adoption of more effective social organiations or more advanced technology which may have been developed elsewhere. The term evolution refers to the original formulation and adoption of qualitative and structural advances in the form of new social attitudes, values, behaviours, or organiations. While the term is usually applied to changes that are beneficial to society, it may result in negative side-effects or consequences that undermine or eliminate existing ways of life that are considered positive.

APPLICATION OF SOCIAL JUSTICE

Social justice is the application of the concept of justice on a social scale. The term appeared before the 1800s, including in the Federalist Papers and Edward Gibbon's The History of the Decline and Fall of the Roman Empireý. The idea was elaborated by the moral theologian John A. Ryan, who initiated the concept of a living wage. Father Coughlin also used the term in his publications in the 1930s and the 1940s. The concept was further expanded upon by John Rawls beginning in the 1960s. It is a part of Catholic social teaching, Social Gospel from Episcopalians and is one of the Four Pillars of the Green Party upheld by green parties worldwide. Some tenets of social justice have been adopted by those on the left of the political spectrum. Social justice is also a concept that some use to describe the movement towards a socially just world. In this context, social justice is based on the concepts of human rights and equality and involves a greater degree of economic egalitarianism through progressive taxation, income redistribution, or even property redistribution. These policies aim to achieve what developmental economists refer to as more equality of opportunity than may currently exist in some societies, and to manufacture equality of outcome in cases where incidental inequalities appear in a procedurally just system.

THEORIES OF SOCIAL JUSTICE

Rawls

The liberal political philosopher John Rawls draws on the utilitarian insights of Bentham and Mill, the social contract ideas of John Locke, and the categorical imperative ideas of Kant. His first statement of principle was made in A Theory of Justice where he proposed that, "Each person possesses an inviolability founded on justice that even the welfare of society as a whole cannot override. For this reason justice denies that the loss of freedom for some is made right by a greater good shared by others. ".

A deontological proposition that echoes Kant in framing the moral good of justice in absolutist terms. His views are definitively restated in Political Liberalism where society is seen "as a fair system of co-operation over time, from one generation to the next. ".

All societies have a basic structure of social, economic, and political institutions, both formal and informal. In testing how well these elements fit and work together, Rawls based a key test of legitimacy on the theories of social contract.

To determine whether any particular system of collectively enforced social arrangements is legitimate, he argued that one must look for agreement by the people who are subject to it, but not necessarily to an objective notion of justice based on coherent ideological grounding. Obviously, not every citien can be asked to participate in a poll to determine his or her consent to every proposal in which some degree of coercion is involved, so one has to assume that all citiens are reasonable.

Rawls constructed an argument for a two-stage process to determine a citien's hypothetical agreement:

- The citien agrees to be represented by X for certain purposes; to that extent, X holds these powers as a trustee for the citien;
- X agrees that a use of enforcement in a particular social context is legitimate; the citien, therefore, is bound by this decision because it is the function of the trustee to represent the citien in this way.

This applies to one person representing a small group as equally as it does to national governments which are the ultimate trustees, holding representative powers for the benefit of all citiens within their territorial boundaries, and if those governments fail to provide for the welfare of their citiens just as to the principles of justice, they are not legitimate. To emphasise the general principle that justice should rise from the people and not be dictated by the law-making powers of governments, Rawls asserted that, "There is... a general presumption against imposing legal and other restrictions on conduct without sufficient reason.

But this presumption creates no special priority for any particular liberty. " This is support for an unranked set of liberties that reasonable citiens in all states should respect and uphold—to some extent, the list proposed by Rawls matches the normative human rights that have international recognition and direct enforcement in some nation states where the citiens need encouragement to act in a way that fixes a greater degree of equality of outcome.

The Basic Liberties Just as to Rawls

- Freedom of thought;
- Liberty of conscience as it affects social relationships on the grounds of religion, philosophy, and morality;
- Political liberties;
- Freedom of association;
- Freedoms necessary for the liberty and integrity of the person; and
- Rights and liberties covered by the rule of law.

Criticism

Many authors criticie the idea that there exists an objective standard of social justice. Moral relativists deny that there is any kind of objective standard for justice in general. Non-cognitivists, moral skeptics, moral nihilists, and most logical positivists deny the epistemic possibility of objective notions of justice. Cynics believe that any ideal of social justice is ultimately a mere justification for the status quo. Supporters of social darwinism believe that social justice assists the least fit to reproduce, sometimes labeled as dysgenics, and hence should be opposed.

Many other people accept some of the basic principles of social justice, such as the idea that all human beings have a basic level of value, but disagree with the elaborate conclusions that may or may not follow from this. One example is the statement by H.G. Wells that all people are"equally entitled to the respect of their fellow-men. " On the other hand, some scholars reject the very idea of social justice as meaningless, religious, self-contradictory, and ideological, believing that to realie any degree of social justice is unfeasible, and that the attempt to do so must destroy all liberty. The most complete rejection of the concept of social justice comes from Friedrich Hayek of the Austrian School of economics:

"There can be no test by which we can discover what is'socially unjust' because there is no subject by which such an injustice can be committed, and there are no rules of individual conduct the observance of which in the market order would secure to the individuals and groups the position which as such would appear just to us. Social justice] does not belong to the category of error but to that of non-sense, like the term `a moral stone'. "

SOCIAL JUSTICE FROM RELIGIOUS TRADITIONS

Methodists

From their founding Methodism was a Christian social justice movement. Under John Wesley's direction, Methodists became leaders in many social justice issues of the day, including the prison reform and abolitionism movements. Wesley himself was among the first to preach for slaves rights attracting significant opposition., Today social justice plays a major role in the United Methodist Church.

Jewish Social Teaching

In To Heal a Fractured World: The Ethics of Responsibility, Rabbi Jonathan Sacks states that social justice has a central place in Judaism. One of Judaism's most distinctive and challenging ideas is its ethics of responsibility reflected in the concepts of simcha, tedakah, chesed, and tikkun olam.

Catholic Social Teaching

Catholic social teaching consists of those aspects of Roman Catholic doctrine which relate to matters dealing with the collective aspect of humanity. A distinctive feature of the Catholic social doctrine is their concern for the poorest members of society.

Two of the seven key areas of "Catholic social teaching" are pertinent to social justice:

- Life and dignity of the human person: The foundational principle of all "Catholic Social Teaching" is the sanctity of all human life and the inherent dignity of every human person. Human life must be valued above all material possessions.
- Preferential option for the poor and vulnerable: Catholics believe Jesus taught that on the Day of Judgement God will ask what each person did to help the poor and needy: "Amen, I say to you, whatever you did for one of these least brothers of mine, you did for me. " The Catholic Church believes that through words, prayers and deeds one must show solidarity with, and compassion for, the poor. The moral test of any society is "how it treats its most vulnerable members. The poor have the most urgent moral claim on the conscience of the nation. People are called to look at public policy decisions in terms of how they affect the poor. "

Even before it was propounded in the Catholic social doctrine, social justice appeared regularly in the history of the Catholic Church:

- The term "social justice" was adopted by the Jesuit Luigi Taparelli in the 1840s, based on the work of Thomas Aquinas. He wrote extensively in his journal Civiltà Cattolica, engaging both capitalist and socialist theories from a natural law viewpoint. His basic premise was that the rival economic theories, based on subjective Cartesian thinking, undermined the unity of society present in Thomistic metaphysics; neither the liberal capitalists nor the communists concerned themselves with public moral philosophy.
- Pope Leo XIII, who studied under Taparelli, published in 1891 the encyclical Rerum Novarum, rejecting both socialism and capitalism, while defending labour unions and private property. He stated that

society should be based on cooperation and not class conflict and competition. In this document, Leo set out the Catholic Church's response to the social instability and labour conflict that had arisen in the wake of industrialiation and had led to the rise of socialism. The Pope advocated that the role of the State was to promote social justice through the protection of rights, while the Church must speak out on social issues in order to teach correct social principles and ensure class harmony.

- The encyclical Quadragesimo Anno of 1931 by Pope Pius XI, encourages a living wage, subsidiarity, and advocates that social justice is a personal virtue as well as an attribute of the social order, saying that society can be just only if individuals and institutions are just.
- Pope Benedict XVI's encyclical Deus Caritas Est of 2006 claims that justice is the defining concern of the state and the central concern of politics, and not of the church, which has charity as its central social concern. It said that the laity has the specific responsibility of pursuing social justice in civil society and that the church's active role in social justice should be to inform the debate, using reason and natural law, and also by providing moral and spiritual formation for those involved in politics.
- The official Catholic doctrine on social justice can be found in the book Compendium of the Social Doctrine of the Church, published in 2004 and updated in 2006, by the Pontifical Council Iustitia et Pax.

SOCIAL JUSTICE MOVEMENTS

Social justice is also a concept that is used to describe the movement towards a socially just world, ie. the Global Justice Movement. In this context, social justice is based on the concepts of human rights and equality, and can be defined as "the way in which human rights are manifested in the everyday lives of people at every level of society". There are a number of movements that are working to achieve social justice in society. These movements are working towards the realiation of a world where all members of a society, regardless of background or procedural justice, have basic human rights and equal access to the benefits of their society.

The Green Party

Social Justice is one of the Four Pillars of the Green Party and is sometimes referred to as "Social and Global Equality" or "Economic Justice". The Canadian party defines the principle as the "equitable distribution of resources to ensure that all have full opportunities for personal and social development". As one of the 10 key values of the party in the United States, social justice is described as the right and opportunity of all people "to benefit equally from the resources afforded us by society and the environment. "

Social Justice in Health care

Social justice has more recently made its way into the field of bioethics. Discussion involves topics such as affordable access to health care, especially for low income households and family. The discussion also raises questions such as whether society should bear health care costs for low income families, and whether the global marketplace is a good thing to deal with health care. Ruth Faden and Madison Powers of the Johns Hopkins Berman Institute of Bioethics focus their analysis of social justice on which inequalities matter the most. They develop a social justice theory that answers some of these questions in concrete settings.

PERIODICALS AND PUBLICATIONS

Social Justice was also the name of a periodical published by Father Coughlin in the 1930s and early 1940s. Coughlin's organiation was known as the National Union for Social Justice and he frequently used the term social justice in his radio broadcasts. In 1935 Coughlin made a series of broadcasts in which he outlined what he termed"the Christian principles of social justice" as an alternative to both capitalism and communism. Some Catholic contemporaries, such as the Catholic Radical Alliance, felt that he misused the term, and was too supportive of capitalism.

DISCIPLINE IN SOCIAL ENGINEERING

Social engineering is a discipline in political science that refers to efforts to influence popular attitudes and social behaviours on a large scale, whether by governments or private groups. In the political arena, the counterpart of social engineering is political engineering.

For various reasons, the term has been imbued with negative connotations. However, virtually all law and governance has the effect of changing behaviour and can be considered"social engineering" to some extent. Prohibitions on murder, rape, suicide and littering are all policies aimed at discouraging undesirable behaviours. In British and Canadian jurisprudence, changing public attitudes about a behaviour is accepted as one of the key functions of laws prohibiting it. Governments also influence behaviour more subtly through incentives and disincentives built into economic policy and tax policy, for instance, and have done so for centuries. In practice, whether any specific policy is labeled as"social engineering" is often a question of intent.

The term is most often used by libertarians, free-market thinkers, and traditionalists as an accusation against anyone who proposes to use law, tax policy, or other kinds of state influence to change existing power relationships: for instance, between men and women, or between different ethnic groups. Political conservatives in the United States have accused their opponents of social engineering through the promotion of political correctness, insofar as it may change social attitudes by defining"acceptable" and"unacceptable" language or acts. The right has itself been accused of social engineering due to its promotion of Abstinence-only sex education, the English-only movement, Sodomy laws and state sponsored school prayer.

Before one can engage in social engineering, one must have reliable information about the society that is to be engineered, and one must have effective tools to carry out the engineering. Both of these only became available relatively recently-roughly within the past one hundred years. The development of social science made it possible to gather and analye information about social attitudes and trends, which is necessary in order to judge the initial state of society before an engineering attempt and the success or failure of that attempt after it has been implemented. At the same time, the development of modern communications technology and the media provided the tools through which social engineering could be carried out.

While social engineering can be carried out by any organiation-whether large or small, public or private-the most comprehensive campaigns of social engineering are those initiated by powerful central governments.

Extremely intensive social engineering campaigns occurred in countries with authoritarian governments. In the 1920s, the government of the Soviet Union embarked on a campaign to fundamentally alter the behaviour and ideals of Soviet citiens, to replace the old social frameworks of Tsarist Russia with a new Soviet culture, to create the New Soviet man. The Soviets used newspapers, books, film, mass relocations, and even architectural design tactics to serve as"social condenser" and change personal values and private relationships. Similar examples are the Chinese"Great Leap Forward" and"Cultural Revolution" programme and the Khmer Rouge's plan of deurbaniation of Cambodia. In Singapore, the government's housing policies attempt to promote a mix of all races within each subsidied housing district in order to foster social cohesion and national loyalty while providing the citiens with affordable housing. Non-authoritarian regimes tend to rely on more sustained social engineering campaigns that create more gradual, but ultimately as far-reaching, change. Examples include the"War on Drugs" in the United States, the increasing reach of intellectual property rights and copyright, and the promotion of elections as a political tool.

The campaign for promoting elections, which is by far the most successful of the three examples, has been in place for over two centuries. Social theorists of the Frankfurt School in Weimar Germany like Theodor Adorno had also observed the new phenomenon of mass culture and commented on its new manipulative power, when the rise of the Nais drove them out of the country around 1930. The Nais themselves were no strangers to the idea of influencing political attitudes and re-defining personal relationships. The Nai propaganda machine under Joseph Goebbels was a synchronied, sophisticated and effective tool for creating public opinion. In a similar vein the Greek military junta of 1967-1974 attempted to steer Greek public opinion not only by propaganda but also by inventing new words and slogans such as: palaiokommatismos, Ellas Ellinon Christianon translated as: Greece of Christian Greeks, Ethnosotirios Epanastasis translated as Nation-saving Revolution meaning coup d'état etc. Social engineering can be used as a means to achieve a wide variety of different results, as illustrated by the different governments and other organiations that have employed it.

The discussion of the possibilities for such manipulation became especially active following World War II, with the advent of television, and continuing discussion of techniques of social engineering-particularly in advertising-is still quite pertinent in the western model of consumer capitalism.

THE O'BRIEN AND GANNON THEORY

The term social engineering has been used in a different context by social scientists Antonis Gannon and Ellis O'Brien. The two believed that peoples attitudes, personalities and other mental attributes are affected by the people surrounding them. The two go on to say that if one were to experiment with how a certain person reacts to different combinations of different people one could hypothetically control how that person behaves, they refer to this as social engineering. This theory was unveiled at Dublin Institute of Technology on the 10th of March 2010.

LITERATURE

George Orwell

A popular novel taught in most high schools is the George Orwell novel Nineteen Eighty-Four, in which the known world is controlled by three perpetually warring superpowers. The story takes place in a brutal dystopia that bombards its population with propaganda, constantly monitoring every citien with ubiquitous TV cameras and police patrols.

Karl Popper

In his classic political science book, The Open Society and Its Enemies, volume I, The Spell of Plato, Karl Popper examined the application of the critical and rational methods of science to the problems of the open society. In this respect, he made a crucial distinction between the principles of democratic social reconstruction and 'Utopian social engineering'

Popper wrote:

- The piecemeal engineer will adopt the method of searching for, and fighting against, the greatest and most urgent evil of society, rather than searching for, and fighting for, its greatest ultimate good.

Popper, the difference between 'piecemeal social engineering' and 'Utopian social engineering' is:

- The difference between a reasonable method of improving the lot of man, and a method which, if really tried, may easily lead to an intolerable increase in human suffering. It is the difference between a method which can be applied at any moment, and a method whose advocacy may easily become a means of continually postponing action until a later date, when conditions are more favourable. And it is also the difference between the only method of improving matters which has so far been really successful, at any time, and in any place, and a method which, wherever it has been tried, has led only to the use of violence in place of reason, and if not to its own abandonment, at any rate to that of its original blueprint.

SOCIAL WORK

Social work has its roots in the struggle of society to deal with poverty and the resultant problems. Therefore, social work is intricately linked with the idea of charity work; but must be understood in broader terms. The concept of charity goes back to ancient times, and the practice of providing for the poor has roots in all major world religions.

PRE-MODERN HISTORY

In the West, when Constantine I legalied the Christian Church, the newly legitimised church set up poorhouses, homes for the aged, hospitals, and orphanages. These were often funded, at least in part, from grants from the Empire. By 590 the church had a system for circulating the consumables to the poor: associated with each parish was a diaconium or office of the deacon. As there was no effective bureaucracy below city government that was capable of charitable activities, the clergy served this role in the west up through the 18th century. During the Middle Ages, the Christian church had vast influence on European society and charity was considered to be a responsibility and a sign of one's piety. This charity was in the form of direct relief as opposed to trying to change the root causes of poverty. The practice and profession of social work has a relatively modern and scientific origin.

MODERN HISTORY

Social work, as a profession, originated in the 19th century. The movement began primarily in the United States and England. After the end of feudalism, the poor were seen as a more direct threat to the social order, and so the state formed an organied system to care for them. In England, the Poor Law served this purpose. This system of laws sorted the poor into different categories, such as the able bodied poor, the impotent poor, and the idle poor. This system developed different responses to these different groups. The 19th century ushered in the Industrial Revolution.

There was a great leap in technological and scientific achievement, but there was also a great migration to urban areas throughout the Western world. This led to many social problems, which in turn led to an increase in social activism. Also with the dawn of the 19th century came a great "missionary" push from many Protestant denominations. Some of these mission efforts, attempted to resolve the problems inherent in large cities like poverty, prostitution, disease, and other afflictions. In the United States workers known as "friendly visitors", stipended by church and other charitable bodies, worked through direct relief, prayer, and evangelism to alleviate these problems. In Europe, chaplains or almoners were appointed to administrate the church's mission to the poor.

During this time, rescue societies were initiated to find more appropriate means of self-support for women involved in prostitution. Mental asylums grew to assist in taking care of the mentally ill. A new philosophy of "scientific charity" emerged, which stated charity should be "secular, rational and empirical as opposed to sectarian, sentimental, and dogmatic. " In the late 1880s, a new system to provide aid for social ills came in to being, which became known as the settlement movement. The settlement movement focused on the causes of poverty through the "three ₹"-Research, Reform, and Residence. They provided a variety of services including educational, legal, and health services. These programmes also advocated changes in social policy. Workers in the settlement movement immersed themselves in the culture of those they were helping. In America, the various approaches to social work led to a fundamental question–is social work a profession? This debate can be traced back to the early 20th century debate between Mary Richmond's Charity Organiation Society and Jane Addams's Settlement House Movement. The essence of this debate was whether the problem should be approached from COS' traditional, scientific method focused on efficiency and prevention or the Settlement House Movement's immersion into the problem, blurring the lines of practitioner and client.

Even as many schools of social work opened and formalied processes for social work began to be developed, the question lingered. In 1915, at the National Conference of Charities and Corrections, Dr. Abraham Flexner spoke on the topic "Is Social Work a Profession?" He contended that it was not because it lacked specialied knowledge and specific application of theoretical and intellectual knowledge to solve human and social problems. This led to the professionaliation of social work, concentrating on case work and the scientific method.

AMERICAN HISTORY

Following European settlement of northern America, the only social welfare was in the area of public health. When epidemics occurred, quarantine facilities were built to prevent contamination. As populations grew, Almhouses were built to house vulnerable people with no other support, including people with a long term illness or older people without families. The first recorded Almshouse was built in 1713 near Philadelphia by William Penn, and was only open to Quakers. A second one was built nearby in 1728, this time with public money. In 1736 New York opened the Poor House of the City of New York and in 1737 New Orleans opened the Saint John's Hospital to serve the poor of the city. Over the next 80 years, the facilities began to change. The precursors to modern hospitals began to form on the grounds of Almshouses, while the Almshouses themselves focused more and more on vulnerable people.

Modern social work in America has its roots in the mass migrations of the 19th Century. Many of the migrants landed in New York and moved to other eastern cities, where mass crowding lead to social problems and ill health. Dr. Eliabeth Blackwell was the United States' first female doctor who set up the New York Infirmary for Indigent Women and Children in 1853. The dispensary was run to assist the poor communities of East Side, and it soon diversified beyond a basic pharmacy, providing social assessments and support to local families. In 1889 Jane Addams was a young medical student who set up Hull House in Chicago to work with poor and immigrant communities. The house was both a community service centre and a social research programme. Precursors to modern social work arose in Blackwell's infirmary and in Hull House as health professionals began to work with social determinants of poor health.

The first professional social worker to be hired in the United States was Garnet Pelton, in 1905 at the Massachusetts General Hospital. Garnet retired after six months due to contracting tuberculosis in the course of her work. She was replaced by Ida Cannon who worked in the role for a further forty years. Dr. Richard Clarke Cabot was the a key advocate in the creation of the role, as he believed there to be a link between tuberculosis and social conditions. Both Pelton and Cannon had trained as nurses before taking up the role. Cabot was in charge of the outpatient ward of the hospital, and together with the newly created social workers, they redefined the way in which health and wellbeing was managed. The economic, social, family and psychological conditions that underpinned many of the conditions that patients presented with were recognised for the first time.

Social workers would work in a complementary relationship with doctors, the former concentrating on physiological health, and the latter on social health. In addition to this, he saw that social work could improve medicine by providing a critical perspective on it while working alongside it in an organisational setting.

This approach soon spread through other American hospitals, and in 1911, there were 44 social work departments in 14 different cities. Two years later, the number of social work departments had grown to 200.

PROFESSIONALISATION

After 1905, most social workers were trained as nurses. The American Association of Hospital Social Workers was set up in 1918 to increase the links between formal education and hospital practice. In 1929 there were ten university courses in medical social work. Around this time, psychiatry and psychology began to compete with social work as the complementary discourse to medicine in hospitals.

Social work practice adapted to this by aligning itself more closely with psychoanalytic ideas, and became less concerned with living conditions and social health. While this detracted from the social concerns, it added a more scientific basis to dealing with patients, and challenging behaviours were more likely to be seen as a mental disfunction than poor moral character. The increase of social spending after World War Two saw another rise in the number of social workers.

Note: In their 2002 article, "What is Humanistic Sociology"—appearing in The American Sociologist—William Du Bois and R. Dean Wright see the creation of the discipline of social work as a political effort within the establishment of sociology to keep its original action-oriented, "change the world" mentality separate from the "rational, masculine science of 'real' sociology.

FREE EDUCATION

Free education is a political term referring to education that is funded through taxation rather than tuition fees. Although primary school and other comprehensive or compulsory education is free in many countries, in the Nordic countries all education is mostly free, including post-graduate studies. In Sweden and Finland, there is no fee for foreign students enrolling at a university, although they may not be eligible for the monthly study allowance and loan most nationals are.

Answers to some of the frequently asked questions about studying in Sweden may be found online.. Denmark also has universal free education, and provides a monthly stipend, the "Statens Uddannelsesstøtte" or "SU", to students over 18 years of age.

Several other European countries, such as England and Germany, have had a history of some form of free education, as has Australia. In the 1970s the Australian Labour Party led by Prime Minister Gough Whitlam introduced reforms which ensured free tertiary education. These reforms were removed later in the 1980s by the Bob Hawke Labour government. Students and radicals opposed the introduction of tertiary fees in the 1980s, and played an important part in forcing the Whitlam government to implement the free education system. Ireland and Argentina provide free education at all levels, including college and university.

In Brail, free education is offered through of the Ministry of Education of Brail that offers scholarships for graduate degrees, master's, doctoral and post-doctoral for the Brailians and immigrants who have Brailian citienship. The best universities and research centers are public institutions, either financed by the local state or by the federal government. These public universities provide a great service to the country in preparing professionals. Graduate students can get paid if they qualify. for the incentive, but competition is extremely fierce. There has been a proliferation in the last 10 years of private universities, which are interested in providing professional training to their undergraduates. These private colleges are not interested in nurturing research centers, since it is not part of their business model to get involved with research. Elsewhere, free education usually comes to students in the form of scholarship and grants, if they cover all or most of students' expenses while at school. Providers of grants and scholarships may be individuals, institutions, advocacy initiatives, etc. They may have economic, humanitarian, charitable or religious motivations. There are examples of steps towards free education being taken across the world primarily in those nations developing rapidly, such as China. In some developing countries like Sri Lanka education is free from the primary level up to the tertiary level. The renowned centers of learning in Libya and Cuba may be attended free of charge.

Free education has long been identified with "sponsored education". This may now evoke images of advertising campaigns, but in the past, especially during the Renaissance, it was common practice among rich dignitaries to sponsor the education of a young man as his patron. In the late 1700s, Thomas Paine was amongst the earliest proponents of universal, free public education, which was considered to be a radical idea at the time. In the United States, government compulsory education was introduced as free or universal education during the late 1800s, and extended across the country by the 1920s. Compulsory education is typically funded through taxes. Aggravated truancy can be prosecuted. Homeschooling or private or parochial schooling is usually a legal alternative.

FREE EDUCATION ON THE INTERNET

Online education has become an option. One of the pioneering Universities to sponsor free education in management is the School of Business and Economics at Umeå University. Free education has become available through several web sites, some of them resembling online universities. Online education faces barriers such as institutional adoption, license/Copyright restrictions and incompatibility, and educator awareness of available resources. Due to the extensive requirements of material for online education, many open community projects have been initiated. Specifically, the Wikimedia Foundation has developed a project devoted to free online educational resources, Wikiversity, and recently, several other sites for specific topics have developed.

MyMCAT was designed as a free community project to aid students wishing to take the MCAT.

BASIC PRINCIPLES IN SOCIAL WORK

RATIONALE

This part discusses the basic principles of social work, and the ethics of a social worker. It gives a clear view of how a social worker is expected to carry out his duties. It also specifies the demands made by social work, and provides important reminders for the social worker.

Guidelines for Social Workers

These are guidelines on how social workers operate:

- *Establishment of a counselling relationship:* The relationship as a process of giving the client an opportunity to grow, develop, and ultimately to understand and discover himself, and make appropriate choices.
- *Acceptance:* Recognize the worth of the individual regardless of his/her cir-cumstances, status, religion, race, politics, behaviour, and wish to foster human dignity and self-respect.
- *Self-determination:* Encourage self-help as a means of growing in self-confidence, and the ability to take on more responsibility for one's own affairs.
- *Freedom to choose:* The client must be able to make appropriate choices, and consider how his/her choice may affect others. Be able to respect and care for clients as individuals without ridicule.
- *Confidentiality:* The relationship is based on trust. You must recognize that what passes between you and your client is confidential. Assume that all information is given in trust, and therefore confidential, unless permission is given to use it in another context.
- *Being empathetic:* You must be sensitive to the client's feelings. Put yourself in the client's position. It helps if you understand your strengths and weaknesses. If you accept yourself as you are, you may be able to accept others.
- *Genuineness:* You must be genuine and not defensive. Be open, real and honest. Studies indicate that positive outcomes can be achieved if the client sees in you empathy, genuineness and a positive regard.

The Art of Building a Helping Relationship:

- Make yourself approachable, genuine and warm.
- Be sensitive, listen attentively.
- Spend time listening to, and talking with, your client.
- Disapprove the act, not the person.

- Be firm and friendly.
- Try not to use threats.
- Explain the rules of the relationship.

Ethics of a Social Worker

The following are the ethics of a social worker:

- Respect the dignity of the individual as the basis for all social relationships.
- Have faith in the capacity of the client to advance towards his/her goals.
- Base your relations with others on their qualities as individuals, without distinction as to race, creed, colour, or economic or social status.
- Recognize that your greatest gift to another person may be to give an opportunity for him/her to develop and exercise his/her own capacities.
- Do not invade the personal affairs of another individual without his/her consent, except in an emergency, where you must act to prevent injury to him/her or to others.
- Believe and accept the differences and individuality of others, and endeavour to build a useful relationship on them.
- Base your opinion of another person on a genuine attempt to understand the whole person, his/her situation, and what it means.
- Constantly try to seek understanding and control yourself, your attitudes, and the prejudices which may affect your relationships.

Demands on Social Work

It is common to find clients who expect much from you. Usually they expect immediate material assistance. For example, if they experience financial difficulties, they expect to be given money. It is important for you to explain to your clients what your roles are, instead of raising false hopes. It is important for you not to take on the personal problems of your clients as your own, as this could cause problems for you. You should present yourself as a person who can assist them to understand their concerns and manage them.

While you, your clients, and the general public, may see social work as the embodiment of social services, you are dependent on public sponsorship. Social work is not about providing solutions to problems, but it provides an arena in which clients can review their concerns, and see how they can manage them best and live an effective life. Social work links clients with services, resources and opportunities, which might provide them with the help they need.

This contributes to problem-solving for clients. It is important to recognize in social work the fact that it is an adaptable service, and one which is more responsive and accountable to a particular locality and its people. Social work is concerned with the provision of welfare services, when people's capacity for responding to the demands of life is strained, when capacity growth seems unattainable, and when important decisions elude resolution.

Social work should assist clients to deal with life, engage in growth-producing activities, and make effective decisions. Naturally when people have a problem, they look for help. Usually, they think they have no capacity to solve their problem unless someone helps them to do so. And even when help comes, they expect the helper to produce the magic which will solve their problems. Social workers must make the role of their work clear when they are approached by a client. Their role is to assist the client to know why they need help and where they can get it.

Expectations of Clients

Naturally, the presence of a social worker, when there is a problem, raises hopes in a client. Clients usually think that someone with a solution to their problem has come. As a result, they may present themselves as people who are completely helpless, even when they are able to do something themselves to resolve their concerns. A social worker should not take over the problem of the client. Instead, he/she must assist the client to re-examine it and consider possible solutions to it.

People who experience difficulties/problems require assistance that should help them deal with them, and live more effectively. It is important that people who experience difficulties/problems are helped to overcome them. Children who experience difficulties require support. As children cannot present their own interests, it is the responsibility of the state, through social welfare services, to take special responsibility for them.

Social work plays a key role in family conflicts with children. It serves children whose parents neglect or abuse them. Social work is also important in schools, because it is in the schools where the inaccessible population is to be found. Social work in schools should be the application of social work principles and methods to the purpose of the school. Goals should centre upon helping pupils attain a sense of competence, a readiness to continue learning, and an ability to adapt to change. Increasingly, the focus of school social work should centre on cognitive areas such as learning, thinking and problem-solving, as well as traditional areas of concern, like relationships, emotions, motivation and personality. It is important for the school social worker to be concerned with the relationship of the school to other social institutions in the community.

ORGANIZATION AND STRUCTURE OF THE FAMILY

What is the difference between a sister and a sister-in-law? There are two types of family relationships. One is brought about by blood ties, and the other is brought about by marital ties. Blood ties are biological relationships established by birth, while marital ties are family relationships established by marriage. Relatives by marriage are also relatives by law (in-laws). There also exists another type of relationship where legally adopted children, who have no biological or marital relationship with the family, are full members of the family.

Types of Families

The two basic types of families are the nuclear family and the extended one. The nuclear family is made up of the father, mother and children living together under one roof. In nuclear families, although individuals have more autonomy and freedom in making their own decisions, they also tend to be burdened by the demands of a busy life, without the support and assistance of a big family. Children's care is often a serious problem, especially if both parents work. Some children grow up in a nuclear family without much knowledge of their grandparents, family origin, history and traditions. When there are problems and stresses, nuclear families tend to have limited help because of the small number of family members. The extended family is made up of all members of a nuclear family, plus the grandparents, aunts, uncles, and/or cousins, all living together as one family.

In traditional African societies, most families are extended. A generation ago in our society, families lived closer and more intimately together. Today, more and more families are becoming nuclear, especially those living in urban areas. Urbanization is, in fact, one of the main reasons for the increase in nuclear families. A lot of people drift to urban areas in search of jobs, and newly-formed couples find it more and more difficult to support the extended family from their meagre resources. Indeed, the extended family has many more members who need to be supported. Apart from this, different needs and personalities of so many people living under one roof tend to cause conflict. But on the other hand, an extended family also means more help and support for one another in times of crisis.

FAMILY COMPOSITION

Now you know how family types develop. The ideal family for a child is one which is intact, meaning both biological parents are present. Unfortunately, in reality, many children today are not so privileged. Many children have either only one parent, live with step-parents or relatives, are abandoned in the streets, or orphaned at a young age without a family to care for them. Each of these forms of family or non-family composition is becoming more and more commonplace today, and each has unique characteristics.

Polygamous Family

In some parts of the world, such as in Muslim countries and some African countries, men are allowed to have more than one wife. These multiple wives may live together in one household, with the husband visiting them occasionally. Even under the best conditions, jealousy, and competition for the husband's attention and wealth, are unavoidable between the wives. In this kind of family, children often have only limited access to their father's attention. They may develop resentment and distrust towards others for taking their father away. Even though they have a biological father, in many ways their life is similar to that of the single-parent family.

Single-Parent Family

The single-parent family is headed by one parent. This single parent is usually the mother. More than 90 per cent of single-parent families are headed by women. There are different reasons why a family has only one parent. Teenage pregnancy, out-ofwedlock pregnancy, marriages dissolved by divorce or separation, the loss of parents through death or desertion, or simply, choice. Most single parents tend to be economically disadvantaged. In addition, they lack emotional support.

Step Family

The step-family is also known as a reconstituted or blended family. Along with the increase in divorce and re-marriage, the number of step-families is growing rapidly. Children end up in a step-family through their parents' remarriage or polygamous marriages. They often have step-brothers and step-sisters, and other step-relatives as well. Family relationships in a step-family are more complicated than in the normal family, as there are often different sets of norms, values, disciplines and expectations.

Arguments, conflicts and abuse among members of a step-family are common. Stepparents need to work harder to love all children equally, whether they are biological children or step-children. A parent's favouritism towards certain children tends to create hard feelings between step-children. The incidence of street children and child abuse sometimes originates here.

Adoptive Family

Some children are adopted by their relatives. In the past, adoptive parents were told to hide the fact of adoption from their children. They believed that if children did not know about the adoption, they would grow up without any problem.

Research, however, showed that when adopted children eventually found out that they were adopted, they often felt cheated and outraged. Nowadays, we believe that it is better to let the child know that he/she was adopted, and that he/she was specially chosen for adoption. We now know that if adopted children are loved and treated with honesty, they will grow up into healthy and well-adjusted adults. Whether they are adopted or not makes little difference. What is important is the adoptive parents' attitude towards the adopted child.

Foster Family

Some children are placed with foster families because they do not have a family of their own, or because their family does not meet their safety and welfare needs. In extreme cases, children are taken out of their biological families and put into foster care because of the severe and abusive conditions in the home. Often, these children are placed in a foster family only for a short time, until social workers are able to help reunite the family again. However, it sometimes happens that children are moved from one foster family to another, because the biological family cannot solve its problems, and is unable to care for the children properly. Because of the transient nature of the placement, children may have difficulty in the foster family. If children are moved too frequently they are not able to form an emotional attachment with foster parents. However, if foster parents are loving and the placement is a stable one, children often benefit from it.

The Child-Headed Family

In your culture who is the head of the family? Recently, a new family composition has emerged. This is the family where a number of children have lost both parents. These children may not have relatives to take care of them, or are too many for someone to take in. In these circumstances, the eldest child becomes the head of the family.

PROBLEMS IN FAMILIES

You have seen how a family develops, and the different compositions of a family. Now, you will learn about problems that arise from these relationships. There are severe problems that need immediate attention. These are where families can no longer cater for the physical, effective and emotional needs of its members. They are called dysfunctional families. There are many causes of dysfunctional families. Some are inter-related and others are isolated. As suggested, describe the problems that affect today's families which concern you. They are: child abuse, teenage pregnancy, alcoholism, drug abuse, domestic violence, death/divorce/separation in the family, homelessness, poverty, and the uprooted family.

Child Abuse

The family is where a child is supposed to receive love and care, to build up a basic trust of the world and of other people. However, the cruel reality is that millions of children throughout the world each year have been abused by the people they love and trust the most-their own parents. This is the ultimate betrayal of trust. There are many kinds of child abuse. There are physical abuse, sexual abuse, emotional abuse, and verbal abuse.

Physical abuse may produce the 'battered-child syndrome'. In this case, a child's growth and development is seriously traumatized by harsh and cruel physical treatment. Emotional abuse and sexual abuse can be even more destructive than physical abuse in the long run. Often, they go undetected and unrecognized for many years, partly because the family tries to keep it a secret, or partly because some people simply do not believe that sexual abuse of a child can happen in the family.

Victims of emotional or sexual abuse often have interpersonal problems as adults. They may go into fits of depression and have outbursts of hostility and anger that they cannot control or understand. Incest is a form of child abuse where the parent or parent-like figure has sexual contact with the child. In many cases, a girl is the victim. The shame and guilt associated with this form of sexual abuse are so severe that they inevitably leave everlasting scars on the child's psychological adjustment. Child neglect is also a common form of maltreatment, and the most destructive. Many deaths, injuries and long-term problems have been due to child neglect. In some cases, for example, infants are starved to death or undernourished. Some are undernourished emotionally-their parents rarely touch, talk or play with them. Finally, many childhood accidents, which are the leading causes of childhood death and serious injury, can be traced to neglect. Because children are dependent upon the care of parents, they usually have nowhere to turn when their own parents abuse them. Often social workers are the only support and hope they have.

Teenage Pregnancy

Adolescence is the stage when someone reaches sexual maturity while he/she is still dependent upon his/her parents for shelter and support. During adolescence, the person's social and emotional development usually lags far behind that of sexual development. In other words, their thoughts may not be as ready for sex as their bodies are. There are two major contemporary issues involved in teenage sexual behaviour. The first one is sexually transmitted diseases, AIDS included, and the second one is teenage pregnancy.

Teenagers may be physically ready to have sexual relationships, though often they do not have the psychological and mental maturity to handle the responsibilities and consequences. Today when AIDS is widespread, teenagers have to be alerted to the danger of sexually transmitted diseases. The second major contemporary issue involved in teenage sexual behaviour is teenage pregnancy.

Although teenagers are physically ready to be parents, they do not have the financial means, nor the psychological maturity, to be responsible parents. Unwanted pregnancies often disrupt family life, and create a major obstacle in a teenagers' life. This is especially so when teenage girls bear the burden of caring for the child. Teenage mothers often drop out of school, are unemployed or settle for low paying jobs. In consequence, their children do not receive adequate care. In the traditional African family, teenage parents could leave children with grandparents. In modern society, however, grandparents are becoming younger and younger, and are themselves working. They have little time to care for their grandchildren. Teenagers and their children tend to be poor and without family support. They usually need social welfare services.

Alcoholism

While alcoholism is generally recognized as a problem, it is not as widely recognized as a family problem. In reality, it is one of the major family problems. The consequences reach far beyond the alcoholic to the spouse, children, and others. Some of the debilitating effects of alcoholism are job loss, alienation of friends, abandonment by family, imprisonment, institutionalization, and even death. Alcoholism is a serious family problem. In most instances, it results in child abuse and spouse beating. When one parent is alcoholic, the lives of all members of the family are seriously affected.

Spouse abuse and beating, financial difficulty, and emotional conflicts associated with alcoholism, all contribute to the long and silent suffering of the spouse. The children of alcoholics are also affected in many ways. The children of mothers who drink heavily during pregnancy can be born with Foetal Alcohol Syndrome. Children with this syndrome tend to have a higher risk of infant mortality, are born prematurely, grow up with delayed motor development, disfigurement, immature physical development, hyperactivity, and learning problems.

In addition, Alcohol Syndrome is the third largest cause of mental retardation. Physical problems may also occur when the father is alcoholic, although the evidence may be indirect and more subtle. Alcoholism also affects the children's emotional development. Those reared in alcoholic families are often neglected, abused, and lack proper care and interaction with their parents. The alcoholic family is often volatile, repressive or inconsistent. One of the most basic needs of children, the need for security, is often unsatisfied. An inadequate sense of security, in turn, diminishes the quality of the children's interactions and personal relationships with others.

Drug Abuse

What may have appeared a distant problem-drug abuse-is now a painful reality in African societies. Abuse of drugs takes place in school premises, in the playground outside school hours, and even in the home. Commonly abused drugs include Indian hemp and, increasingly, hard drugs like Mandrax and cocaine. The effects of drugs can be observed in such things as petty thieving among the young, disobedience, violent individual and group behaviour, sustained delinquency leading to probation, as well as an inability to concentrate on studies.

Drug abuse also leads to the many physical and emotional problems faced by families with an alcoholic member. As a social worker, you will have to recognize the problems and be able to find solutions to them within your school system.

Domestic Violence

Domestic violence often accompanies alcoholism in the family. Domestic violence and spouse beating can be instigated by either the husband or the wife. However, the wife is often the victim of the violence. Beaten wives carry a variety of psychological scars, including an extremely low self-image, a lack of self-confidence and security, a sense of hopelessness and helplessness, and a feeling of guilt that they provoked the alcoholic, and deserved the punishment.

Children from violent families suffer many emotional traumas. Domestic violence happens more often when there are strong gender stereotypes, and unequal status, between men and women. In societies where men are supposed to 'rule' and to 'keep their wives in order' through physical means, there are serious consequences, such as the creation of dysfunctional families. As social workers, we need to be sensitive to the women and children. We need to guard against our own gender biases. We need to be cognizant of the unjust social and environmental forces that make women and children victims of the system. Women's rights are human rights. We have to work towards ways and means of empowering women and girl-children to achieve equality and development, as declared in the Fourth World Conference on Women in Beijing, September 1995.

Death, Divorce and Separation in the Family

Death of a loved one in the family creates deep emotional grief. It is hard for adults to accept the loss of a spouse through death. The financial hardship, that often follows the loss of the wage earner in the family, can be devastating for the surviving spouse. For children, the death of a parent is even more traumatic, as their understanding of death is very limited. They are often confused by the reasons for death, and experience a period of depression.

Even though they often cannot put their sorrow into words, they still have a profound sense of loss. They feel insecure and fearful. Their school performance usually suffers for a year or more after the death of a parent. Many parents prefer not to mention the dead parent in the presence of the child in order to spare the child sorrow. However, the child needs to have a chance to talk about his/her loss, and to express its grief and confusion.

This is the time when the child needs a lot of support, love and communication, in order to deal with death. Divorce is the dissolution of a marriage. It is the disintegration of a legally recognized state of marriage. Separation is when a couple formally live apart without going through the legal procedure of divorce. Divorce and separation signal the death of a family relationship, and therefore, create much emotional trauma in the family similar to that of the death of a spouse. Perhaps divorce and separation are actually more difficult than widowhood, as the couple, who harbour emotional resentment towards each other, may still have to face each other when dealing with their children and making financial settlements.

Studies show that children view the separation and divorce of their parents as extraordinarily stressful. Fewer than 10 per cent were relieved by a divorce decision, despite considerable exposure to intense marital conflict or physical violence between their parents. The stress a child suffers during, and after the divorce, ranks closely to the trauma of losing a parent through death. Typically, children may be flooded with feelings they cannot fully understand or talk about.

These include anger at being caught in a situation they cannot change, guilt from the feeling they may have somehow contributed to the break-up, and sadness over the loss of a parent who no longer lives with the family. In school, a child's behaviour and ability to achieve is affected if the child is under great stress-whatever the cause. The death of a parent, or the divorce of parents, may result in inattention, absent-mindedness, behavioural problems, and withdrawals from class activities. Divorce and separation break the family apart, and result in single families, stepfamilies, and sometimes, homeless children.

Homelessness

War, poverty, unwanted pregnancy, and family break-up, are common causes of child abandonment. In many developing countries, children as young as six or seven years old roam the streets, forming their own gangs, living on begging, stealing and scraping from rubbish dumps, because their families do not want them. In the urban centres of many developed countries, a similar phenomenon has appeared in recent years.

Homeless people are everywhere, young and old alike. They loiter in the streets, sleep on pavements, in train stations or in parks. They have no place to go, nobody to turn to, no job to do, and no money. For adults, the main causes of homelessness are unemployment, alcoholism, mental problems, poverty, old age or illness. Homelessness usually leads to prostitution, early marriages, or loveless affairs in a homeless person's bid to obtain love and affection.

In many parts of the world, war and political turmoil, bloody tribal conflicts and ethnic hostilities, have pushed millions out of their traditional homelands. They are homeless refugees who live marginally on the courtesy of the host countries. However, most are less lucky. They have not only lost their homes but their families as well. The brutal experience of war and the harsh reality of living as a refugee make these people desperately in need of social services.

Poverty

Have you ever been without money? How did you feel? Nothing makes a man more humble and unsure of himself as poverty. It wrecks personal happiness and interpersonal relationships. When a family is poor it means that basic necessities and other needs cannot be provided. Often a poor person seeks refuge in alcohol, which only compounds the problem. As a social worker you have to work with families to improve their economic conditions.

The Uprooted Family

Are you living in the community in which you were born and raised? A number of families, for various reasons, need to move and resettle. This means leaving their community, their relatives and friends and, often, it also requires changing outlooks or ways of doing things. Effective adjustment requires a new set of behaviour, manners and beliefs. An example of uprooted families are refugees. Can you name others?

STRATEGIES FOR SOLVING PROBLEMS IN FAMILIES

Some of the strategies are preventive while others are rehabilitating. Your choice of strategy will depend on the extent of the problem.

Preventive Strategies:

- Provide relevant education to clients.
- Train peer counsellors to give information:.
- Invite speakers to talk about relevant topics. Use traditional community resources, and those from NGOs.
- Avoid total seclusion between boys and girls, by allowing protected interaction and socialization.

Rehabilitation Strategies:

- Provide counselling to the client in order to recover from emotional trauma.
- Provide counselling to family members.
- Seek professional assistance from other specialists.
- Seek assistance from agencies such as NGOs, churches, and law enforcement authorities, where necessary.
- If necessary, recommend foster care.
- Provide options as a solution.

What Schools Can Do to Support Diverse Family Structures:

- Ensure that information about the child's home situation is regularly checked.
- In case of separation, schools should try and inform both parents about the child's progress.

- Know the policy for dealing with possible disputes between parents.
- Be sensitive to significant changes in the child's behaviour.
- If possible, cater for the child's practical needs, *i.e.*, eating well, shelter, clothing, activities to keep the child busy, etc.
- Attempt to break down the stigma felt by many parents and their children, *i.e.*, making cards for father's/mother's day may not be appropriate for some children.
- Avoid the attitude of expecting less from some children, especially if they come from dysfunctional families. All children should receive the same treatment.
- Make information available, especially on financial resources and help.
- Parental involvement should be encouraged. If necessary, start support groups.
- When you talk to groups of parents, do not assume all to be from a two-parent Family.
- Encourage girls to pursue subjects which are likely to make them more financially independent when they grow up.
- Educate children about the responsibilities of parenthood.

TYPES OF REASONING IN SOCIAL RESEARCH

The three forms of scientific reasoning that were distinguished in the previous stage, namely deduction, inductive generalisation and retroduction, perform three different functions in scientific enquiry. Let us summarise the function of each:

- Deductive reasoning is used when a researcher wishes to test an existing theory and has to generate research hypotheses. By definition, theories are usually fairly abstract and general statements that make empirical validation are quite difficult. But if a theory is true, or at least provides a plausible explanation of a certain phenomenon, it must be empirically testable. It must be possible to derive research hypotheses from such a theory in order to collect evidence which would either support or refute such hypotheses. Derivation of hypotheses from theories involves deductive reasoning.
- In survey research, field experiments and most other forms of quantitative research, it has become standard practice to draw samples of cases rather than attempting to gather data from the population. However, once the researcher has collected data from the sample, she usually wishes to generalise her findings to the target population. This 'movement' from sample to population involves inductive generalisation. In fact, some researchers would argue that representative samples are not required if one wishes to generalise beyond the evidence collected. It has become acceptable, also in

qualitative research, to use a form of inductive inference called analytic induction, to generalise from a small number of examined cases to a larger population of similar cases.

- Scientists are rarely satisfied with merely establishing that something is the case. It is not enough to know that there is some pattern, some regularity in human behaviour. We also want to know why people act in specific ways, why certain groups of people hold particular views, why some students perform better than others. We are interested in explanations of phenomena and events in the social word. Such explanations are put forward in the form of new hypotheses or theories. Such a hypothesis or theory is judged to be a good explanation if it provides a plausible account of certain observable phenomena; if it can show that it would be reasonable to expect certain patterns or regularities given that particular theory or hypothesis. But how do scientists come up with plausible explanations? It clearly involves a logical jump beyond the data. One needs to go beyond the evidence at hand and 'think up' an explanation. The kind of reasoning involved here is called retroductive reasoning or 'retroduction' for short.

As suggested, discuss an example of research in the social sciences that illustrates how these three forms of reasoning find expression in actual research. It is worth making an additional point. We argued that the format of the research problem determines what would constitute appropriate evidence to address the problem.

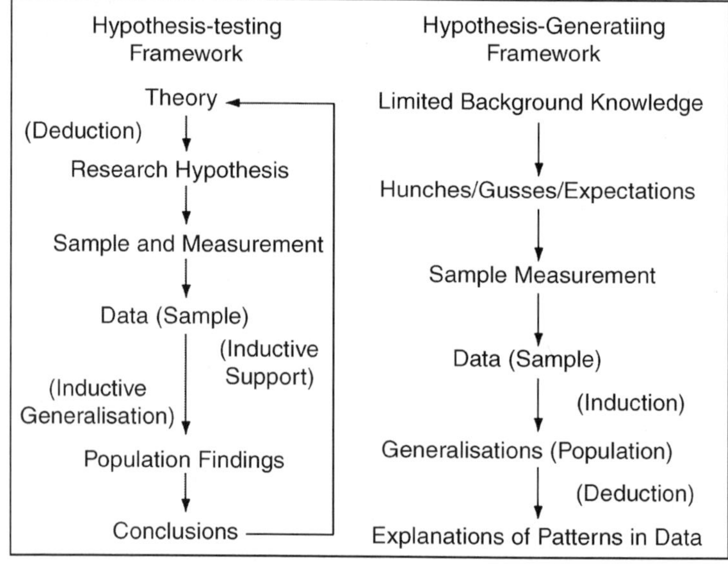

Fig. The Differences between Hypothesis-testing Studies and Hypothesis-Generating Studies

And precisely because reasoning is all about drawing conclusions from evidence, it follows that the form of reasoning is in fact determined by the nature of the research problem. In other words, the manner in which the problem is defined determines the kind of reasoning required in a particular study. Let us illustrate this by looking at the reasoning involved in two different kinds of study: hypothesis-testing studies and hypothesis-generating studies.

Although there are many variations in the statement of the problem and hence also in types of studies.

EXAMPLE: GIORGI'S STUDY ON RELIGIOUS INVOLVEMENT IN SECULARISED SOCIETIES

We begin by reconstructing the main decision-making stages in this study.

Stage 1: The Problem

Giorgi's general interest is in examining the 'secularisation profiles' of various European countries. She is specifically interested in focussing on religious involvement in secularized societies. After discussing certain conceptual issues, Giorgi remarks that the patterns usually associated with the process of secularisation are present in European countries. However, there are also certain cross-national variations that require explanation. Although she does not formulate this clearly, the research question of her study could be formulated as follows: If increasing secularisation can be expected over time in societies that are becoming increasingly industrialised and modernised, why are there still notable differences between countries?

Stage 2: Conceptualisation of the Problem

Giorgi then argues that Martin's general theory of secularisation, which is somewhat unique in that it examines secularisation in its politico-historical context, might in fact suggest an answer to this question. Let us quote Giorgi on what she regards as the core ideas of his theory:

- While never made explicit, one basic assumption underlying Martin's theory is that both religion, especially through its institutional personification in a church, and the nation-state confer identify upon individuals, even if the identity conferred is of a qualitatively different kind. Consequently, even though national or group identity can be mediated through religion, in the typical case, once the state becomes the identity nexus of a society, religion or rather the Church will be marginalized, and this affects individual religious involvement. But there are variations in the way this displacement is brought about, and hence different patterns can be seen to emerge ... Within this context, and in true Weberian style, Martin's general theory set one basic premise: that historical events can and do become crucial in the way societies change and develop; they do so by delimiting the space along which change proceeds ... the most crucial of these historical events for the secularisation process is of course the Reformation that fundamentally divided Europe across religious lines, thus challenging the tradition of the infallible Catholic unity and all that it represented.

The main theses in Martin's theory can be summarised as follows:

- Religion and the nation-state confer identity on individuals.
- Secularisation actually means that the state replaces the Church as the most important social entity or institution in a society.
- Thus, once the nation-state becomes the identity nexus in a society, the role of religion becomes more marginal.
- Secularisation patterns are not identical across societies.
- Historical events are crucial in determining the way societies change.
- The Reformation is the most crucial of historical events as far as the process of secularisation is concerned.

But what was distinctive about the Reformation? Martin, certain elements that had always been present in Christianity–which had always the potential for secularisation–were brought to the surface by Protestantism.

One of the most important of these elements is the individualistic nature of Christianity. With the loss of ritual and symbolism that accompanied the Reformation, secularisation could no longer be held at bay! This leads to the formulation of a final statement namely:

- The Reformation led to a re-emphasis of the rationalistic and individualistic elements that had always been present in Christianity.

If these seven statements, which form the core of Martin's theory, are true, what could be expected to follow from this? Martin in fact derives three more specific theses from this theory. As suggested, confine ourselves to his first theses.

This is Martin's argument as reconstructed by Giorgi:

- Martin associated Protestantism with individual striving, Catholicism with collective class antagonism ...In those countries that adopted the Reformation, argues Martin, and hence Protestantism, the formal separation and effectively the subordination of the Church to the State was smoothly established. In Catholic countries, on the other hand, the Church was forced to oppose any rising political secular ideology, including the State that personified the secular in all its self-willed power... This establishes a spiral of secularisation in Catholic countries, which veers between the two extremes of religiosity and atheism, where atheism is often associated with communism. In these countries, religion thus becomes a major issue in class conflict and political conflict in general. Alternatively, in Protestant countries, the

Church is subordinate to the State from the start, and hence the cleavage between religion and politics is not as drastic as it is in Catholic countries.

Giorgi has now reached the point where she can test a specific hypothesis, which is deductively derived from Martin's theory.

The hypothesis can be formulated as follows:

- One would expect the patterns of religiosity to differ in countries that are predominantly either Catholic or Protestant. More specifically, one would expect greater religious involvement in Catholic countries as opposed to Protestant countries.

This still very general hypothesis is not immediately empirically testable. The key concept in the statement is that of 'religious involvement'. This raises the question of operationalisation.

Stage 3: Operationalisation

Giorgi has in fact argued that religious involvement can be operationalised through the use of four indicators, namely:

1. Church attendance;
2. Self-assessed religiosity;
3. Doctrinal orthodoxy; and
4. Devotionalism.

Each of these concepts is subsequently discussed to specific items in the European Values Study conducted in ten European countries in 1981. The other key question that follows statement is how one decides which countries are predominantly Catholic and which are predominantly Protestant. In fact, the introduction of another category of 'mixed countries' where there are similar proportions of Catholic and Protestant believers. Having operationally defined the key concepts in the statement, Giorgi is now in a position to test the specific research hypothesis, which we can formulate as follows:

- One would expect to find higher proportions of religiously involved people in the predominantly Catholic countries of Europe such as France, Italy and Spain than in the predominantly Protestant countries such as Britain and Denmark. Less clear patterns might be expected to occur in the socalled 'mixed countries'.

Stage 4: Sample and Data

Giorgi has very little to say on the sample and data. This is because she has used existing data collected as part of an international research programme in 1981. It is precisely because this is an extremely well-known study, which has been well documented elsewhere, that she probably assumed that her reader would be willing to accept the fact that the sampling and data collection are of a sufficiently high scientific quality.

Stage 5: Analysis and Interpretation

On the basis of the available data analysed through a simple two-way table, she draws two conclusions:

- Regarding the differences between Catholics and Protestants, as expected, Catholics not only attend church more regularly and profess to be religious in larger numbers than Protestants; they also endorse the religious doctrines to a greater extent than Protestants, and claim a higher degree of devotionalism. However, the non-conformists are probably as religious, if not more so, than Catholics themselves, despite being Protestant.

Since the first 'result' is as expected, no further comment is required. For the same reason, the rather unexpected second result does require an explanation. Giorgi takes up the challenge. She first rejects an explanation in terms of possible biased sampling. The explanation that Giorgi puts forward: "Non-conformists are notorious for their militancy and conservatism in religious matters. If non-conformists comprise one extreme, the non-affiliators comprise the other. Among the latter, religious involvement is very low indeed". This concludes our reconstruction of the Giorgi object. As suggested, now show how, although they are not equally 'visible', all three kinds of reasoning are present in this study.

SUMMARY COMMENTS ON THE EXAMPLE

Deductive Reasoning

Deductive reasoning is exemplified in the derivation of the research hypothesis from Martin's general theory of secularisation. It has the typical form of a conditional: if Martin's theory is true, then the research hypothesis follows. Giorgi assumes the truth of Martin's theory and proceeds to test the truth of the hypothesis derived.

Inductive Generalization

Where an inductive argument is followed there are two stages in this process. First, by inferring from the samples of the countries to the countries themselves, Giorgi generalises beyond the observed data. Although she does not defend this move, it is acceptable, given the status of the European Values Study. The second inductive inference takes place when Giorgi concludes that the findings of her study "support Martin's general theory". This is a clear example of inductive support. Giorgi's study strengthens our belief in the truth of Martin's theory. It does not prove it conclusively but does substantiate it.

Retroductive Inference

Faced with the surprising results about the high religiosity of non-conformists, Giorgi postulates an explanation. She has to 'invent' an explanation that will account for the observable patterns. Her hypothesis, which is the result of retroductive reasoning, not only accounts for the results as they pertain to non-conformists, but also explains why non-affiliators scored very low on religious involvement. This gives her explanation an initial plausibility. But its real strength and true explanatory value will only be tested in future studies.

METHODOLOGICAL AWARENESS IN SOCIOLOGY AND SOCIAL RESEARCH

As suggested, briefly examine how the concept of 'methodological awareness' mediates the relationship between philosophical and theoretical perspectives on the one hand and the practice of social research on the other.

Seale has developed the concept of methodological awareness to describe the way in which practising research can use the competing philosophical positions related to social research as resources to inform and stimulate reflection as to the most appropriate ways of conducting social research.

Seale's idea can be developed to allow for the possibility of various forms of methodological awareness, including the following:

- Principled awareness.
- Pragmaticist awareness.
- Pluralist awareness.

PRINCIPLED AWARENESS

Should the practice of social research be strictly informed by answers to philosophical questions about ontology and epistemology? If so then research strategy, by which we mean epistemology, ontology and the theory-research relationship is the 'foundation' of research practice.

Research practice informed by such 'principled' methodological awareness must be guided by a specific concept of the nature of the social and a specification of the means by which knowledge of the social is obtained and verified. Philosophy is therefore given the position of providing the foundations upon which the project of social research must be based. The implied methodological awareness is of this principled type.

Bryman makes an important statement when he argues that there is no necessary connection between philosophical positions and the practice of social research. He argues that 'practical considerations' prevent such a close relationship between philosophy and research practice.

Bryman recognises that even the most ardent subscriber to a philosophical position may have to compromise on the ideal research design in order to work around the practical difficulties encountered during the conduct of research. Like Bryman, Seale is an experienced social research practitioner, and drawing on his own experience of research, he rejects the traditional view that philosophy lays the foundations for research practices. Rather, he argues we should treat philosophical stances as 'resources' to be drawn upon and evaluated during the research process. When preparing to embark on a project and during the conduct of social research, philosophical positions can be assessed for their relevance to the research question and to research practices.

PRAGMATICIST AWARENESS

One significant constraint on the nature of the research strategy to be adopted, is the research question to be addressed. The form of the research question is not always under the control of the research practitioner, and in these circumstances social researchers may be constrained to choose a strategy that will lead findings that bear directly on the question.

Even if the researcher is able to control the specification of the research question, they must keep one eye on the funding for their next project and may see the audience for research findings as a significant influence. A pragmatic methodological awareness is perhaps becoming more common. It offers the researcher the prospect of choosing the research strategy and research design which offer the most promising outcomes given the nature of the research question and the audience for the research.

PLURALIST AWARENESS

Another methodological awareness that avoids the principled adoption of a research strategy is methodological pluralism. One example of this pluralist tendency is the rise and growth of the multi-methods movement in social research. This position insists that both quantitative and qualitative strategies are equally valid since their different instruments of data collection and analysis capture different aspects of the social world.

The pluralist awareness requires the use of multi-methods in social research whereas the pragmatic awareness insists that this is an empirical question and depends upon the circumstances. We started this stage by using the distinction between quantitative and qualitative research as a learning device. We are now in a position to see how such different research strategies relate to significant philosophical and theoretical debates within academic sociology.

However, the textbook relationship between philosophy and method is the threatened emergence of forms of methodological awareness that challenge the dominance of the principled awareness.

There are a number of influences on the conduct of social research that are encouraging social researchers to adopt a pluralist or pragmatist approach to social research. Rather than be overly concerned with philosophical and theoretical inputs, the modern social researcher may be more concerned with the outputs and the outcomes of their research. What is the best strategy to use if we aim to answer the question: 'What will be the outcome of the research?' Is it likely to have positive consequences for the researchers, the funding agencies and those subjects who might gain from the implementation of research findings? These non-philosophical questions shape the choice of research strategy in social research.

THE BIOGRAPHICAL CONTEXT

The skills of social research are learned by using them alongside others who are more practised in the skills and principles. A period of apprenticeship is required before being deemed a practitioner.

In sociology, most academics are required to have a doctorate. Doctorate research closely approaches the 'craft' model where an aspiring sociologist produces a piece of research that signifies entry into the profession. During apprenticeships, skills are acquired and norms concerning standards are internalised.

If this model is dominant, then the dominant paradigms in sociological research will be reproduced in postgraduate training. Although he was arguing the case for under-graduates, Bechhofer argues that the influence and example of teachers tends to orient sociologists to particular kinds of research topic and, where empirical data are used, to approaches using no quantitative methods or very simple techniques.

It might be said that the preponderance of qualitative methods merely reflects a pragmatic decision by sociologists to avoid using those methods that they have not qualified to use. However, such are the perceived needs of the public and private sector for an increased supply of quantitative social researchers, that the ESRC has taken initiatives to sustain or increase the supply of quantitative social researchers. This demand has become embodied in the research programmes of all PhD students that it funds. Therefore, whatever the theoretical interest of the students concerned they have to complete an advanced unit in quantitative social research.

Undoubtedly the actual practice of social research is influenced by the organisation of training and by the abilities of recruits entering into the profession. Funding agencies have also articulated a need to improve training in quantitative research techniques in order to enhance the capacity to undertake such research that would otherwise remain constrained by institutional factors.

We have sought to clarify the nature of social research. We have distinguished between three aspects of social research: research strategy, research design and research method. There are two main research strategies, quantitative and qualitative, and these are associated with different positions on the philosophy of social science: qualitative social research is for the most part interpretivist, constructionist, and inductive; quantitative social research is often depicted as positivistic, objectivist and deductive.

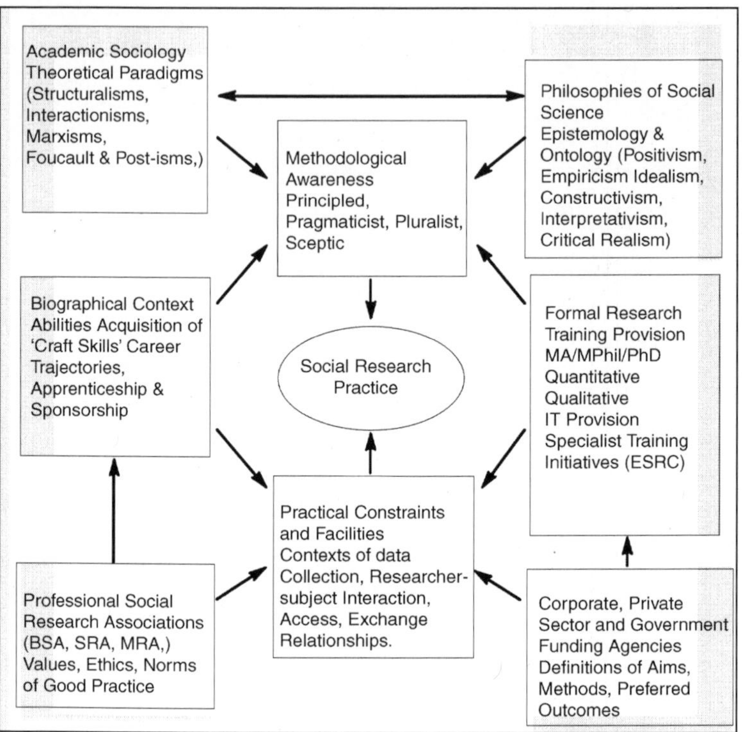

Fig. Mapping the Contested Terrain of Social Research.

CONCLUSIONS

Research design is concerned with the scale of data collection, time order and comparison groups. As Bryman describes, qualitative research is usually small-scale, over time and without comparison groups whereas quantitative social research is often largescale, cross-sectional, and frequently with comparison groups.

Recently, quantitative social research has introduced more time-ordered data collection. Research methods are the forms of data collection and analysis that reflect the major preoccupations of the quantitative and qualitative research strategies. Qualitative social research depicts the social as seen through the eyes of subjects, description in context, emphasis on process, flexibility and limited structure, concepts and theory grounded in data. These preoccupations lend it to use methods such as ethnography and in-depth interviews using analytical techniques such as grounded theory.

In quantitative social research, the pre-occupations are the measurement of concepts to test and refine theories; causal inference and model building; the generalisation of findings, and the replication of studies. These preoccupations are reflected in the use of large-scale standardised sample surveys and multivariate analysis. We sought to understand the factors that influence the choice of research strategy and associated research design and research methods components of social research. We considered the influence of academic sociology with its tendency to adopt specific philosophical and theoretical commitments.

During the paradigm wars, quantitative and qualitative research strategies were depicted as polar opposites and as inherently incompatible strategies. The debate over paradigms assumed the form of a principled methodological awareness defined as the argument that research strategies, designs and methods should follow the implications of theoretical and philosophical positions.

Practising social researchers are much more likely to have a pluralist or pragmatic methodological awareness. The multimethods or pluralist version of methodological awareness argues that all methods capture some aspect of the social and are equally valid as research strategies. Pragmaticist awareness views the choice of method as influenced by the need to secure an appropriate outcome such as the answer to a research question or findings that might improve the social world in some desirable way. Social research is thus more accurately seen as a 'contested terrain': a workplace for social research practitioners where the influence of dominant paradigms, agencies and audiences for social research, practical considerations and the researcher's own biographical context are worked out.

5

Social Work Research in Teaching

INTRODUCTION

A BSW research course was taught in two course parts to meet the needs of a rural state's BSW students. Part one, the traditional class, was taught at the state university on Tuesdays and Thursdays from 9:30 to 11:00 a.m. This class was taught in a very traditional fashion with lecture, group exercises, written assignments, and examinations. Part two, the Block Three Weekends class, was taught at an outreach site approximately 250 miles from the state university in order to offer the course to rural outreach students.

Part two was taught from 8:00 a.m. to 5:00 p.m. on Saturday and Sunday for three weekends. Lecture, group exercises, written assignments, and examinations were used for this course also, but the instructor used strategies to maintain the best learning environment possible. For instance, lectures never exceeded one hour, group activities were used more frequently, and students were required to leave the classroom during breaks.

The same instructor, using the same textbook and the same assignments, taught the courses to maintain comparability between the two courses. Bloom's taxonomy of learning was applied throughout both of these courses as well as the hybrid course. The taxonomy involves three types of knowledge dimensions including Factual, Conceptual, and Procedural knowledge. Factual knowledge involves students learning the basic elements to be acquainted with a subject, such as research.

Conceptual knowledge means that students can understand the interaction of the basic elements and how they interact within the framework or structure of a subject. Finally, Procedural knowledge involves knowing how to do something or in the case of research, how to formulate a proposal for future research. Bloom's taxonomy also includes six different levels of learning.

The levels in ascending order are knowledge, comprehension, application, analysis, synthesis, and evaluation. Knowledge is level one on the taxonomy and is described as "being capable of recalling words, facts, dates, conventions, classifications, principles, and theories." Knowledge is a very concrete type of learning. Evaluation is level six and is described as "being capable of making a critical judgement based on internal and external critieria."

Evaluation is an abstract type of learning when compared to Knowledge. The exams in all of the research courses involved measuring learning at the knowledge level. In contrast, written assignments required demonstration of "Analysis" as the minimum acceptable level of learning. Some assignments such as developing a research proposal or designing a single case research study required demonstration of the Evaluation level of learning.

For all the courses described in this document the types of knowledge just as to Bloom's taxonomy were measured in the following ways. Factual knowledge was measured using examinations containing multiple choice, true/false, and short answer items. Conceptual knowledge was measured through a written assignment. This assignment was an annotated bibliography of four research objects which required the student to identify each component of the object such as research question, methodology, and sampling. The students were required to be able to articulate the relationship between components. For instance, if the study described in one of the objects used random sampling, the student was required to understand and articulate that the results of the study were generalizable. Procedural knowledge was measured by the student submitting another written assignment.

This assignment was an outline for future research on the topic of her or his choice. The outline was required to demonstrate an understanding of the convergence of research regarding the topic, provide a rationale for choices such as method and sampling, and justify the feasibility of the proposed study.

DEVELOPMENT OF HYBRID COURSE

Several factors including reduced resources, ensuring comparability across course parts, and attempting to better serve rural students led to the combination of the two course parts into a hybrid course. The hybrid course was offered on compressed video across the state at multiple sites on Thursdays from 5:30 to 7:00 p.m. and on three Saturdays from 8:00 a.m. to 5:00 p.m. The original plan for the course was to have the all day Saturday sessions in different locations, with the first and third Saturday sessions offered at the state university campus and the second Saturday session offered at the Outreach site. However, because of scheduling difficulties and lack of space at the Outreach site, all 3 Saturday sessions were offered at the state university campus.

STRATEGIES FOR THE RURAL HYBRID COURSE

The rural hybrid course was developed carefully. Assistance from the Center for Teaching Excellence at the university, collaboration with the university's Outreach school, and consultation with other faculty were a part of the process.

Critical decisions made in developing a course that involved both intensive Saturday sessions and compressed video meetings were made thoughtfully and guided by Bloom's taxonomy of learning as explained earlier in the document. The strategies and some educational techniques are presented below.

INTENSIVE SATURDAY SESSION STRATEGIES

The Saturday sessions were used for interactive activities that would have been difficult to conduct on-line or through compressed video. These Saturday sessions also helped the students to get to know each other and the professor. In many rural settings people, including students, tend to distrust outsiders. Seeing the students in person was reassuring to both the students and the instructor for this reason. Interactive group activities such as designing survey instruments, doing qualitative field observations, or selecting sampling and research methodologies for conducting needs assessments with populations at risk in rural areas were used to assist with developing Procedural knowledge as a group.

Lunch was also provided for students in order to build a sense of community and to provide a respite from an all day class. The Saturday sessions were important for developing a sense of cohesiveness in the class and a bond between the students. Cohesiveness was based on the instructor's observations of the class. As the class members got to know each other questions and discussions tended to involve the entire class rather than small groups or clicks within the class.

The class members also referred to themselves as "we" in statements such as "we are very glad to have you hear to teach us on the weekend." Class members frequently spent breaks and lunch periods together rather than splitting into small groups and going their separate ways.

COMPRESSED VIDEO STRATEGIES

There were several strategies that were used to in an attempt to provide the best compressed video experience possible for the students and the professor in the hybrid course. In a compressed video course, Elmos or Power Point may be used for presentations. Elmos are like an overhead except that they broadcast across compressed video and have the capability of showing three-dimensional objects.

Elmos are easiest to read if they are printed on light blue paper and use a minimum font size of 32. Power Point presentations should use high contrast colours for text/background. For example, yellow text with a dark blue background works well. One strategy that was used during the rural hybrid course to make the compressed video portion of the class more student and professor friendly was having students introduce themselves the first day and tell a brief story about their experience with research.

This ensured that every student would use the compressed video technology to speak during the first class. Other strategies were to call on students by name and acknowledge their contributions to class. Yet another strategy is to invite them to respond to class comments and lecture material and be assertive in calling on students to help them learn to use the technology. As with any class, a good sense of humour helps ease tension regarding new material or in this case, a new way of teaching and learning.

QUANTITATIVE COURSE EVALUATION MEASURES

The course evaluations for the BSW Research class in the three different formats are presented in Table One. The Traditional Tuesday and Thursday class from 9:30 to 11:00 and the Three Weekends class 8:00 to 5:00 were during the fall semester of one year. The hybrid course was taught during the fall semester of the following year. It consisted of compressed video 5:30 to 7:00 p.m. on Thursdays and three 8:00 a.m. to 5:00 p.m. Saturdays.

The Course Evaluation forms were those the university used for all courses. The quantitative portion used a Likert type scale with 1 indicating poor and 5 indicating excellent. Individual items included

1. Clarity and course purpose/objective;
2. Distribution of course requirements;
3 Informational content of lectures;
4. Organization of lectures;
5. Presentation of lectures;
6. Varies the mode of presentation; and
7. Overall rating of the course.

Mean scores and standard deviations are presented for each item. A One Way Analysis of Variance was conducted and showed no statistically significant differences between the three classes on the seven variables. Despite the lack of statistically significant differences the means show some differences between the classes that are worth discussing. Variables one and two, clarity and course purpose/objective and distribution of course requirements were both rated lower for the Three Weekends class.

Distribution of course requirement refers to the distribution of exams, written assignments, and assigned activities such as doing qualitative observation over the semester. Since the Three Weekends class only met for six days throughout the semester it was common to have a paper due, an exam to take, and an assigned research activity to do during one weekend. The time to meet with the students was in two 8 hour blocks on three weekends.

The intensive weekend class format was paralleled by an intensive exam, papers, and research exercises schedule. Variables three and four, informational content of lectures and organization of lectures, were rated similarly for all three classes. Variable five, presentation of lectures was rated slightly lower for the hybrid class with a mean of 3.89. Variable six, varies the mode of presentation, was similar for all three classes. Variable seven, overall rating of the course, was rated the lowest for the hybrid class with a mean of 3.71 compared to a mean of 4.17 for the Traditional Tuesdays and Thursdays class and a mean of 4.07 for the Three Weekends class.

ANECDOTAL COMMENTS FROM HYBRID COURSE

Anecdotal comments on the course evaluations for the hybrid course varied. There were several negative comments regarding the compressed video technology such as: "compressed video is a really hard way to learn," "many times the compressed video was not working properly," and "a lot of technological difficulties with compressed video." The hybrid class also included three Saturdays of face-to-face teaching in a traditional classroom.

There were some negative comments about the all day Saturday classes as well. These comments included "Saturday classes are tough, by 3 p.m. we have all had enough," "a Saturday class doesn't seem to give one a break," and "no more Saturday classes." On a more positive note, some students showed enthusiasm for the hybrid course. Comments included "great class," "gets me fired up to do research," *"I was pleased for a first time CV class," and "this class has provided me with life long skills for effective practice."*

PRETEST POSTTEST RESULTS

A Pretest/Posttest instrument designed by Rubin and Babbie was administered at the beginning of the hybrid course on the first Saturday session and at the end of the course during the final Saturday session. It was a 100 item True/False questionnaire that had been tested for reliability and validity. The questions were taken directly from the test bank for the Rubin and Babbie textbook.

One question was "If a purposive sample was used to select participants for a study the results of the study are generalizable." Another example is "Internal validity involves the relationship between the independent and dependent variables." The maximum possible score on the questionnaire was 100. The mean pretest score was 69.18. The mean posttest score was 75.76.

Dependent sample t-tests indicated a significant difference between the pretest and posttest. This instrument measured both Factual and Conceptual knowledge on Bloom's taxonomy of learning. The Factual and Conceptual knowledge was measured by the Rubin and Babbie pretest posttest instrument for this object. Within the course the theory constructs were measured by exams, several small written assignments, and one primary written assignment.

DISCUSSION OF RESULTS

Teaching a hybrid course was a new experience for us as a rural social work educators. It was different teaching research over compressed video. In a traditional classroom, instructors can see the students' faces are able to tell if they aren't getting a particular concept. Over compressed video instructors only get to see the students' faces if one student asked a question and the video technician zoomed in on the person. Instructors could see one person's face clearly, but not the groups' faces.

It was also difficult when there were problems with the video or audio portions of compressed video. If only the video portion was working, instructors communicated via a white dry erase board. If only the audio was working, instructors communicated by voice and instructed the students to look at specific examples in their books. Sometimes it was a bit of a challenge but the challenges were solvable.

The course evaluations confirmed that even though there were challenges the hybrid course and its technology were a viable way to deliver a BSW research class to students in isolated rural areas. Although there were no statistically significant differences between the three classes, the data pose some areas of enquiry for future research. The scores for the hybrid class on variables one and two, clarity and course/purpose objective and distribution of course requirements, were similar to the traditional class scores.

The similar scores for the hybrid course on quantitative course evaluation variables three and four, informational content of lectures and organization of lectures, were encouraging. The instructors attempted to deliver the same information and organized the lecture content in a similar fashion as in the previously offered courses.

The hybrid course score on quantitative variable six, varies the mode of presentation, was also encouraging as it was similar to the other two classes. Teaching research to BSW students requires a substantial amount of lecture because for most BSW students the social work research course is the first research course they have taken. This is especially true for rural BSW students as many of them have no previous college experience and some of them are first generation college students. They are learning new content including the language of research, theories concerning research, research methodologies, and how research relates to social work as a discipline in evaluating practice and furthering social and economic justice.

Variable five, presentation of lectures, was rated lowest for the Hybrid class. This lower rating may be related to the compressed video technology and difficulties experienced with it, the all day Saturday classes, a combination of these variables or other variables not mentioned in the course evaluation. Social work educators should be mindful that a large range of attitudes towards technology, including computers and proficiency with them, still exists among social work students. However, this should not limit their use of technology in the classroom, but rather their approach to students.

Variable seven, overall rating of the course, was rated the lowest among the three classes for the hybrid class. While this is not encouraging, the mean of 3.72 is closer to a score of 5, or excellent, than it is to a score of 1, or poor. The significant difference on the pretest/posttest questionnaire was positive, indicating an increase in research knowledge occurred for the students in the Hybrid course.

LIMITATIONS

There are numerous limitations to this study. The greatest limitation was that this study used a non-randomized sample and had a low number of participants. The sample was one of convenience and the results from this hybrid course are not generalizable to other compressed video or mixed format courses. This study only involved the evaluation of one rural hybrid course that may have had unique qualities because it was the first time it was offered in the combined compressed video and intensive Saturday class meetings format.

Both the professor and the students may have become more familiar with the compressed video technology as it was used during the semester. The course evaluation instrument has not been tested for reliability and validity. The anecdotal comments on the course evaluations may not be representative of the entire class as students who took the time to write comments may have had stronger opinions than students who chose to not write comments.

Finally, although the pretest/posttest scores showed a significant increase in research knowledge, the pre-experimental design did not control for any threats to internal validity. The increase in research knowledge cannot be attributed to the research class.

PRINCIPLES OF TEACHING

- *Share intellectual control with students*: Building a sense of shared ownership is an effective way of achieving high levels of student interest and engagement. It can be achieved in many ways; many of these involve some form of formal or informal negotiation about parts or all of the content, tasks or assessment. Another complementary approach is to ensure that students' questions, comments and suggestions regularly influence, initiate (or terminate) what is done.
- *Look for occasions when students can work out part (or all) of the content or instructions*: Learning is almost always better if students work something out for themselves, rather than reading it or hearing it. This is not always feasible of course, but often it is. It can involve short, closed tasks: *e.g.* 'if the units of density are grams per cm work out the formula by which we calculate the density of a substance from the volume and mass of an object made of that substance'. It can also involve much longer open-ended tasks: e.g.'Here is a photo

of the ruins of Machu Pichu, work out as much as you can, from this photo, about the Incas and their fate'.

- *Provide opportunities for choice and independent decision-making*: Students respond very positively to the freedom to make some decisions about what or how they will work. To be effective, the choices need to be genuine, not situations where there is really only one possibility. These may include choices about which area of content to explore, the level of demand, the form of presentation and how to manage their time during a day or lesson.
- *Provide diverse range of ways of experiencing success*: Raising intellectual self-esteem is perhaps the most important aspect of working with low and moderately achieving students. Success via interactive discussion, question-asking, role-plays and tasks allowing high levelsof creativity often results in greater confidence and hence persistence in tackling other written tasks. Publicly recognising and praising good learning behaviours is useful here.
- *Promote talk which is exploratory, tentative and hypothetical*: This sort of talk fosters link-making and, as our research shows, commonly reflects high levels of intellectual engagement. Teaching approaches such as delayed judgement, increased wait-time, promotion of 'What If' questions and use of P.O.Es are all helpful. The classroom becomes more fluid and interactive.
- *Encourage students to learn from other students' questions and comments*: The conception that they can learn from other students ideas, comments and questions develops more slowly than the conception that discussion is real and useful work. The classroom dynamics can reach new, very high levels when ideas and debate bounce around from student to student, rather than student to teacher.
- *Build a classroom environment that supports risk-taking*: We underestimated the very high levels of perceived risk that accompanies many aspects of quality learning for most students, even in classes where such learning is widespread. It is much safer, for example, to wait for the teacher's answer to appear than to suggest one yourself. Building trusts in the teacher and other students and training students to disagree without personal put-downs are essential to widespread display of good learning behaviours.
- *Use a wide variety of intellectually challenging teaching procedures*: There are at least two reasons for this, one is that teaching procedures that counter passive learning and promote quality learning require student energy and effort. Hence they need to be varied frequently to retain their freshness. The other is that variety is another source of student interest.

- *Use teaching procedures that are designed to promote specific aspects of quality learning*: One of the origins of eedback or knowledge of correct responses also functions as reinforcement to strengthen the responses to be learned was the belief that students could be taught how to learn, in part by devising a range of teaching procedures to variously tackle each of a list of poor learning tendencies, for example failing to link school work to relevant out-of-school experiences. The variety is not random and one basis for selecting a particular teaching procedure is to promote a particular aspect of quality learning.
- *Develop students' awareness of the big picture*: *how the various activities fit together and link to the big ideas*: Many, if not most students, do not perceive schooling to be related to learning key ideas and skills. Rather, they see their role as completing tasks and so they focus on what to do not why they are doing it. Much teacher talk, particularly in skills based areas such as Mathematics, Grammar and Technology reinforces this perception. For these reasons, students (including primary students) commonly do not link activities and do not make links to unifying, 'big ideas'.
- *Regularly raise students' awareness of the nature of different aspects of quality learning*: This is a key aspect of learning how to learn. Students typically have no vocabulary to discuss learning. it is very helpful to build a shared vocabulary and shared understandings by regular, short debriefing about some aspect of the learning that has just occurred. Having a rotating student monitor of a short list of good learning behaviours can be very helpful.
- *Promote assessment as part of the learning process*: Students (and sometimes teachers) typically see assessments as purely summative: something that teachers do to students at the end of a topic. Building the perception that (most) assessment tasks are part of the learning process includes encouraging students learning from what they did and did not do well as well as having students taking some ownership of and responsibility for aspects of assessment. It also includes teachers ensuring that they are assessing for a range of aspects of quality learning (eg if you want students linking different lessons then reward that in your assessment) and for a wider range of skills than is often the case.

CONCEPT OF TEACHING SKILLS

"Teaching constitutes activities that are designed and performed to produce change in student behaviour." Komisar has pointed out that various specific activities included in teaching are introducing, demonstrating, citing, reporting, confirming, questioning, elaborating, etc., which may be considered as constituent skills of teaching. In simple words, teaching constitutes a number of verbal and non-verbal teaching acts like questioning, accepting student responses, rewarding, smiling, movements, gestures, etc. These acts in particular combinations facilitate the achievement of objectives in terms of student growth. A set of related teaching acts or behaviours performed with an intention to facilitate students' learning can be called a teaching skill.

'Teaching skills are specific instructional techniques and procedures that a teacher may use in the classroom'. The Asian Institute for Teacher Educators has defined teaching skills as 'specifically those activities of teaching that are especially effective in bringing about desired changes in students'. Mc Intyre and White have defined the term teaching skills as 'a set of related teaching behaviours which in specified types of classroom interaction situations tend to facilitate the achievement of specified types of educational objectives'.

Teaching Skills

You have already understood the concept of a teaching skill.

Introducing a Lesson

When one introduces a stranger to you, your reactions towards him/her or your responses during the conversation with him/her depend upon the introductory statements that are made about him/her.

Similarly, when a teacher introduces a lesson or a unit, he/she gives a brief introduction about the lesson or the unit, in order to draw the students' attention to it. Generally, an introduction to a lesson includes what the teacher does with or without the help of the students upto the stage of stating the aim of the lesson. Teachers differ from each other in the way they introduce a lesson. Studies have shown that the students' learning of the new lesson or unit largely depends on the way the lesson is introduced. A teacher must possess the necessary skill to introduce a lesson or unit in an effective manner. The components of the skill of introducing a lesson are:

- Desirable behaviours:
  - *Using previous knowledge*: The previous knowledge refers to knowledge already possessed by the students. If any new knowledge is to be added to the previous knowledge, there should be a logical continuity between them. New knowledge should also be relevant to previous knowledge of students. When we present new knowledge to the students, we have to bring their previous knowledge to their conscious level.
  - *Using appropriate devices*: Here, 'device' refers to the technique that a teacher uses while introdu-cing a lesson. Such devices can be:

    a. Use of examples

b. Questioning
c. Lecturing describing narrating
d. Story telling
e. Dramatisation
f. Audio-visual aids and
g. Experimentation. The appropriateness of the use of each of these devices depends on its suitability to the maturity level, age level, grade level, interest, experience of the students and also on the lesson to be taught.

- Undesirable behaviours:
  - *Lacking in continuity*: Continuity refers to the sequence of ideas or information being presented. While introducing a lesson, continuity breaks when the statements made for questions asked by the teacher are not logically sequenced.
  - *Making irrelevant statements*: A statement or a question which a teacher makes while introducing a lesson, is said to be irrelevant when it is not related to the aim of the lesson. Such statements or questions do not contribute to the effectiveness of the skill in terms of establishing rapport with the students. Sometimes such statements also confuse the students.

Explaining

In our day to day life you find persons explaining some idea or phenomenon by going deep into the matter with appropriate examples, logically organising the ideas, using certain non-verbal gestures, etc. You also find persons who cannot explain clearly. They jumble up ideas. They not only confuse the audience but also get confused themselves. This is because they do not present ideas in a logical sequence.

In classrooms right from grade I through higher grades, a teacher explains ideas and concepts. It is a most commonly used skill and is the essence of instruction. When a student does not clearly understand the ideas which his/her teacher tries to convey, he/she generally asks for an explanation. A teacher is said to be explaining when he/she is describing 'how', 'why' and sometimes 'what' of a concept, phenomenon, event, action or condition. Explanation can also be defined as an activity to bring about an understanding in someone about a concept, principle, etc. Explanation involves filling up the gap in one's understanding of the new phenomenon by relating it to his/her past experience. Thus, explanation depends on the type of the past experience, the type of the new phenomenon and the type of relationships between them.

In a classroom, an explanation is a set of interrelated statements made by the teacher related to a phenomenon or an idea, in order to bring about or increase understanding of the students about it. While giving explanation, we generally explain causes of the phenomenon, reasons for the action, various steps involved in arriving at the particular result, or various events that have occurred earlier resulting in the event being explained. All such causes, reasons, steps, events, etc., are called 'antecedents'. Such antecedents result in the phenomenon, event, result or action. Each of these is known as a consequent. Thus an explanation involves giving antecedents to a consequent, which can be diagrammatically presented as follows:

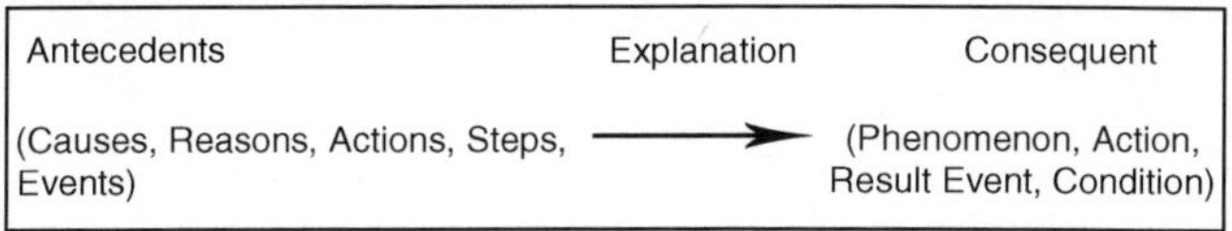

There are various techniques through which we can explain an idea, phenomenon, etc. They are question-answer technique, use of audio-visual aids or by making certain related statement concerning what we have to explain. Sometimes we use all the techniques simultaneously to make explanation more effective. To summarise, the desirable teacher behaviours for effective explanation should include, using only relevant statements, having continuity in statements, using vocabulary which the students know, being fluent in speech, avoiding vague words and phrases, using beginning and concluding statements and testing students' understanding by putting a few questions.

Questioning

Questioning is an important teaching skill that a teacher must learn. A teacher needs to put meaningful questions to the students during the teaching-learning process. You may be curious to know more about 'meaningful questions'.

Let us try to know what makes a question meaningful by considering:

- Structure,
- Process, and
- Product of questioning

Structure refers to the grammatical aspect and the content part of the question.

Various criteria for a well structured question are:

- Grammatical correctness,
- Conciseness,
- Relevance, and
- Specificity.

Increasing Student Participation

You must be aware that when a student participates in the learning process, His/her learning becomes more effective. A student is said to participate when He/she takes active part which is observable by responding to what the teacher asks for, by contributing his/her own ideas related to the topic being taught by the teacher or by reacting to others' ideas in the classroom. Student participation is an observable behaviour of students and includes responding and initiating. When a student is listening to the teacher he/she is not participating, because listening behaviour of the student is not observable.

Student participation in the classroom is essential for the following reasons:

- Students are more attentive towards the lesson when they are participating.
- Students' urges of social recognition and social acceptance are satisfied.
- There will be better understanding on the part of the students when they participate.
- A teacher can evaluate his/her teaching, that is, whether it is being effective in bringing about learning or not.

Skill of increasing student participation involves integrating the various components of the skill, namely, creating set, questioning, encouraging student participation and pausing in such combinations and proportions so as to maximize student participation.

These components are explained below:

- *Creating Set*: 'Set' in a class room may be defined as mental readiness on the part of the students before learning any task. If the students have to participate in the classroom discussion, they should be mentally ready, emotionally as well as cognitively. This can be done by posing to students a problem or situation which they discuss with the help of the teacher.
- *Questioning*: A question is a stimulus in the classroom that elicits student participation in terms of student response. You are aware that a good question is well structured, *i.e.*, precise, direct and grammatically correct. It is also put with proper tone modulation and made audible to all the students. To increase student participation the teacher should:
  - Avoid repeating questions,
  - Avoid answering his/her own questions, and
  - Avoid asking a number of questions.
- *Encouraging Student Participation*: In order to encourage student participation, we use two types of behaviours— verbal and non-verbal. Sometimes we may use both simultaneously. When the student gives the correct response we may say 'yes', 'correct', 'very good' and such other expressions. We may repeat student response to encourage. We may nod, smile-and sometimes pat the student who has responded. When the student gives a wrong response, we may say 'think again', 'it is good that you have attempted' and such other expressions. When the student has not given any response, we may say 'come on', 'try', etc.

- *Pausing*: Pausing can be defined as deliberate silence introduced by the teacher during classroom interaction so as to increase student participation. When the teacher pauses, the students are stimulated to participate. Pausing should be accompanied by non-verbal cues which would elicit more student participation.

Providing Reinforcement

You know that all the students need social approval for their behaviour. When they are answering or responding in the class, they are eager to know whether their answers or responses are correct or not. When the students come to know that the answers given by them are correct, they feel happy and get encouraged. Thus, their participation in the class increases. In such a situation, we say that the student's behaviour of responding correctly is 'reinforced' or strengthened. In other words, it may be said that there is positive reinforcement in the student's behaviour. In providing reinforcement important points to be remembered are as follows:

- Positive reinforcement means strengthening of desirable behaviour. It increases student participation in the class. Positive reinforces are those behaviours of the teacher which encourage students to participate more and more. '
- Negative reinforcement means weakening of undesirable behaviour. It decreases students' partici-pation in the class.
- Negative reinforces are those behaviours of the teacher which discourage the students to participate. Skill of reinforcement involves more and more the use of the positive reinforces and decrease the use of negative reinforces so that the students participate to the maximum.
  - In positive verbal reinforcement the teacher gives positive reinforcement through various verbal (with words) expressions. The teacher makes encouraging remarks such as 'that', 'good', 'right', 'yes', 'correct', 'excellent', 'well done', 'continue', etc.
  - Positive non-verbal reinforcement occurs when the teacher wants to reinforce positively a desired student response. The teacher may use certain non-verbal (without words) expressions like nodding of head, smiling, moving towards the responding student, keeping eyes on the student, writing the response of the student on the blackboard or any other non-verbal action indicating pleasure at the student's response.
  - Negative verbal reinforcement interferes with the learning of the students. It affects learning negatively and decreases the motivation of the students. We should avoid giving this type of reinforcement. The teacher should avoid discouraging expressions such as 'you are not good', 'wrong', 'non-sense', 'incorrect', 'stop

it', 'do something else', etc. The negative remarks of this type should be avoided if the students are to participate more in the class.

- Negative non-verbal reinforcement is given by using such behaviours as moving away from the responding student, keeping eyes on the student with discouraging looks, hard and disapproving stares, not looking at the responding student, tapping foot impatiently and walking around, etc. The teacher should be conscious of such behaviours and avoid them as far as possible if the skill of reinforcement is to be used effectively.

TEACHER

In education, a teacher is a person who provides schooling for others. A teacher who facilitates education for an individual student may also be described as a personal tutor. The role of teacher is often formal and ongoing, carried out by way of occupation or profession at a school or other place of formal education. In many countries, a person who wishes to become a teacher at state-funded schools must first obtain professional qualifications or credentials from a university or college. These professional qualifications may include the study of pedagogy, the science of teaching. Teachers will have to continue their education after they receive their degree from a college or university. Teachers may use a lesson plan to facilitate student learning, providing a course of study which helps cover a standardized test curriculum.

A teacher's role may vary between cultures. Teachers teach literacy and numeracy, or some of the other school subjects. Other teachers may provide help or certain education instruction in craftsmanship or vocational training, the Arts, religion or spirituality, civics, community roles, or life skills. In some countries, formal education can take place through home schooling. Informal learning may be assisted by a teacher occupying a transient or ongoing role, such as a parent or sibling or within a family, or by anyone with knowledge or skills in the wider community setting. Religious and spiritual teachers, such as gurus, mullahs, rabbis pastors/youth pastors and lamas may teach religious texts such as the Quran, Torah or Bible.

PROFESSIONAL EDUCATORS

Teaching may be carried out informally, within the family which is called home schooling or the wider community. Formal teaching may be carried out by paid professionals. Such professionals enjoy a status in some societies on a par with physicians, lawyers, engineers, and accountants. A teacher's professional duties may extend beyond formal teaching. Outside of the classroom teachers may accompany students on field trips, supervise study halls, help with the organization of school functions, and serve as supervisors for extracurricular activities. In some education systems, teachers may have responsibility for student discipline.

Around the world teachers are often required to obtain specialized education, knowledge, codes of ethics and internal monitoring. There are a variety of bodies designed to instill, preserve and update the knowledge and professional standing of teachers. Around the world many governments operate teacher's colleges, which are generally established to serve and protect the public interest through certifying, governing and enforcing the standards of practice for the teaching profession.

The functions of the teacher's colleges may include setting out clear standards of practice, providing for the ongoing education of teachers, investigating complaints involving members, conducting hearings into allegations of professional misconduct and taking appropriate disciplinary action and accrediting teacher education programmes. In many situations teachers in publicly funded schools must be members in good standing with the college, and private schools may also require their teachers to be college peoples. In other areas these roles may belong to the State Board of Education, the Superintendent of Public Instruction, the State Education Agency or other governmental bodies. In still other areas Teaching Unions may be responsible for some or all of these duties.

PEDAGOGY AND TEACHING

In education, teachers facilitate student learning, often in a school or academy or perhaps in another environment such as outdoors. A teacher who teaches on an individual basis may be described as a tutor. The objective is typically accomplished through either an informal or formal approach to learning, including a course of study and lesson plan that teaches skills, knowledge and/ or thinking skills.

Different ways to teach are often referred to as pedagogy. When deciding what teaching method to use teachers consider students' background knowledge, environment, and their learning goals as well as standardized curricula as determined by the relevant authority. Many times, teachers assist in learning outside of the classroom by accompanying students on field trips. The increasing use of technology, specifically the rise of the internet over the past decade, has begun to shape the way teachers approach their roles in the classroom. The objective is typically a course of study, lesson plan, or a practical skill. A teacher may follow standardized curricula as determined by the relevant authority.

The teacher may interact with students of different ages, from infants to adults, students with different abilities and students with learning disabilities. Teaching using pedagogy also involve assessing the educational levels of the students on particular skills. Understanding the pedagogy of the students in a classroom involves using differentiated instruction as well as supervision to meet the needs of all students in the classroom. Pedagogy can be thought of in two manners. First, teaching itself can be taught in many different ways, hence, using a pedagogy of teaching styles. Second, the pedagogy of the learners comes into play when a teacher assesses the pedagogic diversity of his/her students and differentiates for the individual students accordingly. Perhaps the most significant difference between primary school and secondary school teaching is the relationship between teachers and children.

In primary schools each class has a teacher who stays with them for most of the week and will teach them the whole curriculum. In secondary schools they will be taught by different subject specialists each session during the week and may have 10 or more different teachers. The relationship between children and their teachers tends to be closer in the primary school where they act as form tutor, specialist teacher and surrogate parent during the course of the day.

This is true throughout most of the United States as well. However, alternative approaches for primary education do exist. One of these, sometimes referred to as a "platoon" system, involves placing a group of students together in one class that moves from one specialist to another for every subject. The advantage here is that students learn from teachers who specialize in one subject and who tend to be more knowledgeable in that one area than a teacher who teaches many subjects.

Students still derive a strong sense of security by staying with the same group of peers for all classes. Co-teaching has also become a new trend amongst educational institutions. Co-teaching is defined as two or more teachers working harmoniously to fulfill the needs of every student in the classroom. Co-teaching focuses the student on learning by providing a social networking support that allows them to reach their full cognitive potential. Co-teachers work in sync with one another to create a climate of learning.

EXPERIENTIAL LEARNING IN SIMULATED TEACHING

Normal experiential learning that leads to an expert professional in clinical practice is associated with prolonged exposure to that practice. The over-riding idea is that by simulating clinical scenarios, learning is accelerated by the debriefing/feedback session. The expert knowledge is made explicit to the trainee and reinforced with video and verbal feedback.

Simulation training can:

- Prepare students to cope with future roles.
- Provide practice in a safe environment with no risk to patient or student.
- Test/challenge trainee's technical and decision-making skills during realistic patient care situations.
- Be an assessment tool.
- Lead to standardised teaching.

Skills that can be assessed/practiced using simulation:

- Interpersonal and communication skills.
- Critical thinking and decision-making skills.
- Practical skills.
- The use of equipment.

The Best evidence medical education (BEME) collaboration is an international group of individuals, Universities and organisations committed to the promotion of best evidence medical education. They formed a topic group in 2002 that addressed the question: "What are the features/aspects of high fidelity simulators that lead to most effective learning?"

FEEDBACK

The absence of learner feedback was the greatest single factor for ineffective simulation training.

The lack of feedback could lead to:

- Learning of the wrong learning objective.
- Not realising what the desired behaviours should be by not focusing on them.
- Not transferring skills to clinical practice.
- Spending increasing time on only one aspect of training.

PRACTICE

A lack of opportunity for practice is also associated with a poor educational outcome. This could often be attributed to insufficient access to the simulator, as training sessions are usually time dependent, and the simulator is often a hotly contested resource. In addition, each learner is different, and some learners inevitably need longer or more frequent sessions with the simulator to achieve the same educational results as their co-learners.

VALIDITY

Poor validity is associated with a lack of realism. In some simulators novices can out-perform an expert, which questions the validity of that simulation. Typically, this would also lead to a lack of correlation with other outcome measures.

FIDELITY

A common belief is that low fidelity simulation is better than high fidelity. However the group concluded that all levels of fidelity should be used based on the required outcomes. This is discussed by Maran and Glavin, where the progression from low to high fidelity simulation is compared to the progression through medical education. Their conclusion is that the range of fidelity available is almost all potentially useful, but that many simulators are underused due simply to a lack of clear educational goals

'SIMULATOR' LEARNING

Students learn to master the simulator rather than the task. The solution to this is to have multiple outcome measures for the task.

ASSESSMENT

There is current controversy about the use of simulators in high stakes examinations. Issues of domain specificity and itemised versus global scoring systems have bee raised. There is ongoing research into all of these factors though, and it seems certain that simulation will be included as part of high stakes assessment, along with other outcome measures.

IN SUMMARY

If you are thinking of using simulation in teaching you have to think:

- Who am I teaching?
- What am I teaching them?
- What are they expected to learn?

The simulation scenarios should:

- Be as realistic an environment as possible.
- Should involve feedback/debriefing/video sessions.
- Well prepared with a back up plan for equipment failure.
- Involve the observers by getting to make notes on teamwork, situation awareness, communication, etc.

Remember to create a relaxed teaching environment, as simulation can be a stressful experience for students. There follows a brief description of the reasons why simulation has become more popular as a teaching and assessment tool.

MEDICAL SIMULATION

The first recorded use of a medical simulator is that of a manikin created in the 17 Century by a Dr Gregoire of Paris. He used a pelvis with skin stretched across it to simulate an abdomen, and with the help of a dead fetus explained assisted and complicated deliveries to midwives.

In spite of this early start, medical simulators had not really gained widespread use in the following centuries, principally for reasons of cost, reluctance to adopting new teaching methods, and scepticism that what was learned from a simulator could not be transferred to actual practice. All of these reasons are still relevant today, however the combination of improved technology and increased pressures on educators have promoted simulation as one option to address the following problems with traditional clinical skills teaching.

An Alternative to "see one, do one"

In the past, health care professionals learnt on the job, which some still believe is the best way to gain experience. However, there are a number of barriers to this type of traditional clinical teaching.

These include:

- Humanitarian issues – practicing on patients is not ethical. We have moved into an age of where learning on patients is not acceptable if there is an alternative.
- There has been a decrease in the number of inpatients. In part due to an increasing number of day case patients and also the fact that chronic conditions are being cared for in the community. This has led to a decrease in exposure and access of the trainees to ward patients.
- The training time for postgraduate medical education has decreased and will decrease further. With the implementation of new training schemes, experience cannot be built upon over time as before.
- Some situations are so rare that to gain experience would take many lifetimes.
- Legal/litigation issues. The possibility of educational establishments being sued by patients and ex-students for not teaching and assessing clinical skills as laid down by the regulatory bodies could arise.
- Record keeping, reproducibility, assessment and validity are issues all brought to the forefront with clinical governance and revalidation. Simulation is seen as away of addressing some of these issues.
- Students learn more effectively in a non-threatening environment.
- There is increasing emphasis on multidisciplinary learning, and clinical skills' teaching is an ideal forum for this.
- The increase in workload for health care staff means there is less time to spend on traditional clinical teaching, which is compounded by the increase in student numbers.

Recent Recommendations

Simulation training extends from part task trainers, procedural training to the experience of full clinical situations. For example canulation, basic and advanced life support to high fidelity simulators.

However, they also include communication skills, how to take consent, bereavement counseling and IT skills. In 'Tomorrow's doctors: Recommendations on undergraduate medical education.'

GMC July 2002, there are lists of clinical skills that medical students have to be competent in before graduation:

- "The essential skill that graduates need must be gained under supervision. Medical schools must assess students' competence in these skills. The curriculum must stress the importance of communication skills and the other essential skills of medical practice."

In 'Unfinished Business: Proposals for reform of the Senior House Officer grade.' A report by Sir Liam Donaldson, Chief Medical Officer for England, proposed changes in junior doctor training which were considerable. With a shortened training period and the probable division of service commitment from effective training time, the provision of effective skills training and competency-based assessment will have to be addressed.

- "An objective of the foundation programme would be to develop and enhance core or generic clinical skills essential for all doctors (*e.g.*, team-working, communication, ability to produce high standards of clinical governance and patient safety, expertise in accessing, appraising and using evidence as well as time management skills.)"

Multidisciplinary Teaching

As well as increased emphasis on clinical skill teaching, there is increased emphasis on the multidisciplinary approach to learning. Of interest during multidisciplinary teaching are human factors such as decision-making and behavioural interaction, which is thought to be of major importance in the occurrence of critical incidents.

As quoted in 'Working Together – learning Together' A Framework for Lifelong Learning for the NHS. DoH, November 2001:

- "We are taking forward work to develop more pre-registration inter professional education programmes which incorporate common learning in core skills and knowledge. As a minimum we intend to ensure that all health professionals should expect their education and training to include common learning with other professions."

This emphasises that predetermined health care groups deliver many of the skills required by patients during their care, however in the future who delivers these skills may well change.

It is envisaged that simulation teaching could provide packages that any group could access and interact with other groups for relevant multidisciplinary situations.

CHARACTERISTICS OF EFFECTIVE TEACHING STRATEGY

For educational communication to be effective, a proper teaching strategy needs to be adopted. The selection of suitable teaching strategy depends upon the task, context and the teacher's discretion.

Nonetheless, a good strategy:

- Captures and maintain interests;
- Interprets the concepts clearly;
- Encourages critical thinking;
- Applies the learning in problem-solving; and
- Stimulates self-learning.

For this, it is important to select and organise the material taking into consideration learners' abilities, interests and psychological factors into mind. The sequencing of information, *i.e.*, moving from familiar to unfamiliar, simple to complex, general to specific and concerte to abstract needs to be done. Utilisation of illustrations, audio-visual aids, humour, questions use of exercises and assignments for continuous assessment increases the level of interest of students. Short, active responses during the course of the listening facilitate a greater degree of attentiveness and active participation by children.

Communication for Enhancing Children's Competencies

Communication enables development of listening and speaking skills for acquiring new concepts. While planning suitable tasks we need to bear in mind the age level and the interests of the children. The same activity can be varied for different age groups.

While planning suitable listening speaking and comprehension activities for learners, the following questions need to be raised:

- What type of listening activities actually go on in real life?
- What are the particular difficulties likely to be encountered by learners when coping with them?

We would like our children to go through activities which equip them to deal with real life situations effectively. In order to do this we have to create situations in the classroom which are as close to real life as possible.

To do this, we might need to look at:

- *Environment clues*: These include the facial expressions, posture, eye-direction, proximity, gesture and tone of voice of the speaker. In addition, related noises, visual materials such as illustrations, diagrams or maps may be deliberately introduced to make the listening experience as close to real life as possible.
- *Communication in real life*: Communication is interrupted by various stimulus such as person, action, visuals, happenings, etc., in the environment. In real life, stretches of heard speech are broken up by being spoken by different people from different directions. Even when there are long periods of seemingly uninterrupted discourse-talks, instructions, anecdotes, etc., these are often broken down into smaller units by the physical movement of the speaker - pauses, audience reaction, changing environmental clues. More formal stretches of speech - lectures, broadcasts, reports are usually less interrupted.
- *Formal/Informal communication*: It is necessary to draw a distinction between formal and informal communi-cation used in most spontaneous conversations. You would have noticed a range of formality, stretching from the extremely formal (speeches, lectures), to the fairly formal (news reading), to the fairly informal (television interviews), to the very informal (gossip, conversations, phone chats). As teachers, you need to be aware

of these aspects to identify the special characteristics of speech that go with the degree of formality for effective communi-cation.

There is a distinct difference between the auditory effect of a piece of spoken prose and that of informal conversation. The former is characterised by a fairly even pace, volume and pitch. Spontaneous conversation, on the other hand, is jerky, has frequent pauses and overlaps, goes intermittently faster and slower, louder and softer, higher and lower. Hesitations, exclamations, emotional reactions of surprise, irritation or amusement are bound to cause uneven and constantly changing rhythm of speech. Informal speech also contains a lot of colloquial terms, which are often spontaneous. The listener needs to develop some skills to identify the characteristics of this kind of speech. The message of a piece of spontaneous talk is delivered much more slowly, with a lot of repetition and irrelevant talk, than that of a rehearsed or planned speech.

In addition to preparing the activities keeping real life aspects in view, you can use variety of occasions in classroom to impart the skills of listening for:

- Main ideas,
- Important details,
- Sequence of events.

In this context, let us discuss two types of problems that have been identified to be most resistant for instructions:

- *Overuse of preferred information*: Many pupils tend to ignore important information and rely excessively on the facts that appeal to them. Their attention has to be consciously drawn to other relevant facts.
- *Lack of comprehension monitoring*: Many pupils tend to understand narratives, descriptions and explanations one fact at a time, without being able to evaluate the facts or see inconsistencies in the facts. They need to be given several such tasks, initially as reading tasks, where their eyes can move back and forth to detect inconsistencies. Later similar tasks can be given as listening task. The stories they have heard, the places they have visited, the home environment, the programmes they have been listening to on television all provide the backdrop against which they able them to view and give meaning to the various sounds. You can specifically develop tasks which will help children to improve some particular aspects of their listening. Efficient, active attentive listening needs to be taught at all grade levels.

Teacher-Pupils' Communication

Different types of communication serve different purposes. We can utilise these effectively to facilitate teacher-pupils' communication.

Interpersonal Communication

The teacher who values good rapport with children takes time to listen to children. This is where the student and the teacher have a real opportunity to grow and to change together. Generally, teachers say eighty per cent of the words in classroom. S/he may try to maximize informal interactions this would increase interaction amongst students. Endless repetition can be avoided by challenging children to listen carefully. If additional clarification is required, the children should be encouraged to help each other. New topics, instructions and activities need to be planned carefully to correlate with the child's attention span. Variety adds interest, renewed enthusiasm and better listening opportunities in the classroom. They should not become tedious, boring or overwhelming. You also need to reward and commend good behaviour.

Sincere statements to the class at appropriate times might include:

- I appreciate your attention to what was taught.
- I can tell by your answers that you're listening carefully for main ideas.
- I see that you stopped what you were doing to be ready for these directions.

Individual statement of appreciation and observation are always prized by children. Honest, non-judgemental, positive feedback is a reward highly valued by students. These type of comments as quite different from empty praise. It specifically tells students what the teacher values in their task or behaviour. Children will often follow the teacher's example by commenting on good listening by their peers.

Group Communication

Teacher-pupils communication and peer-group interaction falls under group communication. Teachers' skill in organisation and conduction of interaction leads to various outcomes such as sharing of ideas, opinions, information, settlement of differences, problem-solving and so on. Children talk and listen better in informal settings rather than in formal, impersonal settings such settings need to be created.

The length of time for which children can attend to any communication depends in part upon the interest span and amount of time children of a given age can remain physically inactive. The duration of group activities needs to be carefully planned.

To stimulate attentive listening, children need to be motivated. Teacher can use the skill of stimulus variation during communication, such as change in speech pattern (change in tone, volume or speed) of communication can make communication more effective and useful. Interest can be created through a range of post-listening activities which allow children to give personal expression to what they hear - through asking questions, dramatisations, or expressing their ideas with paper, paint and clay. Before beginning a story, the teacher might say, "when I finish the story, let's see if you know what happend to the Rabbit?" Or she may stop occasionally to ask questions that test attentiveness, as "why did the mangoes fall off the tree?" Opportunities to talk over what they listened to or to repeat important points increase the retention of material and give purpose to listening.

MICROTEACHING

Microteaching is a training technique whereby the teacher reviews a videotape of the lesson after each session, in order to conduct a "post-mortem". Teachers find out what has worked, which aspects have fallen short, and what needs to be done to enhance their teaching technique. Invented in the mid-1960s at Stanford University by Dr. Dwight Allen, micro-teaching has been used with success for several decades now, as a way to help teachers acquire new skills.

In the original process, a teacher was asked to prepare a short lesson (usually 20 minutes) for a small group of learners who may not have been her own students. This was videotaped, using VHS. After the lesson, the teacher, teaching colleagues, a master teacher and the students together viewed the videotape and commented on what they saw happening, referencing the teacher's learning objectives. Seeing the video and getting comments from colleagues and students provided teachers with an often intense "under the microscope" view of their teaching. Micro lessons are great opportunities to present sample "snapshots" of what/how you teach and to get some feedback from colleagues about how it was received. It's a chance to try teaching strategies that the teacher may not use regularly. It's a good, safe time to experiment with something new and get feedback on technique.

Techniques

Since its inception in 1963, microteaching has become an established teacher-training procedure in many universities and school districts. This training procedure is geared towards simplification of the complexities of the regular teaching-learning process. Class size, time, task, and content is scaled down to provide optimal training environments. The supervisor demonstrates the skill to be practiced. This may be live demonstration, or a video presentation of the skill. Then, the group members select a topic and prepare a lesson of five to ten minutes. The teacher trainee then has the opportunity to practice and evaluate her use of the skills. Practice takes the form of a ten-minute micro-teaching session in which five to ten pupils are involved

Feedback

Feedback in microteaching is critical for teacher-trainee improvement. It is the information that a student receives concerning his attempts to imitate certain patterns of teaching. The built-in feedback mechanism in micro-teaching acquaints the trainee with the success of his performance and enables him to evaluate and to improve his teaching behaviour. Electronic media gadgets that can be used to facilitate effective feedback is a vital aspect of micro-teaching.

TEACHER MANAGEMENT AND TRAINING

Historically, state governments have not had total control over the management of teachers in publicly-supported schools. While state schools were large in number, a sizeable number of schools were under the management of District Boards, Taluka Boards, Municipal Corporations, and so on. In the early 1970s, many state governments took direct control of these schools, creating a mega system of primary schooling.

This arrangement began to undergo transformation in mid-1990s, following a Constitutional Amendment which called for the empowerment of panchayati raj bodies. Some, but not all, state governments took this opportunity to wholly or partially decentralize the teacher management system. Over time, the unevenness in service conditions of teachers within and between states has increased. In some states, local self-governing bodies are given a reasonably free hand to decide on teacher recruitment at a local level, and operate within a broad framework provided by the state government. While all teachers are technically state government employees, therefore, some teachers are employed by local village level bodies, whilst others are employed by block or district level bodies.

Another significant development during the 1990s, which has the potential to significantly influence the professional development of teachers, is the creation of a system of district and sub-district level teacher resource centres. Following the recommendations of the National Policy on Education 1986, every district in the country was provided with a district-specific teacher education institution, a District Institute of Education and Training. Subsequently, under the District Primary Education Programme, block resource centres and 10-15 cluster resource centres were established in each of the 42 districts which participated in the project. This is now being universalized to reach all districts of the country under SSA.

Availability and Deployment of Teachers

Mere availability of schools does not ensure children's participation. More than schools, motivated teachers play a vital role in ensuring that children attend school regularly and take an active part in the learning process. Though there has been an impressive increase in the number of school teachers in India in the 1990s, the imbalances in intra-state teacher allocation between districts and within districts, and between rural and urban areas continues to be a major concern. An increase in the numbers of upper primary teachers has taken place in rural areas in Andhra Pradesh, Gujarat, Himachal Pradesh, Karnataka, Madhya

Pradesh, and Rajasthan indicating improved completion of the lower primary cycle and increased transition to upper primary classes.

Indeed, in most of states, the percentage increase in upper primary teachers has been more than that of the primary teachers. This indicates a positive trend in transition rates from lower to upper primary classes. However, the allocation of teachers particularly between rural and urban areas continues to be a major concern in many states. In almost all states, trained teachers with higher qualifications are generally concentrated in urban areas.

Several factors, including political and bureaucratic interventions, non-availability of qualified local teachers in remote areas, lack of a proper database on the status of teachers at the school level and the low motivation of urban teachers to serve in rural areas, are obstacles to the rational deployment of teachers. Moreover, teacher transfer is highly influenced by political interventions, and more influential teachers are more likely to be found working in urban schools and schools located in habitations well connected with road or rail transport networks.

The lack of basic facilities also act as de-motivating factors, particularly for female teachers. These factors undoubtedly influence pupil-teacher ratios with the average PTR higher in rural areas than in urban areas.

RECRUITMENT OF PARA-TEACHERS

In the 1990s, a number of states began appointing para-teachers and other types of temporary teachers, mainly at the primary level. This was justified as necessary to meet the additional teacher requirements caused by increased enrolments. However, in some states parateachers have been appointed to fill vacancies left by regular full-time teachers. Available data shows that the relative share of primary and upper-primary parateachers is high in Gujarat, Andhra Pradesh, Himachal Pradesh, Uttar Pradesh, Uttarakhand and Maharashtra.

The trend for appointing para-teachers continues in rural primary and upper primary schools in some states. In Gujarat, for example, more than 43 per cent of rural primary teachers and 31 per cent of rural upper primary teachers are temporary teachers. The Seventh All India Educational Survey, there were 103,270 para-teachers at the primary level, 104,894 para-teachers at the upper primary level, 37,950 at the secondary level, and 33,911 para-teachers at the higher secondary level in 2002. A study conducted under the District Primary Education Programme in 1998, covering 21 para-teacher schools over five states, highlighted that there were distinct advantages if the teacher was a local resident, including better community interactions, teacher punctuality and efficiency of schools.

While acknowledging some short-term advantages of the system, Pandey reiterates that, by accepting the scheme of para-teachers, the central government is encouraging states to evade their responsibility for building a strong cadre of qualified teachers. The trend has also challenged teachers'professional identities. Para-teacher schemes may therefore serve the immediate purpose of universalisation of access to elementary education in far flung rural and hilly areas, but replacing regular teachers with para-teachers is in general detrimental to the quality of education and the effectiveness of schools, and should be avoided if possible. Large-scale non-formal education and alternative schools with para-teachers are often concerned with physical access over quality of provisions.

Meanwhile, investment in improving the capacity of teachers and organizing continuous educational resource support and pedagogic renewal has taken a backseat. The biggest problem with the concept and rationale behind these schemes, as pointed out by the PROBE Report, is that the Shiksha Karmi approach involves the potential risk of institutionalized dualism in the schooling system.

This issue may not be so prevalent when Shiksha Karmis are posted as auxiliary teachers in mainstream schools and are spread evenly through the schooling system. However, Shiksha Karmis tend to be posted in areas where regular teachers are reluctant to go, such as tribal or backward villages. In these deprived areas, Shiksha Karmis tend to be used as low-cost substitutes for non-performing teachers, often managing the entire school on their own. This policy is often supported by regular teachers who, as a result, are more likely to be posted to more attractive areas. This results in deprived children being taught by poorly-qualified, low paid Shiksha Karmis, while those from more privileged families are more likely to be taught by a fully qualified teacher. It is worth noting, however, that regular school teachers are not necessarily better than contract teachers.

Problems relating to classroom processes, pedagogic techniques, classroom management and other constraints which effect para-teachers also impact on the quality of education offered by trained and qualifed teachers. Ramachandran et al in their study on teacher motivation, for example, found that trained teachers indicated several reasons for dissatisfaction, including high teacher-pupil ratios, inadequate infrastructure, erratic disbursement of salaries, being 'forced'to teach children of poor communities and specific social groups who are 'dirty', irregular attendance of children, and illiterate parents, all of which add to teacher workloads.

Tilak also points out that most state governments favour para-teacher schemes and EGS schools as they save huge resources and avoid teacher managerial problems. So while the central government can claim to have gone a long way towards fulfilling the constitutional directive on universal elementary education, little attention has been given to the likely effects on quality of education or the long term implications of the schemes.

As Govinda and Josephine argue:

- The schools, which are targeted for employment of contract teachers, are those where children from the poorer sections of the society study. Thus it would exacerbate inequity in the society by creating classes of government schools with different kinds of teachers for different classes of population.

To avoid such a situation, Govinda and Josephine suggest the creation and nurturing of a professional cadre of teachers governed by well-designed norms and standards as agreed by the state and teachers. A transparent process of recruitment, posting and promotion of teachers is therefore urgently required. Even though the appointment of contract teachers has come in for considerable questioning in public discourses, there are no systematic studies to analyse the long-term impact of such recruitments on the quality of schools on the one hand, and on the development of a professional cadre of teachers, on the other.

This suggests that a focus needs to be placed on the larger implications of policies related to the professional morale of teachers and the manner in which parateacher schemes may jeopardize efforts to build a strong cadre of professionally trained elementary school teachers and the impacts of provision of a second-grade alternative education for children from already deprived and disadvantaged sections of society.

TEACHING, LEARNING AND ASSESSMENT

Teaching and learning in social policy courses normally take place in a combination of all of the following contexts:

- Lectures
- Seminars, classes and workshops
- Tutorials.
- Self-directed study.

Lectures convey substantive information, signpost issues to be considered and provide an introduction to the main themes, debates and interpretations of the subject. Lectures should encourage and enable students to develop skills in listening, selective note-taking, appreciation of how information is structured and presented, and reflection.

The traditional lecture format can be enhanced through the development of new techniques including audio visual aids and electronic presentational methods. Seminars, classes and workshops provide a context for more interactive learning and are usually organised around themes for discussion and/or designated reading. Work in seminars, classes and workshops should be seen as deepening the student's knowledge of a particular subject and their critical awareness of alternative perspectives and communication skills.

It should also provide the opportunity to develop skills in information retrieval and presentation, communication and team working. Tutorials are meetings between a staff member and an individual student or small group. They serve a variety of purposes: assessing personal development and reviewing progress; helping students to develop learning skills and to make informed and realistic choices within their degree course; providing support for individual or group project work, work-related placements or dissertation preparation.

Much students' time is spent in self-directed study, individually or in groups. This may involve preparation for specific assignments required by other parts of the learning process identified in paragraphs 5.1.1-5.1.3. But it also entails reading, discussion and reflection on issues raised in the more formally structured elements of the degree course, including learning resources made available in electronic and other formats. Students reading for a degree in social policy should be provided with full and accurate documentation on their course of study.

Learning outcomes for each unit should also be specified. An indication of relevant reading and other resources and the means of assessment should form part of such documentation. Learning opportunities and teaching methods should reflect the pedagogic objectives of the institution and the course. They should also be kept under review by departments on the basis, for example, of staff selfassessment; student evaluations and the dissemination of good practice from other departments and institutions. The objectives for a degree in social policy are to produce independent learners who are competent in a range of knowledge, resources and skills appropriate to their level of study. Teaching methods and the learning experience should thus be perceived by staff and students alike as designed to encourage progression in the acquisition both of knowledge and of skills.

Such progression should be reinforced by a diversity of teaching and learning and assessment methods during the period of a student's undergraduate career. Thus in terms of knowledge, it is expected that there will be greater opportunities for students to pursue more specialist units in the second and third years of a course in England, Wales and Northern Ireland and in years three and four of an Honours course in Scotland. Opportunities for the formal assessment of a student's independent study-such as the presentation of a dissertation-will normally occur in the student's final year.

In terms of skills, progression should also be a keynote. Thus in level one a course should normally develop basic research, information retrieval and study skills. This should enable the students at subsequent levels to strengthen their analytical, interpretative and communication skills; and by graduation, to demonstrate the problem-solving evaluative and reflective skills intrinsic to the discipline and the attributes for self-managed, life-long learning.

Methods of assessment should:

- Reflect progression within the undergraduate programme;

- Combine the assessment of both knowledge and skills;
- Enable students to demonstrate their level of attainment and to demonstrate their full range of abilities and skills;
- Be relevant to the pedagogic objectives

Unit learning outcomes should reflect the assessment strategy for the appropriate level of the unit within the degree course. Published criteria should be available for all summative methods of assessment and would most appropriately be contained within course handbooks.

These strategies will include some or all of the following:

- Unseen examinations;
- Seen, open book or take away examinations;
- Essays and reports;
- Analytical exercises;
- Individual or group presentations;
- A project-based or work-experience report;
- A dissertation;
- Computer based assessments.

Summative assessment for degree classification purposes should be undertaken wherever possible without any indication of the student's name, though some indicator of level of study should be clearly given in the numbers assigned to candidates.

STANDARDS

In turning to the question of standards, guidance is based on the achievement expected of a BA (or equivalent) single honours graduate in social policy and administration. Students should normally be expected to demonstrate the appropriate level of achievement in all areas of the course, bearing in mind the need for progression through the honours programme. The standard expected of two types of graduate is addressed in this document-a *threshold* graduate and a *typical* graduate.

The former describes the standard achieved by a minimally acceptable honours graduate (*i.e.* at the bottom of the third class). The *typical* level of achievement describes graduates straddling the boundary between the lower and upper second class. This group represents the majority of students; but it is important to note that a significant proportion of graduates will perform above the *typical* level.

Threshold Graduate

Knowledge and Understanding

Threshold graduates will demonstrate a basic knowledge and understanding of the topics in the course of study that they have undertaken, as outlined in part three. *Threshold* graduates will be able to demonstrate a basic understanding of a limited range of social policy issues and be able to offer some critical reflection on ideas that are presented in teaching and in relevant literature.

Subject Specific Skills

Threshold graduates will be able to demonstrate an awareness of the complexities involved in social policy formation, implementation and development. *Threshold* graduates will have well-developed descriptive skills and basic analytic skills. *Threshold* graduates will be able to understand the importance of values in social policy and will appreciate the importance of distinguishing between normative and empirical arguments. *Threshold* graduates will also be able to identify the main strengths and weaknesses of various policies and policy proposals that they encounter. *Threshold* graduates will have a sufficient grasp of research methods and their application to enable them to comment on research evidence and social and economic trends.

Generic Skills

Threshold graduates will be able to demonstrate achievement of the following generic skills.

This will be done in a variety of ways, and not all skills will be directly assessed:

- Communicate a basic line of argument both verbally and in writing
- Identify strengths and weaknesses in the arguments and opinions of others
- Retrieve and synthesise information from varied sources
- Employ basic time-management skills and work to deadlines
- Demonstrate knowledge of, and ability to use, a limited range of Information Technology skills
- Engage in seminar discussions
- Engage in small group work or projects
- Demonstrate ability to prepare and deliver a basic presentation using appropriate technical aids as necessary
- Employ basic independent/self-directed study skills
- Employ basic problem identification and problem solving skills
- Understand and use a standard referencing system and be able to construct a basic bibliography.

Typical Graduate

Knowledge and Understanding

Typical graduates will be able to demonstrate a thorough knowledge and critical understanding of most of the topics that they have studied in their degree course, as outlined in part three. *Typical* graduates will be able to demonstrate an in-depth understanding of a wide range of social policy issues and be able to reflect critically on ideas that are presented in teaching and in relevant literature.

Subject Specific Skills

Typical graduates will be able to demonstrate a critical understanding of the complexities involved in social policy formation, implementation and development. They will have good descriptive and analytic skills. *Typical* graduates will also be able to understand, and reflect upon, the underlying value base of many policy proposals and distinguish clearly between normative and empirical arguments. *Typical* graduates will also be able to identify, and reflect upon the main strengths and weaknesses of various policies and policy proposals that they encounter. *Typical* graduates will be familiar with a range of research methods and will be able to reflect critically on their use in various research studies.

Generic Skills

Typical graduates will be able to demonstrate achievement of the following generic skills.

This will be done in a variety of ways, and not all skills will be directly assessed:

- Demonstrate an ability to develop a strong line of argument both verbally and in writing
- Compare and contrast the strengths and weaknesses in the arguments and opinions of others
- Retrieve, synthesise and analyse information from varied sources
- Employ well developed time-management skills and work to deadlines
- Demonstrate knowledge and application of a wide range of Information Technology skills
- Engage in and take a pro-active role in seminar discussions
- Demonstrate ability to prepare and develop a well focussed presentation using appropriate technical aids
- Employ well developed independent/self-directed study and learning skills
- Employ well developed problem identification and problem solving skills
- Understand and use a standard referencing system (ie Harvard) and be able to construct a complex bibliography.

ACADEMIC STANDARDS-SOCIAL WORK

This benchmark statement fully acknowledges contemporary and forthcoming changes within the context of social work and its regulation across the United Kingdom that may lead to modification of its content over time.

These changes include:

- Establishment of General Councils as regulatory bodies in England, Scotland, Wales and Northern Ireland;

- Articulation of new rules and requirements governing professional and vocational education following the planned disbandment of the Central Council for Education and Training in Social Work (CCETSW) in 2001;
- Formal registration of social workers and certain social care staff;
- Development of occupational standards for social work and social care by the Training Organisation for Social Care (TOPSS) in the countries of the U.K;
- Mapping of social work and social care posts to levels of qualification; and
- Development of care standards, codes of conduct and codes of practice.

NATURE AND EXTENT OF THE SUBJECT

The statement covers social work as an applied academic subject at honours degree level.

It sets out expectations concerning:

- The subject knowledge, understanding and skills of an honours graduate in social work;
- The teaching, learning and assessment methods employed in their education; and
- The standards expected of them at the point of graduation.

Impending legislation to establish regulatory bodies in social work and to introduce statutory registration of social workers, may result in the terms 'social work' and/or 'social worker' becoming protected titles. In this case, honours degrees with titles such as BA (Hons) Social Work are likely to converge with programmes of professional education to comprise integrated academic and professional awards with nomenclature restricted to these circumstances.

Professional social work qualifications in the U.K. are not, however, currently linked to a specific level of academic achievement. The status of qualified social worker can be achieved through study leading to subdegree and post-graduate, as well as degree awards. At present, curriculum design and assessment of practice within integrated awards enables students to meet the Rules and Requirements governing the Diploma in Social Work as determined by CCETSW. Despite the strong link between academic and professional awards, this statement does not attempt to define professional competence at qualifying or registration level.

It is believed that this process should only be undertaken in partnership with other stakeholders including regulatory bodies, employers, professional bodies, providers of practice learning, service users and those who work within social work and social care. The statement also covers honours degrees in the field of social work studies that do not converge with professional awards. These degrees reflect historic and international traditions of social work and social welfare. They are known by a variety of titles such as applied social studies, community studies, human services, social care and social welfare. Excluded from the statement by these definitions is a further range of honours degrees that include counselling, youth and community work and careers guidance.

Honours degree programmes in social work may be studied in full-time, part-time, open and distance learning, workplace-based and post-experience modes. Irrespective of learning mode, however, all honours degree programmes covered by this statement should include structured opportunities for supervised or directed practice in social welfare settings. The statement applies to the United Kingdom but acknowledges and values distinctive country-specific legal, organisational, practice and educational contexts. For example, in Scotland an honours degree normally represents four years of full time study, and in Wales the special provisions of the Welsh Language Act 1993 permeate all aspects of social work.

In addressing the content and standards of honours degrees, the statement takes account of European and international contexts of social work and the desirability of the mutual recognition of social work qualifications within the European sector of the International Federation of Social Workers. Contemporary social work commonly takes place in an inter-agency context, and social workers habitually work collaboratively with others towards inter-disciplinary and cross-professional objectives. Honours degree programmes should, therefore, be designed to help equip students with accurate knowledge about the respective responsibilities of social welfare agencies and acquire skills in effective collaborative practice between these. To facilitate broad access to honours degree programmes in social work, holders of sub-degree and vocational qualifications (normally in social care) may be offered entry with advanced standing by means of approved procedures for the accreditation of prior (experiential) learning.

Honours degree programmes should, however, ensure that all such arrangements enable students to achieve fully the standards set out in this benchmark statement. The term 'service user' is used in this statement to cover the wide and diverse set of individuals, groups and organisations who are involved in, or who benefit from, the contribution of social work to the well being of society. This group will include some that are involuntary or unwilling recipients of social work services. In providing services, social workers should engage with service users in ways that are characterised by openness, reciprocity, mutual accountability and explicit recognition of the powers of the social worker and the legal context of intervention.

DEFINING PRINCIPLES

As an applied academic subject, social work is characterised by a distinctive focus on practice in complex social situations to promote and protect individual and collective well-being. At honours degree level the study of social work involves the integrated study of subject specific knowledge, skills and values and the critical application of research knowledge from the social and human sciences (and closely related domains) to inform understanding and to underpin action, reflection and evaluation. Honours degree programmes should be designed to help foster this integration of contextual, analytic, explanatory and practical understanding.

The specific areas of knowledge and understanding and the relevant subject and other skills to be acquired are defined in sections 3.1 and 3.2 of this statement. Contemporary definitions of social work as a degree subject reflect its origins in a range of different academic and practice traditions. The precise nature and scope of the subject is itself a matter for legitimate study and critical debate. Three main issues are relevant to this: Social work is located within different social welfare contexts.

Within the U.K. there are different traditions of social welfare (influenced by legislation, historical development and social attitudes) and these have shaped both social work education and practice in community-based settings including group-care. In an international context, distinctive national approaches to social welfare policy, provision and practice have greatly influenced the focus and content of social work degree programmes. There are competing views in society at large on the nature of social work and on its place and purpose.

Social work practice and education inevitably reflect these differing perspectives on the role of social work in relation to social justice, social care and social order. Social work, both as occupational practice and as an academic subject, evolves, adapts and changes in response to the social, political and economic challenges and demands of contemporary social welfare policy, practice and legislation.

It follows that, through their education, honours graduates in social work should be:

- Equipped both to understand, and to work within, this context of contested debate about nature, scope and purpose;
- Enabled to analyse, adapt to, manage and eventually to lead the processes of change.

The applied nature of social work as an academic subject means that practice is an essential and core element of learning. The following paragraphs clarify the use of the term 'practice' in the statement. In honours degree programmes covered by this statement, practice as an activity refers to experiential, action based learning. In this sense, practice provides opportunities for students to improve and demonstrate their understanding through the application and testing of knowledge and skills.

Practice activity is also a source of transferable learning in its own right. Such learning can transfer both from a practice setting to the 'classroom' and vice versa. Thus practice can be as much a source of intellectual and cognitive learning as other modes of study.

For this reason, learning through practice should attract full academic credit. The term 'practice' in this statement is used to encompass learning that not only takes place in professional practice placements but also in a variety of other experiential learning situations. All learning opportunities that bear academic credit must be subject to methods of assessment appropriate to their academic level and be assessed by competent assessors. Where they form part of the curriculum leading to integrated academic and professional awards, practice learning opportunities will also be subject to regulations that further define learning requirements, standards and modes of assessment.

Learning in practice can include activities such as observation, analysis and research as well as intervention within social work and related organisations. Practice learning on honours degrees covered by this statement, however, will normally include not only observation and research, but will involve active engagement with service users and others in practice settings outside the university. Such engagement is a compulsory component of honours degrees integrated with professional awards in social work. Social work is a moral activity that requires practitioners to make and implement difficult decisions about human situations that involve the potential for benefit or harm. Social work honours degree programmes, therefore, involve the study, application of and reflection upon ethical principles. Although social work values have been expressed at different times in a variety of ways, at their core they involve showing respect for persons, honouring the diverse and distinctive organisations and communities that make up contemporary society and combating processes that lead to discrimination, marginalisation and social exclusion.

This means that honours undergraduates must learn to:

- Recognise and work with the powerful links between intra-personal and inter-personal factors and the wider social, legal, economic, political and cultural context of people's lives;
- Understand the impact of injustice, social inequalities and oppressive social relations;
- Challenge constructively individual, institutional and structural discrimination;
- Practise in ways that maximise safety and effectiveness in situations of uncertainty and incomplete information;
- Help people to gain, regain or maintain control of their own affairs, insofar as this is compatible with their own or others' safety, well-being and rights.

The expectation that social workers will be able to act effectively in such complex circumstances requires that honours degree programmes in social work should be designed to help students learn to become accountable, reflective and self-critical.

This involves learning to:

- Think critically about the complex social, economic, political and cultural contexts in which social work practice is located;
- Work in a transparent and responsible way, balancing autonomy with complex, multiple and sometimes contradictory accountabilities (for example, to different service users, employing agencies, professional bodies and the wider society);
- Exercise authority within complex frameworks of accountability and ethical and legal boundaries; and
- Acquire and apply the habits of critical reflection, self-evaluation and consultation, and make appropriate use of research in the evaluation of practice outcomes.

6

Research Design Methods

RESEARCH DESIGN AND APPROACH

The activity theory perspective suggests that a focus on teaching, unrelated to students' perceptions about their own learning and its context, is unlikely to be successful in changing outcomes. My approach focuses on the experience of learning Statistics at university from the point of view of the student. Consistent with my theoretical framework based on the ideas of Leont'ev and Vygotsky, I explore the network of relationships between learners, the subject matter and context. My investigation took place at a large and traditional metropolitan university, the oldest in Sydney. The participants were second year Psychology students, all of whom were required to study Statistics. Statistics is introduced in first year Psychology at The University of Sydney, but it is as a compulsory component of the second year course that it plays a major role, contributing one quarter of the final assessment mark. The instruments I used included participant observation, interviews and surveys. My project consists of two investigations.

Study One is entitled "Exploring Mature Students' Learning of Statistics". The context for this study was the Mathematics Learning Centre where I work. The participants in this study were of great interest to me as an educator concerned with ameliorating students' difficulties with Statistics. Study Two is called "Understanding University Students Learning Statistics as a Service Course to Psychology". In this study, I widened the context of my enquiry to include the general Statistics class. For my investigations, I drew on a triad of research tools–naturalistic enquiry, procedures based on the phenomenographic method and quantitative methods for describing data and exploring patterns and relationships. Among the instruments I developed was the Approaches to Learning Statistics Questionnaire.

PSYCHOLOGY STUDENTS AT THE MATHEMATICS LEARNING CENTRE

In Study One we utilise a naturalistic perspective to draw on the rich accounts of five students who were studying Psychology after many years away from the educational setting. My aim is to tell the story of these students in a way that is generalisable to others–that is, we try to uncover recognisable insights. The formal assessment of these students and worked very intensively and closely with them. Hence I was able to develop a close relationship with the participants of Study One and had more access to their perceptions and feelings than is usually the case for university educators in statistics. My analysis is based mainly on interview data, complemented by written expressions from various sources. The five participants were selected "purposively" for their range of experiences and attributes. As is often the case with qualitative research, the data for this study consisted of descriptions, direct quotations and excerpts, obtained by close psychological contact with those being studied.

The study is an example of action research in that my actions as a researcher were inseparable from those designed to assist the students in their learning of Statistics. As I have outlined in Gordon this means that the methodology for the study developed through the "action research spiral".

They describe this spiral as recurring cycles of:

- Planning, acting, observing and reflecting, with each of these activities being systematically and self-critically implemented and interrelated.

VIEW OF PSYCHOLOGY STUDENTS LEARNING STATISTICS

The participants of Study Two were Psychology II Students who took part in a survey during their Statistics lecture, near the end of the first semester. The survey was completed during 20 minutes of the lecture time and was the major source of data for this study. Other data for this study included assessment results and vignettes from interviews with students selected from those who agreed to contribute further to my research.

Background of Phenome Nography as a Research Tool

One major focus of Study Two was to elicit students' conceptions of the subject matter, in the context in which they were studying it. To do this we adopted a phenomenographic approach. The term phenomenography was first used by Ference Marton to describe programmes of research which had the common aim of describing peoples' conceptions. The results of phenomenographic analysis are categories of description of the qualitatively different ways students conceive of the phenomenon being investigated. This focus on describing conceptions is not the sole aim of the investigations in which phenomenography is used as a research tool. Rather it is learning and teaching that are being investigated based on the focusing of conceptions. Conceptions are the lens through which the phenomenographic researcher views learning.

Marton describes phenomenography as a method:

- For investigating the qualitatively different ways in which people experience, conceptualise, perceive and understand various aspects of, and phenomena in, the world around them.

Phenomenography was developed within the framework of education research at the University of Gothenburg, Sweden. It is concerned with the relations between people and the objects of their perceptions or content of their thoughts. Marton calls phenomenography a "research specialization", that is, a combination of a research orientation and a research approach to describing and comparing conceptions and understandings.

The research orientation emphasises the importance of description and the use of categories as forms of expressing the conceptions. The research approach is characterised by the open explorative form of data collection and the interpretative analysis of data. Säljö, a forerunner in the development of the phenomenographic approach, comments that in more recent studies, the term "way of experiencing" is used in preference to the term "conception".

This emphasises that:

- The prime interest of phenomenographic research is in finding and delimiting the variation in ways of experiencing reality.

Hence, in deriving categories of description for students' conceptions of Statistics, I am attempting to find relationships between the students and the subject matter which express their ways of experiencing the subject, Statistics, as they were learning it. Svensson argues that underpinning the phenomenographic specialisation is an assumption that knowledge is fundamentally a "question of meaning in a social and cultural context". Such an approach views phenomena systemically and avoids separating person and context.

As Säljö in an editorial of Learning and Instruction, concludes:

- Human experiences are inescapably cultural in nature, and learning and growth take place within cultural boundaries.

This view of the intertwining of culture, mind and action is consistent with a Vygotskian assumption that there is no duality between self and context; between thinking and acting. The phenomenographic view of knowledge is that it is relational, created through human thinking and activity which relates to the external world–a relation between thought and social and cultural life. Hence my choice of phenomenography as one of my research tools is consistent with the theoretical perspective with which I am framing this investigation.

The relational view of learning furnished by phenomenography has formed the basis of much of the research into student learning in higher education. Phenomenography has been fruitful in exploring students' conceptions and understanding in a number of topics, including physics; literature interpretation; essay writing and computer programming. In summary, this research indicates that learners' experiences should be considered as involving the ways students relate to the learning environment, their goals and intentions, as well as their learning strategies. My colleagues and I have found phenomenographic methods useful to explore the qualitatively different ways in which students experience learning mathematics. Two studies were conducted. In the first study we investigated the conceptions of mathematics and approaches to learning it of students entering university.

In the second investigation we explored these students' conceptions of a fundamental mathematical concept, namely that of a function. Traditionally, phenomenographic studies are built around interviews. However, in these investigations, my colleagues and I extended previous research by constructing categories from the written responses of a large number of students. This developed phenomenography as a research tool. In Study Two, I built on our previous phenomenographic research by looking at the variation in the way second year Psychology students conceived of the nature of the subject matter, Statistics. The phenomenographic perspective provided my basis for identifying categories of description of students' conceptions. These revealed qualitatively different ways of experiencing Statistics. In much research, the categories of description or variables are imposed on the data by an expert researcher.

In Study Two, in keeping with phenomenographic practice, the categories of description were constituted in relation to the data–from interpretations of the survey responses. This does not imply that I, as researcher, viewed the data free of ideas based on prior experience or theoretical orientation.

Indeed:

- The act of categorisation is by its very nature subjective.

Further, my research is deliberately set in the framework of activity theory. However, instead of characterising students' responses to the three open-ended questions in the survey by means of an established taxonomy, the categories emerged in the context of the study. By keeping the questions as general as possible, I tried not to shape students' responses. Rather I tried to explore the students' points of view. This enhances the ethnographic validity of this research, that is, the sense of the research in terms of the lives and awareness of the participants in it. The phenomenographic method analyses meanings constituted within a particular context and content domain. My categories were derived in a particular setting. However, they and their structure as an organised set, may prove useful in contexts other than the one from which they emerged.

In accord with the phenomenographic approach:

- The categories of description are supposed to be replicable, but theway in which they were found is not.

Conceptions may be expressed in different forms of action but they are most accessible through language. Variation in conceptions, expressed by people, immediately brings in the cultural and social context in which these conceptions are reported. The students' reports on their ways of conceiving Statistics, although limited to the students' awareness and abilities in written verbal expression, provided me with a rich source of information for characterising these experiences. This experiential perspective is referred to as a "second order" perspective by Marton.

He contrasts this with phenomenology, based on Husserl's imperative to return to the essence of a phenomenon, through immediate experience and free from conceptual thought–a first order enterprise. Phenomenography is a perspective on how things appear to people–how phenomena are experienced, rather than what they are "in reality" or whether or not such a reality can be described.

Phenomenography was derived from empirical and pragmatic research in education. Its commitment to philosophical foundations is therefore not always clear. The procedures defining its use are neither prescriptive nor indisputable. Indeed, Hasselgren and Beach argue that "there is no genuine consensus method of phenomenography".

To them:

- Phenomenography is research which is simply concerned with how things are understood, the experiences of the process of formation of understandings at individual levels, and their distributions in specific collectivities.

While my way of applying this research tool is individual, I have tried to maintain the essence of phenomenographic research as a way of understanding the multiple realities of students. That is, my appropriation of Marton's term signifies this approach. I view phenomenography as a research tool which bridges the gap between empirical, analytic methods, which are recognised by the research community, and students' subjective awareness of their own diverse conceptions and experiences.

ANALYSIS OF STUDENTS' APPROACHES TO LEARNING STATISTICS

I analysed students' approaches to learning Statistics by means of a questionnaire, the Approaches to Learning Statistics Questionnaire. My questionnaire was modified from the Approaches to learning Mathematics Questionnaire which, in turn, was derived by my colleagues and myself from the Study Process Questionnaire. Biggs refers to three approaches to learning: deep, surface and achieving. He differentiated each of these into two aspects– the motive, or intention, and the strategy. Hence, in the Study Process Questionnaire the items are divided into those referring to motive or intention and those referring to strategy.

Each motive-strategy combination defines a distinct approach to learning– deep, surface or achieving. Early work by Biggs, on samples of students from universities and Colleges of Advanced Education, indicated that the achieving approach was equally related to the surface and deep approaches in tertiary students.

The surface and deep approaches, however, are referred to by Biggs as:

- Independent ways in which students may become involved in learning.

In this project I was concerned with deep and surface approaches to learning. Achieving approaches were of less theoretical interest to me and were not investigated. Considerable research has been done on the Study Process Questionnaire. For example, a literature review on approaches to studying indicates that mature students seem more likely than younger students to adopt deep approaches to learning, while surface approaches decline with age. However, completion rates and possible bias in these studies, for example, in the postal returns of surveys in Biggs' investigations, renders this finding problematic.

Richardson also reviewed the literature on cultural specificity of approaches to studying in higher education. Investigations using the Study Process Questionnaire in countries as diverse as Australia, Nepal, Britain and Nigeria yielded a similar two factor structure for this questionnaire–one indicating a deep approach and the other a surface approach. The research also suggests that orientations towards understanding the meaning of learning materials, that is, deep approaches to learning, reflect a consistent agreement across different cultures with regard to the goals of higher education.

On the other hand, this research indicates that patterns of responses on the subscales measuring surface approaches to learning, are more distinctive to differing cultural contexts. Concern has been expressed about the factor structure underlying Biggs' differentiation of the Study Process Questionnaire into motive and strategy components. In my analysis of the Approaches to Learning Statistics Questionnaire I did not find evidence for a breakdown into intention and strategy factors. I therefore analysed the items of the ALSQ in terms of two subscales: one measuring a general surface approach and the other a deep approach to learning Statistics.

Biggs characterises a surface approach and a deep approach to an academic task by the following.

A surface approach is distinguished by:

- A view of the task as imposed, a demand to be met;
- A fragmented view of the task–parts are unrelated to each other and the task is unrelated to other tasks;
- Worries about the time taken by the task;
- A lack of recognition of any personal meaning in the task;
- Reliance on memorisation and ways of reproducing the details.

A deep approach reflects:

- Interest and enjoyment in the task;
- A search for underlying meaning;
- Efforts to make the learning personally meaningful–relating task to personal experience or to the real world;

- Holistic approach–relating parts of the task to each other and to other knowledge;
- Theorising about the task.

The surface approach and the deep approach, as defined by Biggs, correspond closely with the surface and deep levels of processing distinguished by Marton and Säljö. Later, Marton and Säljö referred to these as surface and deep approaches to learning. In contrast to Biggs, however, Marton and Säljö see surface and deep approaches as the opposite ends of a single continuum, rather than as independent ways of learning. Marton and Säljö showed that students would adopt one of two methods of processing information according to their intentions.

If their aim was merely to memorise and reproduce material, or, as Biggs puts it:

- To display the symptoms of having learned,

They would adopt a surface level of processing; if they wanted to maximise their understanding of the underlying meaning, they would adopt a deep strategy. Hence Marton and Säljö inferred a relationship between strategy and intention. What the student intends to gain from the learning determines the strategy used. In recent research, Marton, Watkins and Tang make the point that while a surface approach to learning is often associated with rote learning, this is not what characterises it.

- Rather, a surface approach is characterised by a focus on the learning material or task in itself and not, as would be the case for the deep approach, on the meaning or purpose underlying it.

Their ideas accord with Leont'ev's proposition that what distinguishes actions are the goals driving them.

RESEARCH METHODS

The goal of the research process is to produce new knowledge, which takes three main forms (although, as previously discussed, the boundaries between them may be fuzzy):

- Exploratory research, which structures and identifies new problems
- Constructive research, which develops solutions to a problem
- Empirical research, which tests the feasibility of a solution using empirical evidence

Research can also fall into two distinct types:

- Primary research
- Secondary research

Research is often conducted using the hourglass model Structure of Research. The hourglass model starts with a broad spectrum for research, focusing in on the required information through the methodology of the project (like the neck of the hourglass), then expands the research in the form of discussion and results.

PUBLISHING

Academic publishing describes a system that is necessary in order for academic scholars to peer review the work and make it available for a wider audience. The 'system', which is probably disorganised enough not to merit the title, varies widely by field, and is also always changing, if often slowly. Most academic work is published in journal article or book form. In publishing, STM publishing is an abbreviation for academic publications in science, technology, and medicine.

Most established academic fields have their own journals and other outlets for publication, though many academic journals are somewhat interdisciplinary, and publish work from several distinct fields or subfields. The kinds of publications that are accepted as contributions of knowledge or research vary greatly between fields.

Academic publishing is undergoing major changes, emerging from the transition from the print to the electronic format. Business models are different in the electronic environment. Since about the early 1990s, licensing of electronic resources, particularly journals, has been very common. Presently, a major trend, particularly with respect to scholarly journals, is open access. There are two main forms of open access: open access publishing, in which the articles or the whole journal is freely available from the time of publication, and self-archiving, where the author makes a copy of their own work freely available on the web.

RESEARCH FUNDING

Most funding for scientific research comes from two major sources, corporations (through research and development departments) and government (primarily through universities and in some cases through military contractors). Many senior researchers (such as group leaders) spend more than a trivial amount of their time applying for grants for research funds.

These grants are necessary not only for researchers to carry out their research, but also as a source of merit. Some faculty positions require that the holder has received grants from certain institutions, such as the US National Institutes of Health (NIH). Government-sponsored grants (*e.g.* from the NIH, the National Health Service in Britain or any of the European research councils) generally have a high status. Research funding is a term generally covering any funding for scientific research, in the areas of both "hard" science and technology and social science. The term often connotes funding obtained through a competitive process, in which potential research projects are evaluated and only the most promising receive funding.

Such processes, which are run by government, corporations or foundations, allocate scarce funds. Total research funding in most developed countries is between 1.5 per cent and 3 per cent of GDP; Sweden is the only country to exceed 4 per cent. Most research funding comes from two major sources, corporations (through research and development departments) and government (primarily carried out through universities and specialised government agencies). Some small amounts of scientific research are carried out (or funded) by charitable foundations, especially in relation to developing cures for diseases such as cancer, malaria and AIDS.

In the OECD, around two-thirds of research and development in scientific and technical fields is carried out by industry, and 20 per cent and 10 per cent respectively by universities and government, although in poorer countries such as Portugal and Mexico the industry contribution is significantly less. The US government spends more than other countries on military R&D, although the proportion has fallen from around 30 per cent in the 1980s to under 20 per cent. Government funding for medical research amounts to approximately 36 per cent in the U.S.

The government funding proportion in certain industries is higher, and it dominates research in social science and humanities. Similarly, with some exceptions (*e.g.* biotechnology) government provides the bulk of the funds for *basic* scientific research.

In commercial research and development, all but the most research-oriented corporations focus more heavily on near-term commercialisation possibilities than "blue-sky" ideas or technologies (such as nuclear fusion). One of the most famous exceptions is the innovation-favouring environment of the 1970s at Xerox Parc, where various ideas including the computer mouse were developed. Similarly, IBM's research into quantum computing has been going on for some years, and it will likely be some years more before it yields commercially available technology.

EXPERIMENTAL QUASI-EXPERIMENTAL DESIGN

The design of any experiment is of utmost importance because it has the power to be the most rigid type of research. The design, however, is always dependent on feasibility. The best approach is to control for as many confounding variables as possible in order to eliminate or reduce errors in the assumptions that will be made. It is also extremely desirable that any threats to internal or external validity be neutralized. In the perfect world, all research would do this and the results of research would be accurate and powerful. In the real world, however, this is rarely the case. We are often dealing with human subjects, which in itself confounds any study. We are also dealing with the restraints of time and situation, often resulting in less than perfect conditions in which to gather information.

There are three basic experimental designs, each containing subsets with specific strengths and weaknesses.

These three basic designs include:

1. Pre-experimental design;
2. Quasi-experimental design; and
3. True experimental design.

PRE-EXPERIMENTAL DESIGN

Pre-experimental designs are so named because they follow basic experimental steps but fail to include a control group. In other words, a single group is often studied but no comparison between an equivalent non-treatment group is made. Examples include the following:

The One-Shot Case Study

In this arrangement, subjects are presented with some type of treatment, such as a semester of college work experience, and then the outcome measure is applied, such as college grades. Like all experimental designs, the goal is to determine if the treatment had any effect on the outcome. Without a comparison group, it is impossible to determine if the outcome scores are any higher than they would have been without the treatment. And, without any pre-test scores, it is impossible to determine if any change within the group itself has taken place.

One Group Pretest Posttest Study

A benefit of this design over the previously discussed design is the inclusion of a pretest to determine baseline scores. To use this design in our study of college performance, we could compare college grades prior to gaining the work experience to the grades after completing a semester of work experience. We can now at least state whether a change in the outcome or dependent variable has taken place.

What we cannot say is if this change would have occurred even without the application of the treatment or independent variable. It is possible that mere maturation caused the change in grades and not the work experience itself.

The Static Group Comparison Study

This design attempts to make up for the lack of a control group but falls short in relation to showing if a change has occurred. In the static group comparison study, two groups are chosen, one of which receives the treatment and the other does not.

A posttest score is then determined to measure the difference, after treatment, between the two groups. As you can see, this study does not include any pre-testing and therefore any difference between the two groups prior to the study are unknown.

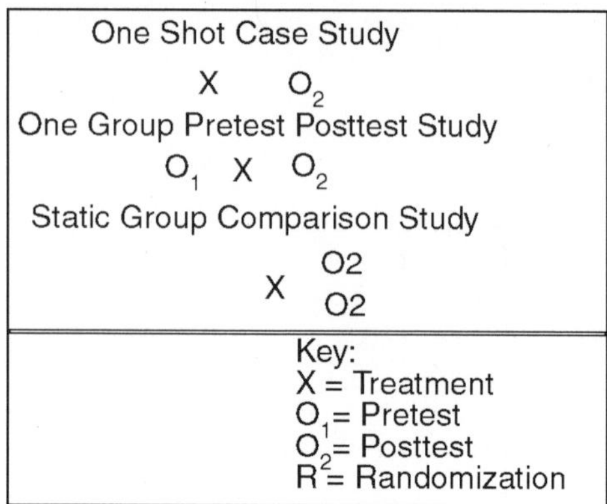

Fig. Diagrams of Pre-Experimental Designs

QUASI-EXPERIMENTAL DESIGN

Quasi designs fair better than pre-experimental studies in that they employ a means to compare groups. They fall short, however on one very important aspect of the experiment: randomization.

Pretest Posttest Non-equivalent Group

With this design, both a control group and an experimental group is compared, however, the groups are chosen and assigned out of convenience rather than through randomization. This might be the method of choice for our study on work experience as it would be difficult to choose students in a college setting at random and place them in specific groups and classes. We might ask students to participate in a one-semester work experience programme. We would then measure all of the students' grades prior to the start of the programme and then again after the programme. Those students who participated would be our treatment group; those who did not would be our control group.

Time Series Designs

Tim series designs refer to the pretesting and posttesting of one group of subjects at different intervals. The purpose might be to determine long term effect of treatment and therefore the number of pre- and posttests can vary from one each to many. Sometimes there is an interruption between tests in order to assess the strength of treatment over an extended time period. When such a design is employed, the posttest is referred to as follow-up.

Non-equivalent Before-After Design

This design is used when we want to compare two groups that are likely to be different even before the study begins. In other words, if we want to see how a new treatment affects people with different psychological disorders, the disorders themselves would create two or more non-equivalent groups. Once again, the number of pretests and posttests can vary from one each to many. The obvious concern with all of the quasi-experimental designs results from the method of choosing subjects to participate in the experiment. While we could compare grades and determine if there was a difference between the two groups before and after the study, we could not state that this difference is related to the work experience itself or some other confounding variable. It is certainly possible that those who volunteered for the study were inherently different in terms of motivation from those who did not participate.

Whenever subjects are chosen for groups based on convenience rather than randomization, the reason for inclusion in the study itself confounds our results.

TRUE EXPERIMENTAL DESIGN

True experimental design makes up for the shortcomings of the two designs previously discussed. They employ both a control group and a means to measure the change that occurs in both groups. In this sense, we attempt to control for all confounding variables, or at least consider their impact, while attempting to determine if the treatment is what truly caused the change. The true experiment is often thought of as the only research method that can adequately measure the cause and effect relationship.

Posttest Equivalent Groups Study

Randomization and the comparison of both a control and an experimental group are utilized in this type of study. Each group, chosen and assigned at random is presented with either the treatment or some type of control. Posttests are then given to each subject to determine if a difference between the two groups exists. While this is approaching the best method, it falls short in its lack of a pretest measure. It is difficult to determine if the difference apparent at the end of the study is an actual change from the possible difference at the beginning of the study. In other words, randomization does well to mix subjects but it does not completely assure us that this mix is truly creating an equivalency between the two groups.

Pretest Posttest Equivalent Groups Study

Of those discussed, this method is the most effective in terms of demonstrating cause and effect but it is also the most difficult to perform. The pretest posttest equivalent groups design provides for both a control group and a measure of change but also adds a pretest to assess any differences between the groups prior to the study taking place.

To apply this design to our work experience study, we would select students from the college at random and then place the chosen students into one of two groups using random assignment.

We would then measure the previous semester's grades for each group to get a mean grade point average. The treatment, or work experience would be applied to one group and a control would be applied to the other.

It is important that the two groups be treated in a similar manner to control for variables such as socialization, so we may allow our control group to participate in some activity such as a softball league while the other group is participating in the work experience programme.

At the end of the semester, the experiment would end and the next semester's grades would be gathered and compared. If we found that the change in grades for the experimental group was significantly different than the change in the grades of our control group, we could reasonably argue that one semester of work experience compared to one semester of non-work related activity results in a significant difference in grades.

NOW WE CAN SAY

The experiment, especially the true experimental design is often the measure of choice when attempting to determine a cause and effect relationship. Utilizing randomization and the pre-testing and post-testing of both an experimental group and a control group allows us to control for more confounding variables than any other research method. These confounding variables, when not addressed, can often result in inaccurate findings.

Controlling for confounding variables is important in research and especially important in the experimental designs. This process helps us assure valid results both internally and externally. The threats to internal validity, those that apply to the experimental situation itself, and external validity, those relating to the generalizability of our results to the real world are also issues of great concern to researchers. As the saying goes: garbage in, garbage out. If we start with a flawed design as suggested, end up with flawed results.

As the degree of control for each of the designs discussed increases, the difficulty in performing the research also increases. Feasibility is always an issue and even when the most stringent control is used, the mere fact that the subjects have agreed to participate in the experiment may have a negative effect on the study's generalizability. Are volunteer subjects truly representative of the population at large? As you can see, there are varying degrees of experimental research, but there is no perfect experiment that controls for all possible variables and assures us of 100 per cent generalizability.

STUDY DESIGN

EFFECT SIZE

In statistics, an effect size is a measure of the strength of the relationship between two variables in a statistical population, or a sample-based estimate of that quantity. An effect size calculated from data is a descriptive statistic that conveys the estimated magnitude of a relationship without making any statement about whether the apparent relationship in the data reflects a true relationship in the population. In that way, effect sizes complement inferential statistics such as p-values. Among other uses, effect size measures play an important role in meta-analysis studies that summarize findings from a specific area of research, and in statistical power analyses.

The concept of effect size appears already in everyday language. For example, a weight loss programme may boast that it leads to an average weight loss of 30 pounds. In this case, 30 pounds is an indicator of the claimed effect size. Another example is that a tutoring programme may claim that it raises school performance by one letter grade. This grade increase is the claimed effect size of the programme. These are both examples of "absolute effect sizes," meaning that they convey the average difference between two groups without any discussion of the variability within the groups. For example, if the weight loss programme results in an average loss of 30 pounds, we do not know if every participant loses exactly 30 pounds, or if half the participants lose 60 pounds and half the participants lose no weight at all.

Reporting effect sizes is considered good practice when presenting empirical research findings in many fields. Effect sizes are particularly prominent in social and medical research. Relative and absolute measures of effect size convey different information, and can be used complementarily.

Types

Pearson r Correlation

Pearson's correlation, often denoted r and introduced by Karl Pearson, is widely used as an effect size when paired quantitative data are available; for instance if one were studying the relationship between birth weight and longevity. The correlation coefficient can also be used when the data are binary. Pearson's r can vary in magnitude from –1 to 1, with –1 indicating a perfect negative linear relation, 1 indicating a perfect positive linear relation, and 0 indicating no linear relation between two variables. Cohen gives the following guidelines for the social sciences: small effect size, $r = 0.1 - 0.23$; medium, $r = 0.24 - 0.36$; large, $r = 0.37$ or larger.

A related effect size is the coefficient of determination. In the case of paired data, this is a measure of the proportion of variance shared by the two variables, and varies from 0 to 1. An r^2 of 0.21 means that 21 per cent of the variance of either variable is shared with the other variable. The r^2 is positive, so does not convey the polarity of the relationship between the two variables.

Effect Sizes Based on Means

A effect size θ based on means usually considers the standardized mean difference between two populations:

$$\theta = \frac{\mu_1 - \mu_2}{\sigma}$$

where μ_1 is the mean for one population, μ_2 is the mean for the other population, and σ is a standard deviation based on either or both populations.

In the practical setting the population values are typically not known and must be estimated from sample statistics. The several versions of effect sizes based on means differ with respect to which statistics are used.

This form for the effect size resembles the computation for a t-test statistic, with the critical difference that the t-test statistic includes a factor of $\sqrt{n}$. This means that for a given effect size, the significance level increases with the sample size. Unlike the t-test statistic, the effect size aims to estimate a population parametre, so is not affected by the sample size.

Cohen's d

Cohen's d is defined as the difference between two means divided by a standard deviation for the data,

$$d = \frac{\bar{x}_1 - \bar{x}_2}{s},$$

What precisely the standard deviation s is was not originally made explicit by Jacob Cohen because he defined it as "the standard deviation of either population Other authors make the computation of the standard deviation more explicit with the following definition for a pooled standard deviation,

$$s = \sqrt{\frac{(n_1 - 1)s_1^2 + (n_2 - 1)s_2^2}{n_1 + n_2}},$$

with $\bar{x}_k$ and s_k as the mean and standard deviation for group k, for k = 1, 2.

$$s_1^2 = \frac{1}{n_1 - 1}\sum_{i=1}^{n1}(x_{1,i} - \bar{x}_1)^2$$

This definition of "Cohen's d" is termed the maximum likelihood estimator by Hedges and Olkin, and it is related to Hedges' g by a scaling:

$$g = \sqrt{\frac{n_1 + n_2 - 2}{n_1 + n_2}}$$

Glass's Δ

In 1976 Gene V. Glass proposed an estimator of the effect size that uses only the standard deviation of the second group:

$$\Delta = \frac{\bar{x}_1 - \bar{x}_2}{s_2}$$

The second group may be regarded as a control group, and Glass argued that if several treatments were compared to the control group it would be better to use just the standard deviation computed from the control group, so that effect sizes would not differ under equal means and different variances.

Under an assumption of equal population variances a pooled estimate for 6 is more precise.

Hedges' g

Hedges' g, suggested by Larry Hedges in 1981, is like the other measures based on a standardized difference,

$$g = \frac{\overline{x}_1 - \overline{x}_2}{s^*}$$

but its pooled standard deviation s * is computed slightly differently from Cohen's d,

$$s^* = \sqrt{\frac{(n_1 - 1)s_1^2 + (n_2 - 1)s_2^2}{n_1 + n_2 - 2}}$$

As an estimator for the population effect size θ it is biased. However, this bias can be corrected for by multiplication with a factor,

$$g^* = J(n_1 + n_2 - 2)g \approx \left(1 - \frac{3}{4(n_1 + n_2) - 9}\right)g$$

Hedges and Olkin refer to this unbiased estimator g * as d, but it is not the same as Cohen's d. The exact form for the correction factor J involves the gamma function,

$$J(a) = \frac{\Gamma(a/2)}{\sqrt{a/2}\Gamma((a-1)/2)}.$$

Distribution of Effect Sizes Based on Means

Provided that the data is Gaussian distributed a scaled Hedges' g,

$$\sqrt{(n_1 n_2 /(n_1 + n_2)}g ,$$

follows a non-central t-distribution with the non-centrality parametre,

$$\sqrt{(n_1 n_2 /(n_1 + n_2)}\theta$$

and $n_1 + n_2$ 2 degrees of freedom. Likewise, the scaled Glass' Δ is distributed with $n_2 - 1$ degrees of freedom.

From the distribution it is possible to compute the expectation and variance of the effect sizes.

In some cases large sample approximations for the variance are used. One suggestion for the variance of Hedges' unbiased estimator is,

$$\hat{\sigma}^2(g^*) = \frac{n_1 + n_2}{n_1 n_2} + \frac{(g^*)^2}{2(n_1 + n_2)}.$$

Cohen's f^2

Cohen's f^2 is an appropriate effect size measure to use in the context of an F-test for ANOVA or multiple regression. The f^2 effect size measure for multiple regression is defined as:

$$f^2 = \frac{R^2}{1 - R^2}$$

where R^2 is the squared multiple correlation.

The f^2 effect size measure for hierarchical multiple regression is defined as:

$$f^2 = \frac{R^2{}_{AB} - R^2 A}{1 - R^2{}_{AB}}$$

where $R^2{}_A$ is the variance accounted for by a set of one or more independent variables A, and $R^2{}_{AB}$ is the combined variance accounted for by A and another set of one or more independent variables B.

By convention, $f^2{}_A$ effect sizes of 0.02, 0.15, and 0.35 are termed small, medium, and large, respectively.

Cohen's $\hat{f}$ can also be found for factorial analysis of variance working backwards using:

$$\hat{f}_{effect} = \sqrt{(df_{effect} / N)(F_{effect} - 1)}.$$

In a balanced design of ANOVA, the corresponding population parametre of f^2 is,

$$\frac{SS(\mu_1, \mu_2, \cdots \mu k)}{K \times \sigma^2},$$

wherein μ_j denotes the population mean within the jth group of the total K groups, and ó the equivalent population standard deviations within each groups. SS is the sum of squares manipulation in ANOVA.

φ, Cramér's φ, or Cramér's V

The odds ratio is another useful effect size. It is appropriate when both variables are binary. For example, consider a study on spelling. In a control group, two students pass the class for every one who fails, so the odds of passing are two to one.

In the treatment group, six students pass for every one who fails, so the odds of passing are six to one. The effect size can be computed by noting that the odds of passing in the treatment group are three times higher than in the control group.

Therefore, the odds ratio is 3. However, odds ratio statistics are on a different scale to Cohen's d. So, this '3' is not comparable to a Cohen's d of 3.

Relative Risk

The relative risk also called risk ratio, is simply the risk of an event relative to some independent variable. This measure of effect size differs from the odds ratio in that it compares probabilities instead of odds, but asymptotically approaches the latter for small probabilities. Using the example, the probabilities for those in the control group and treatment group passing is 2/3 and 6/7, respectively.

The effect size can be computed, but using the probabitities instead. Therefore, the relative risk is 1.28. Since rather large probabilities of passing were used, there is a large difference between relative risk and odds ratio. Had failure been used as the event, the difference between the two measures of effect size would not be so great.

While both measures are useful, they have different statistical uses. In medical research, for example, the odds ratio is favoured for case-control studies and retrospective studies. Relative risk is used in randomized controlled trials and cohort studies.

It is also worth noting that one cannot automatically predict the other, though with small probabilities one can be considered a fairly good estimate of the other.

Confidence Interval and Relation to Non-central Parametres

Confidence interval of unstandardized effect size like difference of means can be found in common statistics textbooks and software, while confidence intervals of standardized effect size, especially Cohen's,

$$\tilde{d} := \frac{\mu_1 - \mu_2}{\sigma}$$

and

$$\tilde{f}^2 := \frac{SS(\mu_1, \mu_2, \cdots \mu_K}{K.\sigma},$$

rely on the calculation of confidence intervals of non-central parametres. A common approach to construct confidence interval of ncp is to find the critical ncp values to fit the observed statistic to tail quantiles $\alpha/2$ and $(1 - \alpha/2)$. SAS and R-package MBESS provide functions for critical ncp. An online calculator based on R and MediaWiki provides interactive interface, which requires no coding and welcomes copy-left collaboration.

T test for Mean Difference of Single Group or Two Related Groups

In case of single group, M(μ) denotes the sample (population) mean of single group, and SD (σ) denotes the sample (population) standard deviation. N is the sample size of the group. T test is used for the hypothesis on the difference between mean and a baseline $\mu_{baseline}$. Usually, $\mu_{baseline}$ is zero, while not necessary. In case of two related groups, the single group is constructed by difference in each pair of samples, while SD (σ) denotes the sample (population) standard deviation of differences rather than within original two groups.

$$t := \frac{M}{SD/\sqrt{N}} = \frac{\sqrt{N}\frac{M-\mu}{\sigma} + \sqrt{N}\frac{\mu-\mu_{baseline}}{\sigma}}{\frac{SD}{\sigma}}$$

$$ncp = \sqrt{N}\frac{\mu-\mu_{baseline}}{\sigma}$$

and Cohen's,

$$d := \frac{M-\mu_{baseline}}{SD}$$

is the point estimate of,

$$\frac{\mu-\mu_{baseline}}{\sigma}.$$

So,

$$\tilde{d} = \frac{ncp}{\sqrt{N}}.$$

T test for Mean Difference Between Two Independent Groups

n_1 or n_2 is sample size within the respective group.

$$t := \frac{M_1 - M_2}{SD_{within}/\sqrt{\frac{n_1 n_2}{n_1+n_2}}},$$

wherein,

$$SD_{within} := \sqrt{\frac{SS_{within}}{df_{within}}} = \sqrt{\frac{(n_1-1)SD_1^2 + (n_2-1)SD_2^2}{n_1+n_2-2}}.$$

$$ncp = \sqrt{\frac{n_1 n_2}{n_1+n_2}}\frac{\mu_1-\mu_2}{\sigma}$$

and Cohen's

$$d := \frac{M_1 - M_2}{SD_{within}} \text{ is the point estimate of } \frac{\mu_1-\mu_2}{\sigma}.$$

So,

$$\tilde{d} = \frac{ncp}{\sqrt{\frac{n_1 n_2}{n_1 + n_2}}}.$$

One-way Anova Test for Mean Difference Across Multiple Independent Groups

One-way ANOVA test applies non-central F distribution. While with a given population standard deviation ó, the same test question applies non-central chi-square distribution.

$$F := \frac{\frac{SS_{between}}{\sigma^2} / df_{between}}{\frac{SS_{within}}{\sigma^2} / df_{within}}$$

For each j–th sample within i–th group $X_{i,j}$, denote,

$$M_i(X_{i,j}) := \frac{\sum_{w=1}^{n_i} X_{i,w}}{} ; \mu_i(X_{i,j}) := \mu_i.$$

While,

$$\frac{SSbetween / \sigma^2}{}$$

$$= \frac{SS(M_i(X_{i,j}); i=1,2,\cdots,K, j=1,2,\cdots,n_i}{\sigma^2}$$

$$= SS\left(\frac{M_i(X_{i,j} - \mu_i)}{\sigma} + \frac{\mu_i}{\sigma}; i = 1,2,\cdots,K, j = 1,2,\cdots,n_i\right)$$

$$\sim X^2\left(df = K - 1, ncp = SS\left(\frac{\mu_i(X_{i,j})}{\sigma}; i = 1,2,\cdots,K, j = 1,2,\cdots,n_i\right)\right)$$

So, both ncp(s) of F and $\div^2$ equate,

$$SS(\mu_i(X_{i;j}) / \sigma; i = 1,2,\cdots,K, j = 1,2,\cdots,n_i).$$

In case of $n := n_1 = n_2 \cdots = n_K$ for K independent groups of same size, the total sample size is N:= n·K.,

$$Cohens\tilde{f}^2 := \frac{SS(\mu_1, \mu_2, \cdots \mu_K)}{K.\sigma^2} =$$

$$\frac{SS(\mu_i(X_{i,j}) / \sigma; i = 1,2,\cdots K, j = 1,2,\cdots n_i)}{n.K} =$$

$$\frac{ncp}{n.K} = \frac{ncp}{N}.$$

T-test of pair of independent groups is a special case of one-way ANOVA. Note that non-central parametre ncp_F of F is not comparable to the non-central parametre ncp_t of the corresponding t. Actually, $ncp_F = ncp_t^2$, and

$$\tilde{f} = \left|\frac{d}{2}\right|$$

in the case.

"Small", "Medium", "Large"

Some fields using effect sizes apply words such as "small", "medium" and "large" to the size of the effect. Whether an effect size should be interpreted small, medium, or big depends on its substantial context and its operational definition. Cohen's conventional criteria small, medium, or big are near ubiquitous across many fields. Power analysis or sample size planning requires an assumed population parametre of effect sizes. Many researchers adopt Cohen's standards as default alternative hypotheses. Russell Lenth criticized them as T-shirt effect sizes

This is an elaborate way to arrive at the same sample size that has been used in past social science studies of large, medium, and small size (respectively). The method uses a standardized effect size as the goal. Think about it: for a "medium" effect size, you'll choose the same n regardless of the accuracy or reliability of your instrument, or the narrowness or diversity of your subjects. Clearly, important considerations are being ignored here. "Medium" is definitely not the message!

For Cohen's d an effect size of 0.2 to 0.3 might be a "small" effect, around 0.5 a "medium" effect and 0.8 to infinity, a "large" effect.

Cohen's text anticipates Lenth's concerns: "The terms 'small,' 'medium,' and 'large' are relative, not only to each other, but to the area of behavioural science or even more particularly to the specific content and research method being employed in any given investigation....In the face of this relativity, there is a certain risk inherent in offering conventional operational definitions for these terms for use in power analysis in as diverse a field of enquiry as behavioural science. This risk is nevertheless accepted in the belief that more is to be gained than lost by supplying a common conventional frame of reference which is recommended for use only when no better basis for estimating the ES index is available."

The last two decades have seen the widespread use of these conventional operational definitions as standard practice in the calculation of sample sizes despite the fact that Cohen was clear that the small-medium-large categories were not to be used by serious researchers, except perhaps in the context of research with entirely novel variables.

STANDARD ERROR

The standard error of a method of measurement or estimation is the standard deviation of the sampling distribution associated with the estimation method. The term may also be used to refer to an estimate of that standard deviation, derived from a particular sample used to compute the estimate. For example, the sample mean is the usual estimator of a population mean. However, different samples drawn from that same population would in general have different values of the sample mean. The standard error of the mean is the standard deviation of those sample means over all possible samples drawn from the population. Secondly, the standard error of the mean can refer to an estimate of that standard deviation, computed from the sample of data being analysed at the time.

The term standard error is derived from the fact that, as long as the estimator is unbiased, the standard deviation of the error is the same as the standard deviation of the estimates themselves; this is true since the standard deviation of the difference between the random variable and its expected value is equal to the standard deviation of a random variable itself.

In many practical applications, the true value of the standard deviation is usually unknown. As a result, the term standard error is often used to refer to an estimate of this unknown quantity.

In such cases it is important to be clear about what has been done and to attempt to take proper account of the fact that the standard error is only an estimate. Unfortunately, this is not often possible and it may then be better to use an approach that avoids using a standard error, for example by using maximum likelihood or a more formal approach to deriving confidence intervals.

One well-known case where a proper allowance can be made arises where the Student's t-distribution is used to provide a confidence interval for an estimated mean or difference of means.

In other cases, the standard error may usefully be used to provide an indication of the size of the uncertainty, but its formal or semi-formal use to provide confidence intervals or tests should be avoided unless the sample size is at least moderately large. Here "large enough" would depend on the particular quantities being analysed.

Standard Error of the Mean

The standard error of the mean is the standard deviation of the sample mean estimate of a population mean. SEM is usually estimated by the sample estimate of the population standard deviation divided by the square root of the sample size:

$$SE_{\bar{x}} = \frac{s}{\sqrt{n}}$$

where,

s is the sample standard deviation, and

n is the size of the sample.

This estimate may be compared with the formula for the true standard deviation of the mean:

$$SD_{\bar{x}} = \frac{\sigma}{\sqrt{n}}$$

where,

σ is the standard deviation of the population.

- *Note* 1: Standard error may also be defined as the standard deviation of the residual error term.
- *Note* 2: Both the standard error and the standard deviation of small samples tend to systematically underestimate the population standard error and deviations: the standard error of the mean is a biased estimator of the population standard error. With n = 2 the underestimate is about 25 per cent, but for n = 6 the underestimate is only 5 per cent. Gurland and Tripathi provide a correction and equation for this effect. Sokal and Rohlf give an equation of the correction factor for small samples of $n < 20$.
- *A practical result*: Decreasing the uncertainty in your mean value estimate by a factor of two requires that you acquire four times as many observations in your sample. Worse, decreasing standard error by a factor of ten requires a hundred times as many observations.

Assumptions and Usage

If the data are assumed to be normally distributed, quantiles of the normal distribution and the sample mean and standard error can be used to calculate approximate confidence intervals for the mean. The following expressions can be used to calculate the upper and lower 95 per cent confidence limits, where $\bar{x}$ is equal to the sample mean, S_E is equal to the standard error for the sample mean, and 1.96 is the.975 quantile of the normal distribution:

$$\text{Upper 95 per cent Limit} = \bar{x} + (S_E.1.96),$$

$$\text{Lower 95 per cent Limit} = \bar{x} - (S_E.1.96),$$

In particular, the standard error of a sample statistic is the estimated standard deviation of the error in the process by which it was generated. In other words, it is the standard deviation of the sampling distribution of the sample statistic. The notation for standard error can be any one of SE, SEM or S_E.

Standard errors provide simple measures of uncertainty in a value and are often used because:

- If the standard error of several individual quantities is known then the standard error of some function of the quantities can be easily calculated in many cases;
- Where the probability distribution of the value is known, it can be used to calculate a good approximation to an exact confidence interval; and

- Where the probability distribution is unknown, relationships like Chebyshev's or the Vysochanskiï-Petunin inequality can be used to calculate a conservative confidence interval
- As the sample size tends to infinity the central limit theorem guarantees that the sampling distribution of the mean is asymptotically normal.

Correction for Finite Population

The formula given for the standard error assumes that the sample size is much smaller than the population size, so that the population can be considered to be effectively infinite in size. When the sampling fraction is large the estimate of the error must be corrected using a "finite population correction"

$$FPC = \sqrt{\frac{N-n}{N-1}}$$

to account for the added precision gained by sampling close to a larger percentage of the population. The effect of the FPC is that the error becomes zero when the sample size n is equal to the population size N.

Correction for Correlation in the Sample

If values of the measured quantity A are not statistically independent but have been obtained from known locations in parametre space x, an unbiased estimate of error in the mean may be obtained by multiplying the standard error by the factor f:

$$f = \sqrt{\frac{1+(n-1)\rho}{1-\rho}}$$

where the sample bias coefficient ñ is the average of the autocorrelation-coefficient $ñ_{ij}$ value for all sample point pairs.

Relative Standard Error

The relative standard error is simply the standard error divided by the mean and expressed as a percentage. For example, consider two surveys of household income that both result in a sample mean of $50,000.

If one survey has a standard error of $10,000 and the other has a standard error of $5,000, then the relative standard errors are 20 per cent and 10 per cent respectively. Intuitively, the survey with the lower standard error would seem to be more reliable since there is less dispersion around the mean.

In fact, data organizations often set reliability standards that their data must meet before publication. For example, the U.S. National Centre for Health Statistics typically does not report an estimate if the relative standard error exceeds 30 per cent.

DESIGN AND THE PURPOSE OF THE RESEARCH

Your research *design* is your plan for providing a sound, and, if possible, conclusive answer to your research question. Designs vary greatly, depending on the research question being addressed and the methods of data collection the investigator chooses to use. Creating a design starts with the purpose of the research.

Most research is done for one of three purposes. The most common purpose is to *describe* some set of variables or relationships among them as accurately as possible. Other purposes of research are to *explore* a topic to learn more about it or to *explain* why certain social patterns or relationships occur as they do.

Some studies combine more than one purpose. For example, while the Sudan Fertility Study was designed primarily as a descriptive investigation, we showed how data from this study were analysed to explain why future fertility rates may decline in northern Sudan. Nevertheless, as suggested, describe each approach separately to show how each purpose affects design decisions. Exploratory research generally requires less rigorous design decisions; so as suggested, start with it.

Exploratory Research

Exploratory research, as the name suggests, is a way of gaining some initial information about a problem or topic. You may be interested in a certain problem, but don't have enough information to write a clear research question. Perhaps you are not sure what the critical variables are or what methods of data collection may work best. Before beginning an investigation, you might decide to explore the problem by doing some informal interviews or by living for a short time with the group you want to study. These techniques are often used in exploratory research.

Example. Julia and Ridha explored experiences of Kuwaiti women during the Iraqi invasion and following occupation of Kuwait in 1990. Twenty women who played various roles, including active opposition to the Iraqi invaders, told of their experiences before, during, and after the invasion. The women reported that they actively sought their own self-development and liberation, but once the conflict ended, their choices and rights tended to become restricted again by traditional male prerogatives.

Exploratory studies, however, seldom provide satisfactory answers to research questions.

One reason is that most exploratory studies are based on samples too small to permit generalizing the results to a larger population. This is certainly true of the study of Kuwaiti women. But exploratory studies can provide valuable, even critical, information for designing larger scale descriptive or explanatory studies.

Descriptive Research

Descriptive research is more specific and focused than exploratory research. The researcher starts with a well defined problem or research question and a clearly defined plan for collecting and analyzing data. Descriptive research is intended to produce clear, well-founded answers to some question or specific, factual information. Surveys are frequently used in descriptive research.

Example. Fattah conducted interviews, using a questionnaire, with 200 randomly selected farm families in Iraq. The questionnaire contained over 200 items about husband-wife decision-making related to the operation of the farm, financial matters, social life, entertainment, training of children, and childcare. She also obtained information on whether the families had a "modern" or "traditional" view of things. These data provided a detailed description of the degree to which wives participated in decision-making with their husbands. Fattah concluded that factors associated with modernism will continue to increase and will enhance the position of women in rural Iraq, which, today, remains male dominated.

Explanatory Research

Explanatory research goes beyond exploratory or descriptive research by trying to find the reasons why certain relationships occur. It seeks to provide explanations for what has been observed. Explanations are based on interpretation of findings in terms of broader concepts and accepted theory.

Example. Using extensive interviews and observation, Dei developed an explanation for how Ghanian villagers survived prolonged drought and related hardships. He found they got through hard times by shifting from farm production for a market economy to shared production with other villagers for household consumption.

A strong sense of community solidarity developed and allowed the villages to survive with what they could produce together. The explanation for their survival was the successful return to earlier farming methods.

Regardless of the purpose of your research, you will also need to decide on a technique for data collection. There are two contrasting yet complimentary techniques - quantitative and qualitative means of collecting data.

QUANTITATIVE AND QUALITATIVE DATA

Many fields of science, particularly the physical sciences, report observations in terms of numbers. Observations reported in numbers are referred to as quantitative data. Social scientists obtain and analyse quantitative data, as you have seen with various studies we have cited. Social scientists also obtain and analyse data in qualitative form. These are observations recorded in words - descriptions of what persons said or did, how they interacted with one another, or what a researcher observed by watching their behaviour. Each technique is useful; each also has certain strengths and weaknesses; each also presents a different set of design decisions.

Some researchers draw a sharp distinction between quantitative and qualitative research. A different view is presented in Types of Data. This discussion shows how quantitative data is based in part on qualitative judgements and that qualitative data can also be described and analysed numerically.

Quantitative Research

A quantitative approach requires a well-developed research design.

Quantitative research is usually based on:

- Careful and precise specification of the question to be answered;
- Identification, definition, and measurement of the key variables;
- Selection and specification of one or more methods of collecting data;
- Development of a sampling plan; and
- Numerical analysis of the data, including use of appropriate statistical tests.

Numbers used in quantitative studies may be as simple as counting the number of"Yes" versus"No" responses to some question. More complex forms of measurement, however, are generally used. The descriptive research by Fattah, for example, used a quantitative design. The many decision-making variables were defined and measures were developed for each. These measures, in the form of questions, were then combined in a questionnaire that was used in interviewing a random sample of farm families.

Quantitative data has important strengths. Using numerical measures provides more precise descriptions of variables. In addition, quantitative research permits use of larger samples. Also, quantitative data can be combined and analysed using various statistical techniques. You are certainly familiar with averages and percentages as ways of summarizing data.

Most of this site focuses on planning and conducting quantitative research and analyzing data based on quantitative variables.

Qualitative Research

Qualitative research, in contrast to quantitative research, seeks to dig deeper into the reasons for behaviour we observe. Generally, researchers doing qualitative research start with a broad idea of what they are looking for. In qualitative studies, researchers often combine informal interviews, in the form of long conversations with people, with systematic observation of their daily activities.

Data are derived continuously from what the persons in the group being studied do and say, how they say they feel about things, and the reasons they give the researcher for what they do. The researcher accumulates a large amount of data, generally in the form of long sets of notes and written descriptions of what was observed. As data are recorded, the researcher tries to interpret what the data mean and to develop an explanation for what has been observed. In this sense, analysis of data proceeds with data collection. Qualitative research is generally a much more flexible process, allowing researcher to take advantage of new lines of enquiry as they develop.

The research studies cited earlier by Julia and Ridha and by Dei were based on qualitative research methods. Research by ElSayed and Ahmed on the "Socio-Cultural Aspect of Kala-azar among the Masalit and Hansa Tribes" further emphasizes use of qualitative techniques.

The authors used small group discussions with villagers, personal interviews with patients, and direct observation of health and sanitation practices in the villages. They found that lack of knowledge about the disease is the main reason for its spread.

Combining Quantitative and Qualitative Techniques

Researchers frequently use both quantitative and qualitative techniques in the same investigation. In this way, researchers benefit from the strengths of each approach and minimize their respective limitations. Altareb, for example, investigated attitudes towards Muslims held by undergraduate students at an American university. He began by conducting focus groups, a qualitative technique, to get an initial understanding of students' attitudes. After this exploratory phase, he developed a quantitative measure of attitudes for the main part of the investigation.

Davidson also combined qualitative and quantitative methods in his investigation of ways families in the Nuba Mountains of the Sudan were adapting to rapidly changing socio-economic conditions in their area. He began by interviewing village elders and then conducted a survey to identify the characteristics of each of the 12 villages in his study area. Following the survey, he carried out in-depth interviews with selected households. This combination of methods provided a rich mix of quantitative data for describing adaptive techniques used by villagers and detailed and qualitative data for understanding how they were adapting to changes.

UNIT OF ANALYSIS

In designing research you also have to decide on what basis you will analyse the data you will collect. This requires a decision about the part *of analysis* for the study.

Units of analysis may consist of individuals, groups, organizations, geographical places, or other entities. Generally the way you state your research question indicates which part will be used as the basis of analyzing the data.

It is easy to confuse part of analysis with the entities you collect data from. Frequently, they are the same. In the Sudan Fertility Survey, for example, the data were collected from women and the data were analysed in terms of the same women.

In this case, the decision was clear. In another study, a researcher might interview factory managers to get information to compare the efficiency of different sized factories. In this case, the part of analysis is factories, not managers because the purpose of the research is to compare factories and managers happened to be the source of data. If you have any doubt, think about the question you are trying to answer. How do the data have to be organized to answer the question?

Individuals as the Part of Analysis

When the purpose of research is to say something about individuals, they become the part of analysis. Individuals are the most frequent part of analysis. They may be any age, either gender, or become the units of analysis because they have a common characteristic. Primary, intermediate and secondary students were the units of analysis in a trend study by Badri and Burchinal.

Many studies are based on collecting data from university students, who then become the part of analysis. Cook, for example, investigated the attitudes of Egyptian university students towards Islam and higher education; Had-Elzein and Ahmed obtained data on perceptions and vision of peace from Sudanese university students.

Married women were the part of analysis in the Sudan Fertility Survey. Mageed, Sulima and Kawther collected data about attitudes towards female genital mutilation from adult men and women. Agricultural technical workers were the part of analysis in a study of worker satisfaction in Kenya. Muneer selected farmers, who became the part of analysis, in his study of the role of cooperatives in western Sudan. Khalafalla selected policy-makers as her sample who also became her part of analysis.

Groups as the Part of Analysis

Research is often conducted by collecting and analyzing data for groups of people. When the purpose is to describe two or more persons as a unit, these groups become the part of analysis. Households, consisting of various numbers of persons, often are used as the part of analysis. Examples include the research by Julia and Ridha on Iraqi farm families and research by Davidson on changes in household life in the Nuba Mountains.

Households were the part of analysis in an extensive study of year-long spending patterns among farm families in Sierra Leon. The sample used by Grotberg and Badri consisted of intact families with a child not older than five and one-half years. The mother-child pairs in these families became the part of analysis in this study. Other units of analysis at the group level include friendship groups, clubs, social groups, and groups of street children.

Organizations as the Part of Analysis

Research often is directed at learning about organizations, such as businesses, firms, ministries of government, universities, political parties, religious bodies, or military units. Although data about each organization may be obtained by interviewing members of an organization, the data would be used to describe and compare features of each organization. For example, Gimbel and associates studied job satisfaction in community-based organizations.

They collected data from employees but analysed their data in terms of characteristics of the organizations. Mohamed analysed operations in a sample of 150 government divisions in the United Arab Emirates.

In a study of safety programmes, Vredenburgh collected data about practices in 62 hospitals. These are only a few of the many management studies based on organizations as the part of analysis.

Geographical Places as the Part of Analysis

Places, such as where people live, can also become the focus of study and therefore be used as the part of analysis. Fishing villages in Uganda were the part of analysis in a socio-economic investigation by Namara. Cities, provinces, and rural versus urban areas are used as the part of analysis in most reports issued by international organizations. Countries frequently are used as the part of analysis. Bulluck compared the extent to which developing countries meet the social needs of citizens. Countries were also used in comparing infant mortality rates throughout sub-Saharan Africa. Wang examined the extent to which women's reproductive rights were protected in 101 countries.

Other Units of Analysis

Although most social research is based on the kinds of units of analysis just mentioned, other things may be selected for analysis. These include the contents of newspapers and magazines; rural development projects; and folk tales.

Table. Summarizes Frequently used Units of Analysis.

1.	*Individuals*: By far the most frequently used
2.	*Groups*: Husband-wife pairs, social groups
3.	Organizations—businesses, offices, factories, government ministries
4.	Classrooms, schools, university student bodies or groups
5.	*Geographical areas*: Villages, communities, cities, regions of a country, entire countries
6.	*Mass media materials*: Newspapers, magazines, television shows

Deciding on the Part of Analysis

Most likely the part of analysis you will use in a study will be clear from the way you defined your problem. If you have any doubts about the part you should use, you will need to resolve this confusion before going on. Otherwise, you may not analyse your data properly and your entire study could be jeopardized. Ask yourself what part you will base your analysis on. This is, as the term implies, your part of analysis. Also, in the process of analyzing your data, you may shift from one part to another.

In the study by Gimbel and associates mentioned under organizations as the part of analysis, the authors used organizations as the part of analysis. However, since they collected data from employees, they could have undertaken other analyses as well. For example, they might have become interested in the level of morale among employees and the length of time each worked for one of the organizations. In this case, they would have shifted to employees as the part of analysis. Our point is simple: just be sure of your part of analysis and that you have data appropriate to that unit.

Collecting Data at the Lowest Possible Part

Also, remember an important rule: Regardless of what you are studying, always obtain data in terms of the lowest part of analysis possible. There is a simple reason for this. You can usually combine data collected at a lower level into a higher level for analysis, but it won't work the other way around. For example, if you intended to analyse data about the production of things by households, collect data about the production activities for each member of the household. Then you can combine the data from each household member for analysis at the level of the entire household. This way you can still do other analyses at the level of members of the household, such as what wives and daughters produced in contrast to husbands and sons, as well as for the entire household. But if you asked only for production of the household as a whole, you would not be able to describe production by separate members of the household.

Design Alternatives

Designing research is a creative process. Designs can be put together in a number of ways. By describing some of

the more frequently used designs, we hope you will get an idea of the various kinds of research questions you can ask and designs you can use in answering them.

To start, designs can be developed for:

- Describing variables as they currently exist;
- For describing changes that have occurred; and
- For describing changes as they occur.

Cross-sectional Designs

Surveys are designed to describe some set of variables as they exist at the time of data collection. Data are collected from a sample over a relatively short period of time. The design used for a survey is also called a *cross-sectional* design because the sample is carefully selected to represent the cross section of some population. Either quantitative or qualitative techniques can be used to collect survey data, although, in general, quantitative techniques are used. The frequently cited Sudan Fertility Survey was based on a survey or cross-sectional design.

The survey design can be expanded to include more than one sample, as suggested, show shortly as part of the discussion of seeking differences between groups with respect to some variable.

7

Methods of Data Collection

INTRODUCTION

QUESTIONNAIRES

Questionnaires are one of the most popular methods of conducting scholarly research. They provide a convenient way of gathering information from a target population.

Advantages and Disadvantages of Written Questionnaires

Questionnaires are easy to analyse, and most statistical analysis software can easily process them. They are cost effective when compared to face-to-face interviews, mostly because of the costs associated with travel time. This is especially true for studies involving large sample sizes and large geographic areas. Written questionnaires become even more cost effective as the number of research questions increases.

Questionnaires are familiar to most people. Nearly everyone has had some experience completing questionnaires and they generally do not make people apprehensive. They are less intrusive than telephone or face-to-face surveys. When respondents receive a questionnaire in the mail, they are free to complete it on their own time-table. Unlike other research methods, the respondent is not interrupted by the research instrument. On the other hand, questionnaires are simply not suited for some people. For example, a written survey to a group of poorly educated people might not work because of reading skill problems. More frequently, some people are turned off by written questionnaires because of misuse.

Written questionnaires reduce interviewer bias because there is uniform question presentation. Unlike in-person interviewing, there are no verbal or visual clues to influence a respondent to answer in a particular way. Many investigators have reported that interviewer voice inflections and mannerisms can bias responses. Written surveys are not subject to this bias because there is no interviewer. On the other hand, the lack of an interviewer limits the researcher's ability to probe responses. Structured questionnaires often lose the "flavour of the response", because respondents often want to qualify their answers. By allowing frequent space for comments, the researcher can partially overcome this disadvantage.

A common criticism of mail surveys is that they often have low response rates. Low response is the curse of statistical analysis, and it can dramatically lower confidence in the results. While response rates vary widely from one questionnaire to another, well-designed studies consistently produce high response rates.

When returned questionnaires arrive in the mail, it's natural to assume that the respondent is the same person you sent the questionnaire to. A number of researchers have reported that this may not actually be the case. Many times business questionnaires get handed to other employees for completion. Housewives sometimes respond for their husbands. Kids respond as a prank. For a variety of reasons, the respondent may not be who you think it is. In a summary of five studies sponsored by the British Government, Scott reports that up to ten per cent of the returned questionnaires had been completed by someone other than the intended person.

Response Rate

Response rate is the single most important indicator of how much confidence can be placed in the results of a mail survey. A low response rate can be devastating to the reliability of a study. Fortunately, "low response rates are not an inherent shortcoming of mail surveys", and the researcher must do everything possible to maximize response. Much of the research in questionnaire methodology has centred around techniques to maximize response. However, Jones and Lang point out that increasing the response rate does not necessarily improve the precision of survey results.

Following up on Non-respondents

One of the most powerful tool for increasing response is to use follow-ups or reminders. "Traditionally, between 5 and 65 per cent of those sent questionnaires respond without follow-up reminders. These rates are too low to yield confident results". The need to follow up on non-respondents is clear.

Researchers can increase the response from follow-up attempts by including another copy of the questionnaire. The most important consideration is that the investigator "designs the follow-up procedure by taking into consideration the unique characteristics of the people in the sample." The most successful follow-ups have been achieved by phone calls.

Many researchers have examined whether postcard follow-ups are effective in increasing response. The vast majority of these studies show that a follow-up postcard increases response rate, and a meta-analysis by Fox, Crask, and Kim reveals an aggregate gain of 3.5 per cent. The postcard serves as an effective reminder for subjects who have forgotten to complete the survey.

Non-response Bias

Many studies have attempted to determine if there is a difference between respondents and non-respondents. Some researchers have reported that people who respond to surveys answer questions differently than those who do not. Others have found that late responders answer differently than early responders, and that the differences may be due to the different levels of interest in the subject matter. One researcher, who examined a volunteer organization, reported that those more actively involved in the organization were more likely to respond.

Demographic characteristics of non-respondents have been investigated by many researchers. Most studies have found that non-response is associated with low education. However, one reseacher reported that demographic characteristics such as age, education, and employment status were the same for respondents and non-respondents. Another study found that non-respondents were more often single males.

Most researchers view non-response bias as a continuum, ranging from fast responders to slow responders. In fact, one study used extrapolation to estimate the magnitude of bias created by non-response. Another group of researchers argue that non-response should not be viewed as a continuum, and "that late respondents do not provide a suitable basis for estimating the characteristics of non-respondents".

Goal Definition

Most problems with questionnaires can be traced back to the design phase of the project. Well-defined goals are the best way to assure a good questionnaire design. One of the best ways to clarify the study goals is to decide how the information will be used.. Study goals should be committed to writing. When the goals of a study can be expressed in a few clear and concise sentences, the design of the questionnaire becomes considerably easier. The questionnaire is developed to directly address the goals of the study.

One important way to assure a successful survey is to include other experts and relevant decision-makers in the questionnaire design process. Their suggestions will improve the questionnaire and they will subsequently have more confidence in the results.

General Layout and Format Considerations

The physical appearance of a written survey may largely determine if the respondent will return it. Therefore, it is important to use professional production methods for the questionnaire—either desktop publishing or typesetting and keylining. Every questionnaire should have a title that is short and meaningful to the respondent. The rationale is that a questionnaire with a title will be perceived as more credible than one without.

Well-designed questionnaires include clear and concise instructions on how they should be completed. These must be very easy to understand, so use short sentences and basic vocabulary. The questionnaire itself should have the return address printed on it since questionnaires often get separated from the reply envelopes.

Questionnaires should use simple and direct language. The questions must be clearly understood by the respondent, and have the same meaning that the researcher intended. The wording of a question should be simple, to the point, and familiar to the target population.

Surprisingly, several researchers have found that longer questions elicit more information than shorter ones, and that the information tends to be more accurate. However, it is generally accepted that questionnaire items should be simply stated and as brief as possible. The rationale is that this will reduce misunderstandings and make the questionnaire appear easier to complete. One way to eliminate misunderstandings is to emphasize crucial words in each item by using bold, italics or underlining.

Uncommon words, jargon, and abbreviations may be included in a questionnaire provided that they are familiar to the population being investigated. Slang is often ambiguous, and should be excluded from all questionnaires.

Questionnaires should leave adequate space for respondents to make comments. One criticism of questio-nnaires is their inability to retain the "flavour" of a response. Leaving space for comments will provide valuable information not captured by the response categories. Leaving white space also makes the questionnaire look easier and this might increase response.

Researchers should design the questionnaire so it holds the respondent's interest. The goal is to make the respondent want to complete the questionnaire. One way to keep a questionnaire interesting is to provide variety in the type of items used. Varying the questioning format will also prevent respondents from falling into "response sets".

The Order of the Questions

Questionnaires should begin with a few non-threatening and easy to answer items. If the first items are too difficult or threatening, there is little chance that the person will complete the questionnaire. People generally look at the first few questions before deciding whether or not to complete the questionnaire. The researcher can encourage response by starting with a few interesting and nonthreatening questions.

Likewise, the most important items should appear in the first half of the questionnaire. Respondents often send back partially completed questionnaires. By putting the most important items near the beginning, the partially completed questionnaires will still contain important information.

Items on a questionnaire should be grouped into logically coherent parts. Grouping questions that are similar will make the questionnaire easier to complete, and the respondent will feel more comfortable. Questions that use the same response formats, or those that cover a specific topic, should appear together.

Each question should follow comfortably from the previous question. Writing a questionnaire is similar to writing anything else. Transitions between questions should be smooth. Questionnaires that jump from one unrelated topic to another feel disjointed and are not likely to produce high response rates.

Most investigators have found that the order in which questions are presented can affect the way that people respond. One study reported that questions in the latter half a questionnaire were more likely to be omitted, and contained fewer extreme responses. Carp suggested that it may be necessary to prevent general questions before specific ones in order to avoid response contamination. McFarland reported that when specific questions were asked before general questions, respondents tended to exhibit greater interest in the general questions. A few researchers, however, have found that question-order does not effect responses. Bradburn and Mason reported that interviews involving self-reports and self-evaluations were unaffected by question order. Clancey and Wachsler found that responses to questions were similar regardless of where the questions appeared in a questionnaire. Bishop et al. reported that question-order effects existed in interviews, but not in written surveys. Ayidiya and McClendon reported mixed results, where some questions were subject to order effects, and other similar questions were not.

Anonymity and Confidentiality

As a general rule, long questionnaires get less response than short questionnaires. However, some studies have shown that the length of a questionnaire does not necessarily affect response. "Seemingly more important than length is question content." A subject is more likely to respond if they are involved and interested in the research topic. Questions should be meaningful and interesting to the respondent.

Colour of the Paper

One study found that the colour of the paper. Nevertheless, Berdie, Anderson and Neibuhr suggest that colour might make the survey more appealing. Another early study examined the ink and paper colour combinations that provide the greatest legibility. The authors suggest three different ink colours for white paper: black, grass green, and lustre blue. The only other recommended combination is black ink on yellow paper. Some investigators have examined the effect of using a green paper compared to white paper. Two studies reported no significant differences in response rates, while another reported a 9.1 per cent difference. A meta-analysis of these studies calculated an average aggregate increase of 2.0 per cent when using a green questionnaire.

Incentives

Many researchers have examined the effect of providing a variety of non-monetary incentives to subjects. These include token gifts such as small packages of coffee, ball-point pens, postage stamps, or key rings, trading stamps, participation in a raffle or lottery, or a donation to a charity in the respondent's name. Generally, non-monetary incentives have resulted in an increased response.

There can be little doubt that monetary incentives increase response. Only a few investigators have reported no increase in response. The overwhelming majority have reported increased response by including monetary incentives.

Church conducted of meta-analysis of 38 prior studies that used some form of an incentive. Monetary and non-monetary incentives were effective only when enclosed with the survey. The promise of an incentive for a returned questionnaire was not effective in increasing response. The average increase in response rate for monetary and non-monetary incentives was 19.1 per cent and 7.9 per cent, respectively.

Many researchers have found that higher monetary incentives generally work better than smaller ones. Armstrong proposed a diminishing return model, where increasing the amount of the incentive would have a decreasing effect on response rate. A meta-analysis performed by Fox, Crask, and Kim applied Armstrong's diminishing return model to fifteen studies. An incentive of 25¢ increased the response rate by an average of 16 per cent, and $1 increased the response by 31 per cent.

It is not known whether the effects of incentives disappear after follow-up mailings. Kephart and Bressler found that a 25¢ incentive significantly increased response, however, the effect disappeared after one follow-up mailing. Another study using a 25¢ incentive reported a significant difference, and the difference continued to be significant even after three follow-up mailings. James and Bolstein reported that four mailings without an incentive produced a better response than one mailing with an incentive. However, incentives of $1 and $2 with follow-ups produced a significantly better response than the same number of follow-ups with no incentive.

Nederhof used a ball-point pen as an incentive and reported that "the effect of non-monetary incentives on response rates disappears after the first mailing."

It is not clear whether offering to share the results of the research provides sufficient incentive to affect response. Mullner, Levy, Byre, and Matthews report that mentioning the offer in a cover letter did not increase response, while two older studies found that it did.

Notification of a Cutoff Date

Several researchers have examined the effect of giving subjects a deadline for responding While a deadline will usually reduce the time from the mailing until the returns begin arriving, it appears that it does not increase response, and may even reduce the response. One possible explanation is that a cutoff date might dissuade procrastinators from completing the questionnaire after the deadline has past. A meta-analysis by Fox, Crask and Kim revealed an aggregate increase in response rate of 1.7 per cent, which was not significant.

Reply Envelopes and Postage

A good questionnaire makes it convenient for the respondent to reply. Mail surveys that include a self-addressed stamped reply envelope get better response than business reply envelopes, although they are more expensive since you also pay for the non-respondents. Some investigators have suggested that people might feel obligated to complete the questionnaire because of the guilt associated with throwing away money--that is, the postage stamp. Others have pointed out that using a business reply permit might suggest advertising to some people. Another possibility is that a business reply envelope might be perceived as less personal.

Armstrong and Lusk performed a meta-analysis on 34 studies comparing stamped versus business reply postage. They calculated that stamped reply envelopes had a 9 per cent greater aggregate effect than business reply envelopes. In a subsequent meta-analysis on nine studies, Fox, Crask, and Kim reported an aggregate effect of 6.2 per cent.

The Outgoing Envelope and Postage

There have been several researchers that examined whether there is a difference in response between first class postage versus bulk rate.. A meta-analysis of these studies revealed a small, but significant, aggregate difference of 1.8 per cent. Envelopes with bulk mail permits might be perceived as"junk mail", unimportant, or less personal and thus will be reflected in a lower response rates.

A few researchers have also examined whether metreed mail or stamps work better on the outgoing envelope. The results of these studies suggest a small increase in response favouring a stamped envelope. A meta-analysis of these studies revealed that the aggregate difference was slightly less than one per cent. Many researchers have reported increased response rates by using registered, certified, or special delivery mail to send the questionnaire. The wisdom of using these techniques must be weighed against the consequences of angering respondents that make a special trip to the post office, only to find a questionnaire.

It is not clear whether a typed or hand-addressed envelope would affect response. One study, conducted at the University of Minnesota, reported that students responded better to hand-addressed postcards, while professors responded better to typed addresses. This researcher could find no studies that examined whether gummed labels would have a deleterious effect on response rate, although we might predict that response rate would be less for gummed labels because they have the appearance of less personalization.

This researcher could also find no studies that examined whether the colour of the envelope affects response rate. First impressions are important, and the respondent's first impression of the study usually comes from the envelope containing the survey. Therefore, we might predict that colour would have a positive impact on response because of its uniqueness.

The "Don't Know", "Undecided", and "Neutral" Response Options

Response categories are developed for questions in order to facilitate the process of coding and analysis. Many studies have looked at the effects of presenting a "don't know" option in attitudinal questions. The "don't know" option allows respondents to state that they have no opinion or have not thought about a particular issue.

Holdaway found that the physical placement of the "undecided" category could change response patterns. Respondents were more likely to choose the "undecided" category when it was off to the side of the scale. This study also reported different response patterns depending on whether the midpoint was labeled "undecided" or "neutral".

Bishop also found that the physical location of the middle alternative can make a difference in responses, and that placing the middle option at the last position in the question increased the percentage of respondents who selected it by over 9 per cent. Bishop states that "offering respondents a middle alternative in a survey question will generally make a significant difference in the ceases that would be drawn." The middle option of an attitudinal scale attracts a substantial number of respondents who might be unsure of their opinion.

Poe et al. studied the "don't know" option for factual questions. Unlike attitude questions, respondents might legitimately not know the answer to a factual question. Their findings suggest that the "don't know" option should not be included in factual questions. Questions that excluded the "don't know" option produced a greater volume of accurate data. They found no difference in response rate depending on the inclusion or exclusion of the "don't know" option. Poe's finding directly contradict several previous authors who advocate including a "don't know" response category when there is any possibility that the respondent may not know the answer to a question.

Question Wording

The wording of a question is extremely important. Researchers strive for objectivity in surveys and, therefore, must be careful not to lead the respondent into giving the answer a desired answer. Unfortunately, the effects of question wording are one of the least understood areas of questionnaire research.

Many investigators have confirmed that slight changes in the way questions are worded can have a significant impact on how people respond. Several authors have reported that minor changes in question wording can produce more than a 25 per cent difference in people's opinions.

One important area of question wording is the effect of the interrogation and assertion question formats. The interrogation format asks a question directly, where the assertion format asks subjects to indicate their level of agreement or disagreement with a statement. Schuman and Presser reported no significant differences between the two formats, however, other researchers hypothesized that the interrogation format is more likely to encourage subjects to think about their answers. Petty, Rennier and Cacioppo found that the interrogation format caused greater polarization in subjects' responses, suggesting that there was greater cognition than the assertion format.

Other investigators have looked at the effects of modifying adjectives and adverbs. Words like usually, often, sometimes, occasionally, seldom, and rarely are "commonly" used in questionnaires, although it is clear that they do not mean the same thing to all people. Simpson and a replication by Hakel looked at twenty modifying adjectives and adverbs. These researchers found that the precise meanings of these words varied widely between subjects, and between the two studies. However, the correlation between the two studies with respect to the relative ranking of the words was.99.

John Hoyt conducted a study on how people interpret quantifying adjectives. The results show that some of the adjectives had high variability and others had low variability. The following adjectives were found to have highly variable meanings: a clear mandate, most, numerous, a substantial majority, a minority of, a large proportion of, a significant number of, many, a considerable number of, and several. Other adjectives produced less variability and generally had shared meaning. These were: lots, almost all, virtually all, nearly all, a majority of, a consensus of, a small number of, not very many of, almost none, a damn few, hardly any, a couple, and a few.

Sponsorship

There have been several studies to determine if the sponsor of a survey might affect response rate. The overwhelming majority of these studies have clearly demonstrated that university sponsorship is the most effective. A meta-analysis of these studies revealed an aggregate increase in response rate of 8.9 per cent. Dillman suggested that this may be due to the past benefits that the respondent has received from the university. Another possibility is that a business sponsor implies advertising or sales to potential respondents.

Prenotification Letters

Many researchers have studied prenotification letters to determine if they increase response rate. A meta-analysis of these studies revealed an aggregate increase in response rate of 7.7 per cent.

Dillman proposed that prenotification letters might help to establish the legitimacy of a survey, thereby contributing to a respondent's trust. Another possibility is that a prenotification letter builds expectation, and reduces the possibility that a potential respondent might disregard the survey when it arrives.

The prenotification letter should address five items:

1. Briefly describe why the study is being done.
2. Identify the sponsors.
3. Explain why the person receiving the pre-letter was chosen.
4. Justify why the respondent should complete the questionnaire.
5. Explain how the results will be used.

Cover Letters

The cover letter is an essential part of the survey. To a large degree, the cover letter will affect whether or not the respondent completes the questionnaire. It is important to maintain a friendly tone and keep it as short as possible. The importance of the cover letter should not be underestimated. It provides an opportunity to persuade the respondent to complete the survey. If the questionnaire can be completed in less than fifteen minutes, the response rate can be increased by mentioning this in the cover letter.

Flattering the respondent in the cover letter does not seem to affect response Altruism or an appeal to the social utility of a study has occasionally been found to increase response, but more often, it is not an effective motivator.

The cover letter should address seven items:

1. Briefly describe why the study is being done.
2. Identify the sponsors.
3. Mention the incentive.
4. Mention inclusion of a stamped, self-addressed return envelope.
5. Encourage prompt response without using deadlines.
6. Describe the confidentiality/anonymity policy.
7. Give the name and phone number of someone they can call.

Personalization in a Cover Letter

There are no definitive answers whether or not to personalize cover letters. Some researchers have found that personalized cover letters can be detrimental to response when anonymity or confidentiality are important to the respondent.

The literature regarding personalization are mixed. Some researchers have found that personalized cover letters with hand-written signatures helped response rates. Other investigators, however, have reported that personalization has no effect on response.

Signature on the Cover Letter

The signature of the person signing the cover letter has been investigated by several researchers. Ethnic sounding names and the status of the researcher do not affect response. One investigator found that a cover letter signed by the owner of a marina produced better response than one signed by the sales manager. The literature is mixed regarding whether a hand-written signature works better than one that is mimeographed. Two researchers reported that mimeographed signatures worked as well as a hand-written one, while another reported that hand-written signatures produced better response. Another investigator found that cover letters signed with green ink increased response by over 10 per cent.

Postscript on the Cover Letter

It is commonly believed that a handwritten postscript in the cover letter might increase response. One older study did find an increase in response, however, two more recent studies found no significant difference.

Questionnaire Construction

A questionnaire is a series of questions asked to individuals to obtain statistically useful information about a given topic. When properly constructed and responsibly administered, questionnaires become a vital instrument by which statements can be made about specific groups or people or entire populations.

Questionnaires are frequently used in quantitative marketing research and social research. They are a valuable method of collecting a wide range of information from a large number of individuals, often referred to as respondents. Adequate questionnaire construction is critical to the success of a survey. Inappropriate questions, incorrect ordering of questions, incorrect scaling, or bad questionnaire format can make the survey valueless, as it may not accurately reflect the views and opinions of the participants.

A useful method for checking a questionnaire and making sure it is accurately capturing the intended information is to pretest among a smaller subset of target respondents.

Questionnaire Construction Issues

- Know how you will use the results of your research before you start. If, for example, the results won't influence your decision or you can't afford to implement the findings or the cost of the research outweighs its usefulness, then save your time and money; don't bother doing the research.
- The research objectives and frame of reference should be defined beforehand, including the questionnaire's context of time, budget, manpower, intrusion and privacy.
- How and from where you select the respondents will determine whether you will be able to generalize your findings to the larger population.
- The nature of the expected responses should be defined and retained for interpretation of the responses, be it preferences, facts, beliefs, feelings, descriptions of past behaviour, or standards of action.
- Unneeded questions are an expense to the researcher and an unwelcome imposition on the respondents. All questions should contribute to the objective(s) of the research.
- If you"research backwards" and determine what you want to say in the report then even though you don't know the exact answers yet, you will be certain to ask all the questions you need - and only the ones you need - in such a way to write your report.
- The topics should fit the respondents' frame of reference. Their background may affect their interpretation of the questions. Respondents should have enough information or expertise to answer the questions truthfully.
- The type of scale, index, or typology to be used shall be determined.
- The level of measurement you use will determine what you can do with and conclude from the data. If the response option is yes/no then you will only know how many or what per cent of your sample answered yes/no. You cannot, however, conclude what the average respondent answered.
- The types of questions should fit the statistical data analysis techniques available and your goals.
- Questions and prepared responses to choose from should be neutral as to intended outcome. A biased question or questionnaire encourages respondents to answer one way rather than another. Even questions without bias may leave respondents with expectations.
- The order or "natural" grouping of questions is often relevant. Prior previous questions may bias later questions.
- The wording should be kept simple: no technical or specialized words.
- The meaning should be clear. Ambiguous words, equivocal sentence structures and negatives may cause misunderstanding, possibly

invalidating questionnaire results. Double negatives should be reworded as positives.

- If a survey question actually contains more than one issue, the researcher will not know which one the respondent is answering. Care should be taken to ask one question at a time.
- The list of possible responses should be collectively exhaustive. Respondents should not find themselves with no category that fits their situation. One solution is to use a final category for "other ________".
- The possible responses should also be mutually exclusive. Categories should not overlap. Respondents should not find themselves in more than one category, for example in both the "married" category and the "single" category - there may be need for a "not living with spouse" category.
- Writing style should be conversational, yet concise and accurate and appropriate to the target audience.
- Many people will not answer personal or intimate questions. For this reason, questions about age, income, marital status, etc. are generally placed at the end of the survey. This way, even if the respondent refuses to answer these "personal" questions, he/she will have already answered the research questions.
- "Loaded" questions evoke emotional responses and may skew results.
- Presentation of the questions on the page and use of white space, colours, pictures, charts, or other graphics may affect respondent's interest or distract from the questions.
- Numbering of questions may be helpful.
- Questionnaires can be administered by research staff, by volunteers or self-administered by the respon-dents. Clear, detailed instructions are needed in either case, matching the needs of each audience.

Table. Methods of collection

Method	Benefits/Cautions
Postal	This method has a low cost. Survey participants can choose to remain anonymous. It is not labour intensive.
Telephone	Questionnaires can be conducted swiftly. Rapport with respondents High response rate Be careful that your sampling frame doesn't skew your sample, For example, if you select the phone numbers from a phone book, you are necessarily excluding people who only have a mobile phone, those who requested an unpublished phone number, and individuals who have recently moved to the area because none of these people will be in the book.

Electronic	This method has a low cost, and on most surveys costs nothing for the participants and little for the surveyors. Questionnaires can be conducted swiftly. Survey participants can choose to remain anonymous. It is not labour intensive. Questions can be more detailed, as opposed to the limits of paper or telephones. This method works well if your survey contains several branching questions. Sample may "self select" and thus not be representative of the population.
Personally Administered	Questions can be more detailed, as opposed to the limits of paper or telephones. Rapport with respondents High response rate Usually a convenience sample so you cannot generalize your results.

Types of Questions

- *Contingency questions*: A question that is answered only if the respondent gives a particular response to a previous question. This avoids asking questions of people that do not apply to them.
- *Matrix questions*: Identical response categories are assigned to multiple questions. The questions are placed one under the other, forming a matrix with response categories along the top and a list of questions down the side. This is an efficient use of page space and respondents' time.
- *Closed ended questions*: Respondents' answers are limited to a fixed set of responses. Most scales are closed ended. Other types of closed ended questions include:
  - *Yes/no questions*: The respondent answers with a "yes" or a "no".
  - *Multiple choice*: The respondent has several option from which to choose.
  - *Scaled questions*: Responses are graded on a continuum. Examples of types of scales include the Likert scale, semantic differential scale, and rank-order scale.
- *Open ended questions*: No options or predefined categories are suggested. The respondent supplies their own answer without being constrained by a fixed set of possible responses.

  Examples of types of open ended questions include:
  - *Completely unstructured*: For example, "What is your opinion of questionnaires?"
  - *Word association*: Words are presented and the respondent mentions the first word that comes to mind.
  - *Sentence completion*: Respondents complete an incomplete

sentence. For example, "The most important consideration in our decision to buy a new house is..."

- *Story completion*: Respondents complete an incomplete story.
- *Picture completion*: Respondents fill in an empty conversation balloon.
- *Thematic apperception test*: Respondents explain a picture or make up a story about what they think is happening in the picture

Question Sequence

- Questions should flow logically from one to the next.
- The researcher must ensure that the answer to a question is not influenced by previous questions.
- Questions should flow from the more general to the more specific.
- Questions should flow from the least sensitive to the most sensitive.
- Questions should flow from factual and behavioural questions to attitudinal and opinion questions.
- Questions should flow from unaided to aided questions.
- The three stage theory, initial questions should be screening and rapport questions. Then in the second stage you ask all the product specific questions. In the last stage you ask demographic questions.

RESEARCH AND DATA-COLLECTION

Feedback is a vital part of any organizations growth. Weather you conduct regular focus groups to elicit information from key players or, your account manager calls up all your marquee accounts to find out how things are going – essentially they are all processes to find out from your customers' eyes – How are we doing? What can we do better? Online surveys are just another medium to collect feedback from your customers, employees and anyone your business interacts with. With the advent of Do-It-Yourself tools for online surveys, data collection on the internet has become really easy, cheap and effective.

SENDING OUT A SURVEY TO CUSTOMERS CAN DOUBLE SALES

We all are well aware of a simple fact in marketing - Acquiring a new customer is 10 times more difficult and expensive than retaining an existing one.

This is one of the fundamental driving forces behind the wide-spread adoption and interest in CRM and related customer retention strategies. In a research study by Rice University Professor Dr. Paul Dholakia and Dr. Vicki Morwitz, published in Harvard Business Review, the experiment concluded that the simple fact of asking customers how a company was performing by itself proved to be a great customer retention strategy.

In the research study, conducted over the course of a year, one set of customers were sent out a satisfaction and opinion survey and the other set was not surveyed. After a year, twice the number of people continued and renewed their loyalty towards the company in the group that took the survey.

The research study offered a couple of interesting rationales based on consumer psychology, behind this phenomenon:

- *Satisfaction Surveys Reinforce the Customers Desire to be Coddled and Reinforce Positive Ffeelings*: This stems from part of the human psychology that wants to "appreciate" a product or service they already like. The survey feedback loop is merely a tool to express this. The survey is a vehicle to "interact" with the company and reinforces the customer's commitment to the company.
- *Surveys may Increase Awareness of Auxiliary Products and Services:* Surveys can be considered vehicles of communication - both inbound as well as outbound. Most people consider surveys as a data collection exercise. When conducting consumer surveys, they can also serve as a medium for disseminating information. It is important to note a few caveats here.
- In most countries including the US, "selling under the guise of research" is illegal.
- However, we all know that information is disseminated while collecting information.
- Additional disclaimers may be added to the survey to make users aware of this fact. Eg: "As suggested, be collecting your opinion and informing you about products and services that have come online in the last year..."
- Induced Judgements:
- The very process of asking people their opinion can induce them to form an opinion on something they otherwise would not have considered. This is a very subtle and powerful argument. This argument is analogous to the "Product Placement" strategy currently used for marketing products in mass-media like movies and television shows. One example is the extensive and exclusive use of the "mini-Cooper" in the blockbuster movie "Italian Job." This strategy is questionable and should be used with great caution.
- Surveys should be considered as a critical tool in the customer relationship dialog. The best thing about surveys is its ability to carry "bi-directional" information. The research conducted by Paul Dholakia and Vicki Morwitz shows that surveys not only get you the information that is critical for your business, but also enhances and builds upon the established relationship you have with your customers.
- Recent advances in technology have made it incredibly easy to conduct real-time surveys and opinion polls. Online tools make it easy to frame

questions and answers, and create surveys on the Web. Distributing surveys via e-mail, web site links or even integration with online CRM tools like Salesforce.com have made online surveying a quick-win solution.

SURVEY MODE: PHONE VS. ONLINE VS. IN-PERSON INTERVIEWS

Essentially there are four choices for data collection – in-person interviews, mail, phone and online.

There are pros and cons to each of these modes:

- In-Person Interviews
- *Pros:* In-depth and a high degree of confidence on the data
- *Cons:* Time consuming, expensive and can be dismissed as anecdotal
- Mail Surveys
- *Pros:* Can reach anyone and everyone – no barrier
- *Cons:* Expensive, data collection errors, lag time
- Phone Surveys
- *Pros:* High degree of confidence on the data collected, reach almost anyone
- *Cons:* Expensive, cannot self-administer, need to hire an agency
- Web/Online Surveys
- *Pros:* Cheap, can self-administer, very low probability of data errors
- *Cons:* Not all your customers might have an e-mail address/be on the internet, customers may be wary of divulging information online.

In-Person interviews always are better, but the big draw-back is the trap you might fall into if you don't do them regularly. It is expensive to regularly conduct interviews and not conducting enough interviews might give you false positives. Validating your research is almost as important as designing and conducting it. We've seen many instances where after the research is conducted – if the results do not match up with the "gut-feel" of upper management, it has been dismissed off as anecdotal and a "one-time" phenomenon.

To avoid such traps, we strongly recommend that data-collection be done on an "ongoing and regular" basis. This will help you compare and contrast how perceptions change depending upon how you market your product or service. The other issue here is sample size. To be confident with your research you have to interview enough people to weed out the fringe elements.

A couple of years ago there was quite a lot of discussion about online surveys and their statistical validity. The fact that not every customer had internet connectivity was one of the main concerns. Although some of the discussions are still valid, the reach of the internet as a means of communication has become vital in the majority of customer interactions. The US Census Bureau the number of households with computers has doubled between 1997 and 2001.

In 2001 nearly 50 per cent of the households had a computer. Nearly 55 per cent of all households with an income of more than 35,000 have internet access, and this jumps to 70 per cent for households with an annual income of 50,000. This data is from the US Census bureau for 2001. There are primarily three modes of data-collection that can be employed to gather feedback – Mail, Phone and Online. The actual mode used for data-collection is really a cost-benefit analysis.

There is no slam-dunk solution but you can use the table to understand the risks and advantages associated with each of the mediums:

Survey Medium	Cost Per Response	Data Quality/Integrity	Reach (All US Housholds)
Paper	$20 – $30	Medium	100 %
Phone	$20 - $35	High	95%
Online/ E-mail	$1 - $5	Medium	50-70%

Keep in mind, the reach here is defined as "All US Households." In most cases, you need to take a look at how many of your customers are online and make a determination. If all your customers have e-mail addresses, you have a 100 per cent reach of your customers. Another important thing to keep in mind is the ever-increasing dominance of cellular phones over land-line phones. United States FCC rules prevent automated dialing and calling cellular phone numbers and there is a noticeable trend towards people having cellular phones as the only voice communication device. This introduces the inability to reach cellular phone customers who are dropping home phone lines in favour of going entirely wireless. Even if automated dialing is not used, another FCC rule prohibits from phoning anyone who would have to pay for the call. Almost all cellular phone services in the US charge for incoming airtime.

Multi-mode Surveys

Surveys where the data is collected via different modes (online, paper, phone etc.) is also another way of going. It is fairly straightforward and easy to have an online survey and have data-entry operators to enter in data (from the phone as well as paper surveys) into the system. The same system can also be used to collect data directly from the respondents.

RESEARCH METHODS FOR DATA COLLECTION AND ANALYSIS

This subject guide is called Social research methods, but the term 'research methods' in this guide is reserved for those research instruments that are constructed to either guide or standardise data collection. Qualitative social research uses a variety of data collection methods. The classic method is ethnography: studying people by description of the culture and action. In participant observation studies the researcher attempts to take the place and play out the roles of someone who belongs to the social group being studied. The participant observation may be covert, or undertaken with the understanding of those being observed. Qualitative research also involves non-participant or more artificial settings such as the interview and the focus group. The research methods chosen by qualitative social researchers reflect five specific methodological commitments:

1. Depicting the social world as seen through the eyes of subjects
2. Description in context
3. Emphasis on process
4. Flexibility and limited structure
5. Concepts and theory grounded in data.

Qualitative research methods allow the researcher to discover how the social world is constructed by the people studied. The aim of the research may be to report how the culture of the people observed challenges popular but false stereotypical perceptions. Qualitative research may reveal aspects of the social world that may or may not be recognised by those being studied. The sociologist might reveal the taken for granted assumptions that are often found or hidden rules governing decision-making.

For example, in the 1970s, Zimmerman studied a welfare agency in which the following rules applied:

- Whatever a client said that bore on their ineligibility for welfare benefits was taken at face value, believed and not subject to further investigation.
- Whatever a client said that bore on their eligibility for welfare benefits was not believed unless there was documentation supplied to support the truth of the statements made.

The commitment to seeing the social world through the eyes of the subject reflects a commitment to understanding the social world via gaining access to the subjective meanings by which it is understood by participants. The outcome of qualitative social research is an enhanced 'interpretative understanding' of the social world.

The qualitative researcher's commitment to description-in-context reflects the belief that all action is to be understood as a reflection of the qualitative context in which it takes place. Describing the context in detail is required to comprehend what might otherwise be incomprehensible behaviours. Qualitative social research is distinctive in its concern with social processes. Whereas quantitative research often takes cross-sectional snapshots of the social world at one moment in time, the design features of qualitative research reflect a concern to see how social processes emerge within the wider context. The use of techniques such as participant observation illustrates this commitment to process. A strong example of this tradition comes under studies of 'becoming', or more formally, in the study of status passage.

Whether it is concerned with becoming a marijuana user, a qualified medical practitioner, or a Moonie, qualitative research is keen to establish stages in the process of transition from one social status to another. Qualitative research designs are characterised by flexibility and limited structure: the idea is to let analysis and findings emerge from the data over the time-period of the study. Research questions, concepts and theory may not be defined or may only be defined as 'working framework' that is subject to change during the unit of the project. This approach is crystallised in Blumer's famous call for 'sensitising concepts' in social research.

Concepts and theory are grounded in data because any premature closure of concept formation and theory development is to be avoided. Quantitative social research is most often associated with social surveys. Survey analysis is used most frequently to collect information from large samples of individuals. These samples are selected to be representative of whole populations.

Quantitative social research can also take other forms. Government administrative systems routinely collect data and this can be analysed using social research methods. Government statistics are compiled on an area basis and researchers can attempt to establish descriptive and causal findings from an analysis of the data.

Quantitative techniques can also be used in the structured observation of social settings and in the content analysis of large text files such as newspaper archives. Even qualitative social researchers can advocate some limited use of counting. In using these data sources, quantitative social researchers are often seen to exemplify the following preoccupations:

- Measurement of concepts to test and refine theories
- Causal inference and model building
- Generalisation of findings
- Replication of studies.

Measurement is important in quantitative social research because it is the only way of demonstrating the contingent relationships between concepts.

To establish that social class influences life expectancy, it is necessary to measure class by placing individuals within a social class classification scheme. If we then use data measuring the age at which people die, it is possible to see if there are social class differences in the mean age at death. Without measurement, it is impossible to establish contingency.

Where there is a lack of measurement, we are unable to test the related theoretical ideas. A practical example concerns car insurance. If insurance companies could get accurate estimates of how well people drive, then they would use this data to predict accident rates and thus determine insurance premiums.

Instead they use a number of proxy measures of driving ability such as age, number of previous claims, number of driving convictions etc.

In social research we measure education by the qualifications gained but this is not necessarily a precise guide to knowledge and skills. Measurement and the establishment of contingency are not sufficient since such contingencies may reflect chance or spurious relationships between concepts. To establish the validity of a contingency relationship, quantitative social research must establish that the findings meet the criteria of causal inference.

A valid model is a set of contingent relationships between concepts that has been established by both measurement and causal inference. What are these criteria of causal inference?

They are association, time order and lack of spuriousness:

- *Association*: For the units being studied the values of one variable are dependent on the values of another.
- *Time order*: Or a change in the values of one variable at results in a change in the value of the other
- *Lack of spuriousness*: Establishing that the contingent relationship between the dependent and the independent variable is not the product of a third common or antecedent variable.

Quantitative social research requires quite complex multivariate analysis to establish that the contingent relationship between two variables is 'true' or to establish in what contexts it is true. Thus we might want to conclude that in most advanced industrial societies there is a close relationship, controlling for other influences between educational achievement and occupational status. There are two further preoccupations to consider.

Quantitative social research often uses research designs based on systematic sampling techniques that ensure that the findings relating to a sample can be generalised to the wider population from which the sample was drawn. Using techniques of statistical inference and significance tests, the degree of confidence in the generalisation can be established. Test results show whether confidence is established at the 95 per cent, 99 per cent or 99.9 per cent levels. Such tests can only be used with systematic random sampling and this is usually found only in quantitative social research.

The transparency of data collection techniques and methods of analysis in quantitative social research means that the replication of studies is relatively straightforward. Although replication remains rare in practice, the possibility of confirming or rejecting the findings of previous studies is possible.

In qualitative social research, improvements are being made to increase the degree of transparency and the archiving of qualitative data does facilitate replication of the data analysis stage. Quantitative social research is variable-centred. It seeks to test and develop theoretical models of concepts by measurement and causal inference.

In measuring concepts such as education, these social objects reflect real underlying causal forces. If they did not then there would be no contingent relationships between measured social objects. In measurement, the research is reifying social constructs, making them object-like and the validity of measurement is confirmed where contingent relationships can be established and thus useful research findings result since our knowledge of the forces of the acting is enhanced.

Table. Example Research Methods by Research Strategy

Research Method Components	Qualitative Research Strategy	Quantitative Research Strategy
Methods/instruments of data collection	Aims to maximise openness of response in interviews/ unstructured interview/focus groups.	Aims to standardise meaning of response in survey questionnaires and records of official activities.
Data analysis strategy	Revealing implicit meanings. Coding text to categories and modelling connections and/or sequences to convey plausibility.	Estimating descriptions and (causal) associations between variables to meet criteria for inference

The research strategies are linked to research designs and to the criteria that are applied to evaluate the validity of social research findings. As are some of the more technical aspects of research design.

DATA COLLECTION (ENSURING RELIABILITY)

The wide range of observer effects identified in the stage illustrates how reactivity may influence the collection of data in social research. Although it is usually practically impossible for any researcher to identify and control for all of these effects, he still has a responsibility to plan and execute a study in a manner that will minimise the combined effects of various threats to validity. We now turn to some of the methods that the researcher can use to control for some of the effects. Our discussion does not address specific techniques, which may be found in the publications cited. Our primary concern is with the broad issues.

TRIANGULATION

A first general principle in data collection is that the inclusion of multiple sources of data collection in a research project is likely to increase the reliability of the observations. Denzin coined the term triangulation to refer to the use of multiple methods of data collection. Campbell and Fiske suggested a similar strategy which they called multiple operationism. Both of these concepts refer to the use of a variety of methods and techniques of data collection in a single study. The underlying assumption is that, because various methods complement each other, their respective shortcomings can be balanced out. It is important to bear in mind that specific types of data collection are designed for collection of certain types of data. In a classic article in 1962, Morris Zelditch distinguished between three types of information: frequency distributions, incidents or events, and institutionalised norms and status. For each of these types of information there is a prototypical method of data collection, which encompasses the use of surveys for information concerning incidents and the use of informants or interviews for information on norms and status. Zelditch's classification also illustrates the fact that each type of method has specific limitations. By employing different methods of data collection in a single project we are, to some extent, able to compensate for the limitations of each.

We focussed on the fact that not all methods are equally reactive. It is hence an important principle to supplement the more reactive methods such as direct observation, with less reactive methods, such as the use of documentary sources. Two examples of triangulation will illustrate the advantages of such an approach.

We have specifically indicated that items that address issues relating to race and sex are likely to result in considerable response variability, particularly when there have been no controls for the race and gender of the interviewer. In the event of such a variation occurring in response to sensitive questions, more reliable information is likely to be obtained by doing a follow-up study using in-depth interviews. Similarly, where historical events are being investigated and memory decay may play an important part, the reliability of the information can probably be increased by the use of documentary sources like diaries and letters.

Ensuring Anonymity

As indicated by Schuman and Presser, respondents tend to be reluctant to provide interviewers with information on sensitive matters. A similar problem surfaces in studies of sensitive behaviour such as so-called deviant behaviour. Douglas indicated that subjects tend to be unusually reluctant or unwilling to participate because they regard the investigation as an invasion of their privacy.

The fact that his investigations concerned situations of a sensitive nature–massage parlours and nudist beaches–obviously contributed to this kind of response! One possible strategy to reduce the effect of such responses would be to emphasise the anonymity of responses and observations where possible. Rather than face-to-face interviews, it may for instance be possible to use postal or telephone surveys. Nevertheless, respondents are not necessarily convinced that the latter approaches actually ensure their anonymity. In the case of studies on so-called deviant behaviour, the assurance that the investigator will not identify the respondents in any way, must be regarded as a minimum requirement for establishing greater validity.

Establishing Rapport

As opposed to anonymity one could use a strategy of trying to establish the best possible interpersonal relationship or rapport with the respondent. This strategy is obviously time consuming, and it might hence not always be practical. Douglas reported that a year had elapsed before they discovered that one of their most trustworthy participants had been using a 'nom de plume' all along.

The advantage of a strong interpersonal relationship between researcher and participant is that it neutralises initial distrust. It can also serve as a control for role selection effects. If the respondent trusts the interviewer, there is no longer any need for any kind of role playing. The establishment of good rapport can also serve as a control for context effects.

Covert Research

A more drastic strategy is to make use of some form of covert research. Covert observation may assume a variety of guises. Basically, it amounts to the researcher deceiving the participant about the actual purpose of the research or about the identity of the researcher. In such cases all possible measures are taken to ensure that the participant does not become aware of the fact that he or she is part of a research project.

A good example of this type of research is Simon Holdoway's study of police brutality. Because he suspected that he would not obtain reliable data in any other way, Holdoway resorted to covert research. He went as far as joining the police force, undergoing the necessary training, and spending several months serving as a policeman on patrol duty. With a single exception, nobody knew that his eventual aim was to conduct a sociological study of police activities. Covert research is particularly applicable in studies where participant observation or in-depth-interviewing is used.

These are studies in which it is essential for the researcher to establish close ties with the group being investigated while keeping his/her actual identity from them. Other types of covert research are encountered where researchers disguise the fact that research is being conducted.

An example of this method is found in the study conducted by Schwartz and Skolnick in which letters of application for employment were manipulated to investigate the effect of a criminal record on 'suitability for appointment'. Experimental designs in the natural context where some form of disguise is used, the reader can refer to Campbell.

One of the most common examples of deception in laboratory experiments is to be found in so-called blind and double-blind designs. In blind experimental designs the participants do not know whether they are part of the experimental group or the control group, whereas in double-blind experimental designs there is the additional requirement that the experimenters do not know whether they are dealing with the experimental group or the control group. Effective covert research is obviously a useful strategy for countering the general guinea-pig effect.

Where research participants are unaware of the fact that they are being studied they cannot react to the fact of being investigated. Covert research also controls for expectancy effects. In the example of the double-blind experimental design, one of the most important causes of expectancy effects is eliminated.

Although the use of covert strategies like disguise, deception or withholding information is one of the most effective ways of minimising or even eliminating error, there are fundamental ethical objections to the wholesale use of this approach. Covert research necessarily implies that the subject is deceived, or that his/her right to privacy is infringed on, or that he/she has to be lied to. The dilemma confronting the researcher is hence how to weigh the moral interests of the subject against the interests of science.

A number of authors have proposed suggestions on ways to neutralise the negative ethical implications of covert research. One approach involves requesting the subject's permission to use the information gathered, immediately after completion of the study while obviously still ensuring the subject's anonymity.

Martin Bulmer's Social research ethics may be consulted for an excellent exposition of the ethical implications of participant observation and covert research.

Control Group

It has always been the norm to use control groups in experimental studies wherever possible. Apart from the experimental group to which the specific experimental treatment is applied or in which given interventions are made, a comparable control group, which does not undergo the experimental treatment, is used.

In an attempt to ensure that the experimental and control groups are comparable, techniques such as random assignment of participants to either the experimental or control groups or matching of participants in the two groups is used. This enables the researcher to draw causal inferences with a higher degree of validity. A control group facilitates control for participant effects such as maturation, history and selection effects. However, researchers who intend to use an experimental approach are cautioned to study carefully the most important participant effects that are likely to occur in different types of experimental design and the measures that may be taken to eliminate these.

Training

Adequate training of experimenters, interviewers, research assistants and fieldworkers is a precondition for any research. One of the specific aims in such training is to counteract researcher effects. In our discussion of researcher effects, we noted the negative consequences of researcher orientation effects, and particularly those associated with researcher expectation effects.

The likelihood of obtaining reliable data is increased when interviewers are given clear instructions regarding the aims of the project, and the importance of accurate and consistent interviewing is emphasised.

Thorough prior training is also likely to eliminate or reduce the occurrence of some of the other researcher effects that we have not discussed, such as inaccurate noting of responses, coding errors, classification errors and many more.

Selection of Fieldworkers

The cause of one of the more important researcher effects can be found in the distance between researchers and participants. Although various factors such as context or level of motivation result in greater degrees of distance between researchers and participants, researcher characteristics such as gender, race, age, and style of dress are some of the most important factors that fall under this rubric.

An obvious solution to this problem is to exercise due care in the selection of fieldworkers. Fieldworkers who share as many characteristics of the sample as possible ought to be given preference.

Replication Studies

In conclusion, one can hardly overemphasise the importance of the principle of replication. As Barber notes, a variety of factors contribute to the situation where exact replication in the social sciences is virtually impossible. Following Lykken's lead, Barber argues in favour of more constructive replication by stressing that more investigators should try to confirm empirical relationships claimed in earlier reports while the replicator formulates his own methods of sampling, measurement and statistical analysis.

Constructive replication implies that the researcher wishes to control the findings of an earlier study by investigating the same problem for a different sample and/or by using a different research design. A good example of such studies is included.

DATA COLLECTION (DATA SOURCES, REACTIVITY AND CONTROL)

One of the distinctive features of the social sciences is that, to a greater of lesser degree, the participants in social research, to wit, individuals or groups, are aware of the fact that they are 'objects' of investigation. Depending on the nature of the particular data source and the manner in which it is collected, human beings are aware of this situation when they participate in research and they tend to react to it. In the literature on methodology, this phenomenon has been known as reactivity since 1957.

This term will be applied in a broad sense to refer to the phenomenon that human beings react to the fact that they are participants in research. This reaction manifests itself in a variety of forms, for example, resistance to being interviewed or to completing questionnaires, supplying inaccurate information as a result of apathy, wilfulness, modifying behaviour or information to create a better impression, or deliberately misinforming the researcher. However, it is important to note that, depending on the nature of the data source, reactivity is an important variable. In accordance with Manheim's scheme, data sources in the social sciences can be divided into two main categories, with two subcategories in each, namely:

1. Human behaviour and human characteristics.
2. Products of human behaviour and of human characteristics.

Human Behaviour and Human Characteristics

Mannheim distinguishes between two main categories: on the one hand, verbal behaviour, which includes verbal or written responses to questions posed by the researcher and on the other, all observable behaviour and characteristics. The first category includes all forms of human behaviour which only become accessible by means of indirect observation such as questionnaires, interviews or projective tests.

The second category includes all forms of individual behaviour, social interaction, and observable characteristics such as gender, number of individuals, physical locality, non-verbal behaviour and stature.

Direct observation methods are generally used to collect data in this category. Examples would include structured or controlled observation in experimental situations, and participant observation in non-structured situations. The distinction drawn between structured and unstructured observation is clearly not equally applicable in all situations. Nonetheless, it provides a rough systematisation of data-collection techniques, which is useful for the remainder of the discussion.

Products of both Human Behaviour and Human Characteristics

Mannheim divides this category into two subcategories, namely physical traces and archival sources. Physical traces are defined as any physical evidence that has been left from earlier human behaviour. In accordance with Webb's subsequent refinement of this category, physical traces are further subdivided into erosion measures and accretion measures. Examples of erosion measures would include wear on floor tiles at museum exhibits, erosion of library books and patterns of attire such as shoes, which may be employed as indications of human activity. Examples of accretion measures would include for example, the number of empty liquor bottles per week in refuse cans, the placing of buildings and pot shards.

Archival or documentary sources refer to the extensive collections of records, documents, library collections or mass media material that have been amassed. Those sources would also include well-known material such as census data, life statistics, ecological and demographic data, personal documents like diaries, autobiographies and letters, and case studies.

Other types of archival sources include mass media material like newspaper reports, the content of radio and television programmes, and film material. Webb *et al.* also refer to less well-known material such as inscriptions on tombstones, sales records, suicide notes, nursing records on patients, and voting records. Webb and Banks were the first researchers to focus on the existence of 'differential reactivity'.

Data sources where human beings are directly involved are regarded as highly reactive sources, whereas those where human beings are only indirectly involved are far less likely to be regarded as reactive sources. Reactivity becomes the largest single threat to the validity of research findings when human behaviour or characteristics are the sources of data or information.

With the exception of covert observation, and irrespective of whether data is collected by means of indirect or direct observation, human respondents or research participants are aware of the researcher and usually react to this situation in some or other way. Obviously the products of human activities such as documents or texts cannot react to the fact that they are being researched.

It should nevertheless be borne in mind that the products of human behaviour are the result of decisions and cognitive processes. These products are the sedimentations or 'residues' of the human spirit. An example is manifested in the fact that when studying a text, the researcher has to be mindful of the original intention or aim of the author and of the researcher's own historicity.

The fact that human beings are rational beings is obviously also manifested in the products of human behaviour. Although data sources in the second category, where human involvement is only indirect, are unlikely to display reactivity to any marked degree, the possibility cannot be ignored. In the remainder of this part, we shall discuss the threats to the validity of findings in which human beings are directly involved. How do researchers respond to the high level of reactivity of some data sources? Typically they resort to some form of 'control'. The researcher could for instance attempt to reduce the effect of error by imposing a greater degree of structure on the observations, or by exerting more control on the research situation. Traditionally, the strongest form of control has been experimental research design.

Randomisation is one such form of control. It involves the assignment of research subjects or participants to experimental and control groups on a random basis to control for the possible effects of individual differences. As Krathwohl aptly points out, 'random assignment makes groups comparable in all of the variables we think might present problems and also in all other things we had not expected'. Unfortunately, it is also true that such measures of experimental control are intrusive. Quite frequently, the participants of such research are isolated in a laboratory situation that is removed from their natural environment so as to limit the effects of external nuisance or confounding variables. Banks focussed on the interesting phenomenon that these control measures vary positively with the degree of reactivity of the specific observation technique employed. This means that the greater the number of controls the researcher builds into the research situation, the more likely the participants are to be reactive.

Because laboratory conditions such as isolation and random assignment to treatments do not typically form part of the everyday life of the subjects, it is likely to result in artificial and atypical patterns of behaviour. As Groenewald quite justifiably states, this presents a dilemma for the researcher. While, on the one hand, it is desirable to use observation techniques that elicit as little reactivity as possible in order to ensure the highest level of validity it is, on the other, equally desirable to employ observation techniques that make it possible to exercise as much control as possible.

Data-collection sources in which direct observation methods like systematic and participant observation, or indirect observation methods like questionnaires and interviews are used, can be controlled by the use of appropriate statistical techniques. We have, however, already indicated that these data sources are also highly reactive. The second main category of data sources, namely physical and archival sources, does not really allow for any 'strong' measures of control. In a certain sense, the data is already given.

The researcher can of course select which data sources to use. He may also be able to sample such sources in a content analysis study. But he has no direct control over the 'production' of the data.

By definition, documentary and archival sources have already been produced. What is important is that the researcher should take steps to ensure the authenticity of such sources. Although physical and archival sources do not allow for much control, the good news is that these data categories are low on reactivity and for this reason do not pose as big a threat to the eventual validity of the findings.

The fact that reactivity and control are positively correlated illustrates a point which we made earlier in this book, namely that methodology in general, and research design in particular, inevitably involve compromises. The researcher must constantly weigh the advantages and disadvantages of a number of issues against each other, and eventually decide on whatever measures are, as a whole, likely to increase the validity of his findings most.

THE REQUIREMENT OF RELIABILITY

The key validity criterion for data collection is 'reliability'. This is the requirement that the application of a valid measuring instrument to different groups under different sets of circumstances should lead to the same observations.

Smith defines reliability by posing the following question:

- Will the same methods used by different researchers and/or at different times produce the same results?

As suggested by this definition, reliability demands consistency over time. In this sense, reliability refers to the fact that different research participants being tested by the same instrument at different times should respond identically to the instrument. But what are the possible sources of error during data collection?

I shall argue that the reliability of data is affected by the following:

- The researchers, 'experimenters', 'interviewers' or 'observers';
- The individuals or 'subjects' who participate in the research project;
- The measuring instruments such as questionnaires, scales, tests, interviewing schedules and observation schedules; and
- The research context or the circumstances under which the research is conducted.

Our discussion here and in the next stage will be confined to the effects of the researcher, the research participant and the research context on the reliability of the data. Each of these terms will be used in the widest sense possible. The term researcher includes project leaders, interviewers, experimenters, participant observers and fieldworkers. Participants include individuals being observed, questioned or a group of people who are being either observed or questioned. The research context refers to both the broad spatio-temporal circumstances under which research is conducted and the specific spatio-temporal setting.

A further distinction is drawn between the characteristics and orientations of the researcher and the participant. Researcher or participant characteristics refer to attributes such as gender, nationality, age, socio-economic status and educational level. These characteristics are known as organismic variables. Researcher or subject orientations have reference to attitudes, opinions, expectations, preferences, tendencies and values.

In accordance with common usage in the literature on experimental design, we shall refer to the consequences of the nuisance variables associated with each of the four variables as 'effects': researcher effects, participant effects, measuring instrument effects and context effects. Researcher effects are the negative consequences relating to validity that are directly attributable to the researcher. Similarly, measuring instrument effects are the negative consequences or lack of validity that may be directly attributed to some aspect of the measuring instrument.

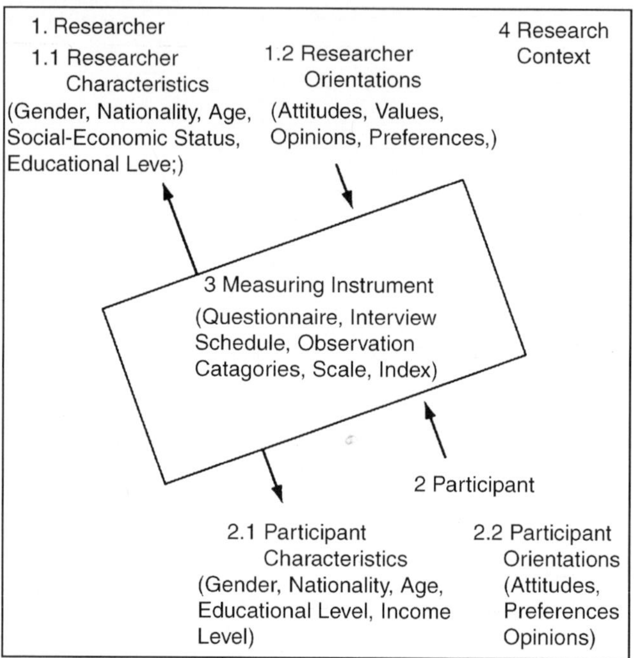

Fig. Factors that Affect the Reliability of Data

These distinctions are schematically presented in figure. Reliability is a precondition for measurement validity. It is clearly impossible to expect accurate measurements, for instance when using a scale to measure your weight, if the instrument does not consistently produce similar readings. Some of the readings will be accurate and some not. At the same time, reliability is not the only precondition for measurement validity. You can have a scale that consistently gives you the wrong readings! This means that the readings are reliable but invalid. The relationship between reliability and validity can be illustrated by the analogy between a measuring instrument and a gun. An accurate and reliable gun will repeatedly hit the target in the centre. The shots are clustered and on target. If some shots are clustered but not on target, the gun is reliable but not very accurate. If the gun is not consistent the shots will be all over the target and therefore inaccurate or invalid.

CONCLUDING COMMENTS

The objective of data collection is to produce reliable data. This means that such data is consistent over time and place. But, there are a number of potential sources of error that could result in the production of unreliable data.

These sources of error or observation effects have been classified into three categories, namely effects that are due to the researcher, those that result from the reactivity of the participant and those that follow from certain factors in the environment.

We have also shown that, in many cases, measures to control these effects lead to higher levels of reactivity and hence to lower reliability. Social researchers have no choice but to strike a compromise between control and creating reactivity, in order to produce the highest degree of reliability possible.

DATA COLLECTION (SOURCES OF ERROR)

The term 'observation effects' is used in a broad sense to include researcher, participant and context effects. These are sometimes also referred to as 'confounding' variables: that is, elements that pose a threat to the reliability of data collected. The aim in this stage is to identify different kinds of confounding variables or sources of error and give examples from various kinds of studies. Although the examples are mainly derived from the experimental and survey research literature, they have a wider application.

RESEARCHER EFFECTS

Our discussion of researcher effects is divided into two parts; in the first, we discuss effects associated with researcher characteristics, and in the second, those associated with researcher orientations.

Researcher Characteristics

Some of the most important researcher effects associated with specific researcher characteristics or attributes relate to the affiliation of the researcher, the image projected by the researcher to the research participants, and the distance between the researcher and the participants owing to differences between certain characteristics in the researcher and in the participants. The latter category is hence not only an effect of researcher characteristics, but also arises from the interaction between characteristics in the researcher and those in the participants.

Affiliation of the Researcher

The researcher's association with a specific organisation may result in biased responses. If the interviewer is employed by a highly influential organisation that is known for the quality of its research, respondents are likely to be better motivated to answer questions seriously and truthfully. Universities and large research organisations usually have reputations of this nature.

However, should the interviewer be associated with an organisation that elicits suspicion or with a completely unknown organisation, respondents are likely to react more negatively to the interview situation. Atkin and Chaffe found that the affiliation or presumed affiliation of interviewers played an important role in research related to government control of violence in television programmes. In cases where the respondents, who were parents, thought that the interviewer represented some government body, they were more inclined to give extreme responses to questions.

Image of the Researcher

In an important study, Jack Douglas discusses the problems surrounding conflict in research. A tacit assumption in research has always been that participants naturally wish to cooperate with the researcher, and that they would obviously provide valid and reliable information. However, Douglas maintains that the assumptions of what he calls 'the investigative paradigm' are far more realistic.

The investigative paradigm is based on the assumption that social life is pervaded by profound conflicts of interest, values, feelings and actions. Based on a variety of studies that he conducted, including some in massage salons and on nudist beaches, Douglas found that suspicion and mistrust were the rule rather than the exception: In an important study, Jack Douglas discusses the problems surrounding conflict in research.

A tacit assumption in research has always been that participants naturally wish to cooperate with the researcher, and that they would obviously provide valid and reliable information. However, Douglas maintains that the assumptions of what he calls 'the investigative paradigm' are far more realistic. The investigative paradigm is based on the assumption that social life is pervaded by profound conflicts of interest, values, feelings and actions. Based on a variety of studies that he conducted, including some in massage salons and on nudist beaches, Douglas found that suspicion and mistrust were the rule rather than the exception:

- One manifestation of mistrust was in avoidance or evasive responses. Rather than being the exception, I suspect such evasiveness is the common situation in field research: People rarely tell the whole truth as they see it about the most important things, but they are generally being evasive or misleading rather than lying. A field researcher must understand this and the reasons for it: Primarily a fear of exposure, of being caught in a lie, and an unwillingness to appear less than absolutely 'moral' to an academic stranger.

A researcher is often seen as a stranger, an outsider, or an intruder. In the research conducted by Douglas these issues were probably given greater prominence as a result of the sensitive nature of his research. It seems fairly obvious that women in massage salons would regard the researcher as suspect since the possibility of him being a policemen cannot be excluded. The examples that we have discussed have all related to fairly general perceptions of the researcher as a suspect or stranger. At a considerably lower level Brislin *et al.* use the term rudeness as an all-embracing term to refer to the researcher as someone who interrupts the normal activities of the respondents. However, a variety of issues like the affiliation of the researchers, their interests and cultural background, and the time and place of the research all contribute to the image of the researchers: the positive or negative perception that the participants are likely to have of them.

Distance between Researcher and Participant

A large body of research has been conducted in an attempt to establish which effects result from differences between the researcher and the participant. In some of the most important findings the existence of racial effects, gender effects, status effects, urban-rural effects, and even style-of-dress effects have been indicated.

We shall consider a few of these studies. In a recent study Campbell found race-of-interviewer effects similar to those found in earlier studies by Schuman and Hatchet and also by Hyman. He concluded that racial differences between interviewer and participant may lead to a significant degree of bias. However, this bias is limited to the items in which the race of the respondent is explicitly mentioned by the interviewer. The direction of the observed bias is also constant in the sense that respondents consistently provide responses that are favourable to the race to which the interviewer belongs. In a study on pre-marital sex, Zehner found that the responses of male participants were not influenced by the gender of the interviewer.

In comparison, female participants tended to be far more reticent when they were interviewed by female interviewers. However, in his study on controversial issues related to sexual intercourse, Rangonetti found no significant differences between the answers provided by those who were interviewed by male and female interviewers respectively. What he did find was that, irrespective of the gender of the interviewer, respondents were significantly more open in their responses when they were interviewed by a single interviewer than in a group interview situation. Mendras attempted to establish whether differences in rural and urban background between the interviewer and the participant had an influence on response bias. Giles and Chevasse in turn attempted to establish whether the interviewer's style of dress had any influence on participants' responses.

Their conclusion was that style of dress could have an even greater influence on response than the perceived status of the interviewer! In a more recent publication, Sudman and Bradburn found that the distance created between participant and interviewer as a result of interviewer and participant characteristics should not be seen as an issue separate from the content of the questions posed. It has already been noted that racial differences are only found when the content of the question includes a reference to the race of the respondent, and that gender factors were found to be sensitive in Zehner's study only when the items referred 150 to sexually sensitive themes.

Sudman and Bradburn, the perceived threat of a question is of greater importance than the other issues. People are simply reluctant to reply to questions that deal with sexual behaviour, alcohol consumption, traffic offences, possession of firearms and the use of drugs. It is hence hardly surprising that when questions are posed that relate to sexual behaviour, which is a sensitive topic, and these questions are posed by members of a specific gender, gender effects will be observed. The same would apply if questions on race relations were to be asked by interviewers from a race group other than that of the interviewee.

Researcher Orientations

From research conducted over a broad spectrum it can be concluded that the final data is clearly influenced by the prejudices, expectations, attitudes, opinions and beliefs of the researcher, and that this applies equally to an interview, a laboratory or a field situation. Hyman attempted to systematise the influence of researcher orientations by identifying three types of orientation effects in interview situations:

1. Bias-producing cognitive factors in the interviewer;
2. Attitude structure expectations; and
3. Role expectations.

In the first category Hyman included the cognitive factors that could result in specific expectations in terms of respondents' answers and are unique to the interviewer. These factors include specific beliefs and perceptions. As an example, Hyman quotes the following passage in which a female interviewer discusses her attitudes towards respondents:

- When asked whether she could make guesses about the attitudes of the respondents, she replied: "I often get fooled. On Russian questions I perhaps unconsciously make guesses. But if I do that I'm likely to write down what I think. Therefore I try not to". But when the issue is pursued by asking her whether there are any characteristic types of respondents, she says: "Once they start talking, I can predict what they'll say ...".

Hyman justifiably maintains that expectations of this nature may constitute an important source of bias if the interviewer allows herself to be led by them in her further probing, classification of responses and so on. Under the second category that Hyman refers to as attitude-structure expectations, he notes the fact that some interviewers tend to believe that the attitudes of respondents are likely to display a uniformity of structure. This leads to a situation where the interviewer expects the respondent to answer later questions in a schedule in accordance with responses provided earlier on. This situation is clearly reflected in a statement like: "Once they start talking, I can predict what they'll say ...".

The third category of orientation effects, which could perhaps more appropriately be referred to as expectancy effects is defined as follows: we might conceive of role expectations to denote the tendencies of interviewers to believe that certain attitudes or behaviours occur in individuals of given group memberships, and therefore to expect answers of a certain kind from particular persons. Role expectations, which frequently lead to the development of rigid stereotypes, are especially prevalent in cases where men have certain views of female roles, where whites have specific perceptions about blacks, youth about the aged, or the inverse, and so on.

As an illustration of this phenomenon, Hyman refers to the remark by a male interviewer who said: "I just don't think the average woman has as much social consciousness as the average man". Rosenthal and his coworkers systematically studied similar expectancy effects in experimental studies. One of the best-known studies on experimenter expectancy effects was conducted by Rosental and Fode with laboratory rats. The experimenters were undergraduate psychology students who were led to believe that they would acquire practice in established experimental procedures. One half of the experimenters were told that the rats that they would use had been bred from exceptionally intelligent blood stock, while the other half were also inaccurately informed that their rats were less gifted. In actual fact the rats had been randomly selected from a homogeneous rat colony and there was no reason to expect that there was any difference in their intelligence.

The final results confirmed the expectancy effect: the first group of experimenters, who had expected their rats to learn more quickly, reported that this had indeed been the case, whereas the second group with the supposedly dull rats reported that their rats had acquired the skills less quickly. In a recent review of the literature on interviewing techniques, Campbell *et al.* comment on a similar orientation effect which they refer to as reinforcement and feedback.

They emphasise the fact that several studies have shown that, when the interviewer provides positive feedback for instance by saying uh-uh or good, this has a definite influence on subsequent responses. In some cases the interviewer's systematic approval of a response could have a biasing effect on the information obtained.

PARTICIPANT EFFECTS

The mere fact that human beings are being studied leads to atypical behaviour. It is probably safe to claim that the first description of participant effects in the literature of the social sciences is to be found in the publication by Roethlisberger and Dickson. Four researchers, Mayo, Roethlisberger, Whitehead and Dickson, did a research project at the Hawthorne factory of the Western Electric Company in 1927. The original intention was to study the effects of working conditions such as temperature, lighting, rest periods and hours of work, on worker productivity by observing six female workers.

The interesting and unexpected finding was that the workers' performance increased irrespective of the variable being manipulated. Irrespective of whether working hours were increased or reduced or rest periods lengthened or shortened, productivity consistently increased.

The researchers interpreted their findings as meaning that the employees felt flattered to have been able to participate in the experiment! It has subsequently become common practice to refer to this type of participant effect as the Hawthorne effect.

Participant Characteristics

In the preceding part, we considered the influence of some of the betterknown participant characteristics such as gender, racial group and status in the interaction between researcher and participant. We now turn briefly to another three well-known subject effects: memory decay, the omniscience syndrome and interview saturation.

Memory Decay

Smith, the researcher has to accept the fact that there is a natural decay in the ability to remember events that have positive correlations with:

- The length of time that has elapsed since the occurrence of the event;
- The irregular occurrence of the event;
- The relative unimportance of the event; and
- Decreased accessibility to relevant data relating to the event.

The Omniscience Syndrome

Some respondents appear to believe that they can answer any question. The researcher must be sensitive to this type of effect to avoid the inclusion of responses that are not authentic.

Interview Saturation

Pareek and Rao justifiably maintain that some members of society, and particularly those who live in metropolitan areas, have become so strongly conditioned to market surveys that they tend to answer questions mechanically and superficially.

Apart from the fact that this type of attitude can be identified in the interview situation, initial refusal or reluctance on the part of the respondent is usually also a good indication of over-saturation.

Participant Attitudes

Role Selection

One of the most radical participant effects is the participant's perception of his or her role in the research setting. Webb *et al.* justifiably maintain that:

- By singling out an individual to be tested the experimenter forces upon the subject a role-defining decision–What kind of person should I be as I answer these questions or do these tasks?.

Webb *et al.* also maintain that the role selection effect is likely to be manifested in a variance between 'don't know' responses and the measurement of imaginary attitudes and opinions. If, for example, the instructions to the interviewee were to read: "You have been selected as part of a scientifically designed sample ... It is important that you should answer all the questions ...", the importance and uniqueness of the respondent are obviously emphasised. When instructions like these play an important role in the interview situation, it is not at all difficult to predict that fewer 'don't know' responses will be found, and that more imaginary attitudes and opinions will be measured.

Level of Motivation of the Participant

One of the most important variables that can influence the validity of the data collection process either positively or negatively, is the participant's level of motivation. The level of motivation is clearly influenced by a variety of factors such as interviewer characteristics, contextual factors and the manner in which the questions are phrased.

Two issues may be emphasised in this context: the degree of interest that the topic has for the interviewee, and the extent to which he or she is likely to feel threatened by the questions that are posed. It has been empirically demonstrated that the more interesting the respondent finds the topic, the more highly motivated he or she will be and this in turn results in an increase in the response rate. As indicated earlier, the level of threat posed by the questions will have an important bearing on people's willingness to respond to them, and also on their level of motivation. Questions that relate to highly private issues are likely to be perceived as threatening by the majority of respondents, and they are likely to respond unreliably. For this reason Cannell and Kahn maintain that the interviewer must make the interviewing experience and task sufficiently meaningful, rewarding and enjoyable to attain and maintain the necessary respondent motivation.

Response Patterns

One of the most important types of observer effect in interviewing is the occurrence of systematic response patterns that are generally referred to as 'response sets'. A number of authors, including Cronbach, Kolson and Green, and Webb *et al.*, have addressed this matter. Kolson and Green focus on the fact that children are inclined to gamble when they are unsure of the meaning of items. Similar response patterns noted, particularly when the meaning of an item is obscure, include a tendency to endorse only the extremes on scaled items or to check the midpoints of the scale. For purposes of our discussion, we shall highlight two well-known types of response patterns: social desirability and the acquiescence response set.

The Hawthorne effect is clearly an example of a social desirability tendency. Selltiz and Cook most individuals will try to give answers that make them appear well-adjusted, unprejudiced, rational, open-minded and democratic. Rosenberg was also able to confirm that individuals who attained high scores on Marlow-Crone's Social Desirability Scale were more inclined to supply extremely positive responses than those with low scores on the scale.

The tendency to answer either yes or no to virtually all the items in a questionnaire or scale is referred to as the acquiescence response set. As early as 1937, Sletto found that respondents were more likely to agree with a statement than to disagree with its inverse. Schuman and Presser were able to confirm earlier findings on this topic.

Apart from the fact that they were able to confirm the existence of this type of response pattern, which can produce differences that range between ten and fifteen per cent, they also found indications that this phenomenon is more likely to occur amongst respondents with a low level of education than amongst for instance university graduates.

However, these researchers maintain that we have not yet built up a large enough body of research on the phenomenon of the acquiescence response set to be able to provide an adequate interpretation of the reasons underlying this type of response pattern.

CONTEXT EFFECTS

When discussing the research context one can distinguish between broader spatio-temporal factors that are determined by historical, socio-political, and economic factors, and the narrower research setting within which the research is conducted. With regard to the former the researcher must be sensitive to the following types of factors:

- The period during which the research is conducted. It is particularly relevant in the case of longitudinal research where changes in behaviour or attitudes are investigated and significant changes could be the result of external events such as elections, civil unrest, or increased unemployment.
- Cultural factors such as habits, traditions, customs and institutions. The anthropological literature abounds with examples in which researchers, to their own detriment, have failed to take local

conventions and customs into account in the design and execution of their research.

- Political factors such as the existence of interest groups, lack of freedom, and intimidation.

The importance of this issue is associated with the perceived 'neutrality' of each setting. In the first two, the respondent is familiar with the setting, but the researcher is not. However, the third and fourth categories are neutral territories. Studies on the influence of the research setting have shown that the researcher's impressions of the participant's home or place of work frequently led to significant data bias. The respondent's role is also directly influenced by the research setting. In the domestic setting a woman's role as a mother may be more noticeable, whereas her role as employer or supervisor may be more noticeable in the workplace.

8

Quantitative Research

INTRODUCTION

Believing that the research question was even more fundamental than the paradigm one felt allegiance to, several years ago we began to discuss the qualitative-quantitative debate from that perspective. The dichotomy and the debate disappeared, and the ideas presented here began to develop. This book describes our stance at a point in time, not the conclusions of our ideas, which continue to emerge, to grow, and to build from our work as researchers and as teachers.

While clearly a work in progress, which continues to evolve, the framework of an interactive continuum presented here has been enlightening to colleagues and students who operate within the current world of often-misunderstood and frequently debated paradigm shifts. At the conclusion of this chapter, the reader should be able to:

- Describe the history of qualitative and quantitative research methods and the debate about their relative values
- Describe the typical purpose and outline of qualitative research
- Describe the typical purpose and outline of quantitative research
- Discuss the advantages and disadvantages of a dichotomy versus a continuum conceptualization of research design

Qualitative and quantitative researches have philosophical roots in the naturalistic and the positivistic philosophies, respectively. Virtually all qualitative researchers, regardless of their theoretical differences, reflect some sort of individual phenomenological perspective. Most quantitative research approaches, regardless of their theoretical differences, tend to emphasize that there is a common reality on which people can agree.

From a phenomenological perspective, Douglas and Geertz believe that multiple realities exist and multiple interpretations are available from different individuals that are all equally valid. Reality is a social construct.

If one functions from this perspective, how one conducts a study and what conclusions a researcher draws from a study are considerably different from those of a researcher coming from a quantitative or positivist position, which assumes a common objective reality across individuals. There are different degrees of belief in these sets of assumptions about reality among qualitative and quantitative researchers. For instance, Blumer (1980), a phenomenological researcher who emphasizes subjectivity, does not deny that there is a reality one must attend to.

The debate between qualitative and quantitative researchers is based upon the differences in assumptions about what reality is and whether or not it is measurable. The debate further rests on differences of opinion about how we can best understand what we "know," whether through objective or subjective methods.

William Firestone (1987), in an article in the "Educational Researcher", differentiates qualitative from quantitative research based on four dimensions: assumptions, purpose, approach, and research role. Regarding assumptions, Firestone asks: is objective reality sought through facts or is reality socially constructed? Related to purpose, he asks: is it looking for causes or for understanding? To determine approach, he asks whether the research is experimental/ correlational or a form of ethnography. Lastly, related to the researcher's role, he asks whether the researcher is detached or immersed in the setting.

Shaker (1990), in a discussion of programme evaluation models, presents them as a metaphorical journey—moving from quantitative perspectives in the past to more recent naturalistic and qualitative assumptions. While positing a chronological continuum, Shaker would not seem to oppose our notion of question-driven research and evaluation. While he describes the "new identity" for evaluation as being "based on naturalistic approaches," he places this in the context of a "pragmatic commitment to finding methods that yield results in practice as we find it, rather than as we wish it to be".

The qualitative, naturalistic approach is used when observing and interpreting reality with the aim of developing a theory that will explain what was experienced. The quantitative approach is used when one begins with a theory (or hypothesis) and tests for confirmation or disconfirmation of that hypothesis.

It is important here to set the stage for abandoning the dichotomy. To do so, we examine a few of the key events in the chronicle of scientific evolution that established the debate in the first place. As long as one view of how we can explain the workings of the world reigns supreme, there is no debate.

The debate rests on a dichotomy characterized by a lessening of the dominance of one paradigm over another, leveling the playing field so that the debate could occur. In fact, the debate may be but one more phase in the ebb and flow of an everchanging philosophy of knowledge. For example, in The Enlightened Eye, Eisner (1991) cautions against the dichotomy and asserts that qualitative and quantitative research can be combined. He warns against qualitative researchers merely adopting a "soft form of positivism".

The genesis of the current qualitative-quantitative debate in educational research occurred as far back as 1844, when Auguste Comte claimed that the methods of natural science could be justified in studying social science. Science, in this view, is the collection and study of facts that can be observed through sensory input. These are the traditional data investigated by natural scientists—the physicists, the chemists, the biologists.

This view holds that true science is accumulated through the study of phenomena that can be physically sensed, observed, and counted. The "unknowables," as Herbert Spencer described them in his 1910 essay, those things that cannot be sensed but might rely on reason or thought, are banished from scientific investigation. Both Comte and Spencer were positivists.

Interestingly, this "positivism" was a move away from a more speculative, more "unknowable" view. It was a move away from relying on theological and metaphysical explanations of the world. It was a move towards what could be "positively" (confirmed through sensory data) determined. The philosophy maintained a grip on social science from the late 1800s through the early 1900s.

In the early 1900s, John Dewey, among others, questioned the absolutism of this position, viewing science as not separate and distinct from problem solving. His pragmatism considered science less rigidly than did the positivists. In his Sources of a Science of Education (1929), written some time after his initial speculations, he pointed out that practice should be the ground of our enquiry. Because of the value placed on experience for learning and the emphasis on practice, he appreciated the deeper complexity of what educational and social scientists study.

During the same period, a group of scholars who made up what became known as the famous Vienna Circle met and developed a new philosophy of science, logical positivism. Supporting Comte's positivism, they combined it with the symbolic logic of mathematics. Hypotheses derived using the rigour of mathematics (the symbolic) could be combined with fact gathering (the positivism) to test their confirmability (which was eventually modified to disconfirmability).

Although counter to an impetus by Dewey to diffuse the positivistic assumptions made by researchers, this hypothetico-deductive system was dominant in the middle years of the 20th century in psychology and sociology. Education, which borrowed traditions of enquiry from these disciplines, was affected as well. The respect for precision in measurement, mathematically systematic tests of hypotheses, and a quest for value-free science solidified this paradigm.

During the 1940s and 1950s, the quantitative paradigm dominated the social science and the educational research scene. Behaviourists and organizational theorists utilized empirical fact gathering and hypothesis testing almost exclusively in studying educational and social phenomena. In the mid- 1960s, while the quantitative perspective continued to prevail, a shift began as skepticism towards the domination of logical positivism and the evident chasm between human social systems and mathematical logic grew. New epistemologies began to emerge that acknowledged, for example, the value-laden nature of human social interactions. That human beings construct reality for themselves and that knowledge itself is transmitted in social ways were beginning to be assumed. Questions arose about the tenability of applying natural science methodology to these complex human dynamics.

In 1962, in The Structure of Scientific Revolutions, the most significant work on this issue, Thomas Kuhn explored the shifts in science's dominant paradigms. His doctorate in theoretical physics led him to look back into the history of science as he sought to know more about its foundations. He describes how, by randomly exploring the literature, he was exposed to Jean Piaget and, in the late 1950s, to a historical analysis of social science and psychology. Kuhn's study of methodology drove him to leave physics and become a historian of science.

He conceptualizes the notion of paradigms, "universally recognized scientific achievements that for a time provide model problems and solutions to a community of practitioners," and proposes that competing paradigms emerge chronologically when the dominant one no longer serves the explanatory needs of the scientific community.

For the most part, using the context of physics from the perspectives of Sir Isaac Newton and Albert Einstein, Kuhn explains these periods of competition, or scientific revolutions, in the natural sciences. He acknowledges that competing paradigms can possibly coexist on equal footing following such a revolution, or "paradigm shift," although, he cautions, it may be only rarely possible. He proposes that the predominant paradigm affects researchers not only methodologically but also in how they see the world. Kuhn's conceptualization of "paradigm" has been reinterpreted by others since his work, and many definitions are incorporated in the literature of the 1990s.

The quantitative paradigm continued to reign over social science and, according to Culbertson (1988), prevailed in education until the mid-1980s. At that time the logical positivists were losing supremacy. (The strong traditional bias towards quantitative science might even be based on Americans' preference for facts we can observe and count, a sense that that's what science "is.")

Concurrent with Kuhn's early notions of paradigms in the 1960s, society was undergoing radical changes. While some began to question the efficacy of the positivists' tools in explaining human organizational and social phenomena, education was moving into a more complex social context. Culbertson points to such 1960s and 1970s issues as racial integration, poverty, equal opportunity, schools as tools in global economic competition, the Soviet Union's threat to our math and science pre-eminence, and the need to account for the success and failure of the nation's children and posits that, in this context of increased complexity, some began to search for policy tools that the quantitative paradigm did not seem sufficiently able to explain.

That education served economic, political, and policy ends enhanced the opportunity for scholars interested in the culture of schools to begin to use anthropological strategies in their enquiry. These same interests fed the scholars' attempts to approach their research from the perspective of the critical theorists, as well as that of the feminists. Although always an important issue, the policy makers' interest in the world of classroom practice grew, and they increasingly expressed concerns that research and practice were unconnected and that this disconnection was in part due to the use of tightly controlled laboratory-like quantitative assumptions. A move among some social scientists in the direction of deriving theory from practice, rather than the other way around, characterized this change as well.

Graduate programmes preparing educational and social science researchers as well as professional journals have increasingly directed their attention towards qualitative research. Allotting time and space to what had been considered the "alternative" paradigm led to wide discussions in the journals and at professional meetings. The editors of the American Educational Research Journal, for example, announced in 1987 that particular emphasis on qualitative methodology would be forthcoming as they evaluated manuscripts.

This was a major legitimation of the paradigm for educational researchers. A plethora of books, articles, and presentations on the trustworthiness of the qualitative paradigm materialized. Some extolled the virtues of qualitative research as the only avenue to "truth," while others claimed that only by holding onto the quantitative traditions can we have confidence in our knowledge base.

In many forums the debate was manifest. Which is more scientific: the deductive methods of the logical positivists (quantitative researchers) or the inductive methods of the naturalists (qualitative researchers)? Can the results of qualitative research be generalized as are the results of quantitative research? Can science be value laden (qualitative) or only legitimate if value free (quantitative)? What epistemological assumptions are violated by adopting one paradigm or the other?

While to some the debate has ended, to others, especially those we encounter in researcher-preparation programmes, the debate has either not yet materialized to the full extent of its fury or continues unabated. Our strong sense is twofold. First, we continue to prepare students for an "either-or" world, a dichotomous world that no longer exists. We still prepare students who leave our colleges and universities with a monolithic perspective. Either they become well-trained statisticians, or they become cultural anthropologists, methodologically weak in asking research questions and in justifying either one or the other set of strategies. Second, researchers in education and in the social sciences have not yet constructed a way to ensure their success in utilizing both paradigms. The interactive continuum model in this book serves as a kind of framework directed towards both those needs.

The dichotomy of qualitative and quantitative research is one we deny but one we exploit here for heuristic purposes. The dichotomy, while not an ontological construct, does allow us to separate the idea. We slice it thin to examine it and make the case in this chapter that it does not exist in the scientific research realm.

All research in education stands on basic underlying assumptions. This is true for quantitative methods as well as qualitative methods. To the extent that these assumptions withstand the scrutiny of scientific enquiry, the methods can be supported, taught to novice researchers, and used professionally and ethically without reservation. Since the mid-1980s when quality in all educational professions came under public review, it has become particularly crucial to delineate the foundational bases of educational research. Within the realm of this book, such bases will be examined.

COMBINE QUALITATIVE AND QUANTITATIVE RESEARCH

Qualitative studies in psychology can be fascinating and insightful but they may leave readers with a quantitative disposition worrying about the generality of their findings. Quantitative studies, on the other hand, whilst providing data from larger and more representative samples, seem more mechanical and arid to qualitative researchers. But both methods have advantages and disadvantages and the results from different methods can complement each other.

This paper considers these issues in the context of studying the problems that students face in essay writing. It contrasts the recent results from a qualitative study with those from a quantitative one (described in this paper). At the time of writing we have copies of four of Street and Lea's articles in front of us. Only in the major one are we told how many students, lecturers and institutions were involved in their study:

'The analysis of the research data has concentrated on the differing interpretations and understandings of academic staff and students with regard to academic writing within two contrasting university settings. 10 interviews were conducted with staff in the older university and 21 students were interviewed, either individually or in small groups. At the new university 13 members of academic staff and 26 students were interviewed.'

But these are the only numerical data given. We are not told, for example, what proportion of the students are men or women, traditional-entry or mature students, and what disciplines they are studying. And there are no quantitative data to qualify their results. The actual results are of great interest. Street and

Lea differentiate between three different, but overlapping, sources of difficulty for students writing essays and reports, and how their institutions deal with them.

These are:

- Difficulties with 'interpretation' *e.g.*, knowing what is expected within and between different departments, and even between different tutors within the same department. These are largely ignored by many tutors, but students' ignorance of these matters is criticised in their feedback.
- Difficulties with 'deficits' *e.g.*, grammar, spelling, punctuation and style. These are mainly dealt with by study skills courses, and handouts/guides for students.
- Difficulties stemming from 'institutional failings' - *e.g.*, the inability of staff to mark written work within a reasonable time span and with sufficient detail because of limited staff resources and the large numbers of students. These difficulties are ignored, defended or deplored by different members of staff.

Street and Lea place their greatest emphasis on the second area of difficulty - one that has not really been explored in previous research on essay writing (although see Hinkle, 1997). But are they right to do so? How widespread are the difficulties faced by their 47 students, and which do they find the greatest burden? We cannot answer questions such as these because of the qualitative nature of their reports.

Nonetheless, the findings, the commentary and the suggestions are so interesting that we set out to gather some more - quantitative - evidence to try to build upon this pioneering study.

Questionnaire Method

We devised a questionnaire on essay writing that addressed the three concerns discussed by Street and Lea. Thus there were questions about students' experiences of difficulties connected with 'deficits', 'interpretation' and 'institutional failings'. The questions were largely based upon the comments and discussion provided in Street and Lea. We gave this questionnaire to 102 *second-year* psychology students attending a lecture at Keele University at the beginning of their first-semester.

These students were asked to complete the questionnaire with reference to the difficulties that they might have faced when writing their essays and reports in their *first-year* at Keele. Students at Keele typically study two principal subjects and two subsidiary subjects in their first-year, so they would have had to write essays/reports in four different subject matters during the year. (It is this kind of complexity that Street and Lea had in mind in their study and which has not been commented on before.)

In our study the responses from two overseas students who had not been at Keele in their first-year, and from six students studying conductive education (who did not follow a normal subsidiary programme) were deleted, making a total of 94 respondents. (The total number of students in this cohort was 146 - so our data come from 64 per cent of the class.)

METHODOLOGICAL DILEMMAS

We draw on our participation in a specific commissioned workplace research project, focusing on the new language of work, as a typical site of such collaboration. Our reflexive commentary on our work aims to bring to the surface a range of methodological, political and epistemological tensions in commissioned research in the contemporary world that puts pressure on academics to produce particular kinds of knowledge. We anticipate that through this reflexive process we can explore ways of developing methodological practices that open up, challenge, incite and disrupt what might be regarded as inevitable non-negotiables or closures. Collaborative research has been thought to involve compliance on the part of the academic but we argue that academics can be strategically optimistic about collaborative research, when working with notions of hybridity.

The chapter begins by positioning our commentary within the inevitable tensions of the current economic, political and social context. This is followed by a reflexive commentary on the project itself; here we analyse the texts produced both as part of and as end-products of the research process. The analysis reveals a shift in our understanding of ourselves as researchers as we struggle from a position of compliance to one of productive disruption. We present this new position as a site for further exploration of the methodological possibilities of collaborative research.

The experiences and issues addressed are both specifically Australian and also global, since most industrial and industrialising countries are also engaging in similar restructuring and workplace training reforms. Globalisation and the accompanying dismantling of borders and boundaries (be they national, commercial, or disciplinary), together with the foregrounding of vocational and workplace education and training as keys to national competitiveness and success in the global economy, are familiar themes in 'global' economic discourse.

The Australian National Training Authority, for example, sees vocational education and training as 'now well-positioned to contribute significantly to a socially progressive and economically powerful Australia in the 21st century'.

Collaborative partnerships between government, industry and the university have been hailed by politicians as a significant cornerstone in recent workplace training reforms. The collaboration of these three partners is seen as a critical part of the technology for increasing the knowledge and skills of

Australia's workforce. The alliance of government, industry and education has allowed for 'collaborative' policy construction and implementation heavily supported by commissioned research and curriculum development funding. However, such partnerships are not unproblematic.

Fuelled by the dominance of economic goals that tie together production, performativity and the master discourse of economic rationalism, workplaces are the common site of interest of all the partners. But with such partnerships, a number of dilemmas surface at local levels. These relate to tensions around the different histories and positions of the participants who, in the contemporary moment, are located within the dominant discourse of economic rationalism—with which they engage with varying degrees of resistance and compliance.

These tensions were particularly evident in the Commonwealth government commissioned project in which we were involved. The project had two stages. First, a research stage examined changing work culture and practices in enterprises that were undergoing restructuring in the context of post-Fordism. The second stage developed training programmes on spoken and written language competencies relevant to communicating in these 'new' workplaces.

Before moving to details it is important to discuss the significance of this particular project in terms of the contemporary moment. This collaborative project exemplifies the intersection of a number of social changes. The first is to do with the nature of the 'new' workplace and 'new' work practices. Post-Fordist workplaces are characterised by the introduction of new technologies, ongoing job training and increased consultative and participatory processes at all levels of the workplace.

Many enterprises are currently implementing flattened hierarchies in which work roles are becoming less differentiated and where the notion of teamwork or working in teams underpins the new relationships (with team members ranging from operator level workers to managers). The contemporary privileging of social relationships at work and the construction of workers as social subjects have foregrounded the role of language at work.

Spoken and written language were once invisible at work, only noticed if there was a communication breakdown, particularly in the case of non-English speaking background employees. Yet now, with the textualisation of the new workplace and the accompanying privileging of the relational, 'communication' has a central place in workplace and training discourses. Communication in the workplace not only encompasses a range of spoken and written language practices, but is now regarded as the key to 'effective' work practices and thus to productivity increases.

This new interest in communication in workplaces is accompanied by what has become known in contemporary cultural analysis as the 'linguistic turn', where theorists from a variety of disciplines:

... have declared language to bring facts into being and not simply to report on them... Meaning of any object resides not within that object itself but is a product of how that object is socially constructed through language and representation.

The interdisciplinary interest in the relationship of language to social and cultural process, and thus to the production of knowledge, has opened up interest in language and discourse analysis as methods for studying social change.

The project was possible not only because of the increasing recognition of the importance of language in the changing contemporary workplace but also because of the growth of significant academic expertise in discourse analysis. Our own location, in such a climate and given our own particular academic training in applied linguistics, positioned us as particular kinds of researchers.

In Fairclough (1992) terms our research could be seen as part of the 'technologization of discourse' where, as institutional agents, we consciously intervened in discursive practices in order to bring about change. The research focused on describing and developing efficient, effective practices of the new workplace and our task was to influence the practices of workplace trainers.

This contingent coalition of interests is highlighted in the recent book, The New Work Order: behind the language of the new capitalism, whose authors lay out their project as follows:

Framed within a socio-cultural studies perspective, we want to determine what particular social identities workers are expected to construct and display, and what related social practices they are expected to learn, demonstrate and value. What ways of talking, listening, reading, writing, acting, interacting, believing and valuing are expected in newly organised and reconstructed workplaces, and how close or far are these from an egalitarian ideal of empowerment?

Governments, industry and educational institutions are all emphasising the importance of language, literacy and numeracy skills. One Commonwealth government department commissioned report, for example, states that:

... economic and industrial imperatives, access and equity considerations, and current thinking in the fields of adult learning and language and literacy development, all call for programmes which can develop the language, literacy and numeracy competence of the job as part of vocational skills development.

Thus, the discursive construction of the 'new worker' includes the foregrounding of spoken and written language skills and the integration of these into competency standards. New education and training in these areas has developed into an industry of its own as government-funded language and literacy projects; industry funded programmes; university consultancies; and private providers all develop and offer diagnoses, curricula and training to help workers at all levels in the workplace attain the standards required to ensure increased productivity levels.

This is the background to the project. The development of our research methodology was appropriate to the government and industry agendas and desired outcomes. As academics, however, our research work was problematised by the tensions and ensuing collisions that became evident among the different players. Our principal research interest was to understand the complexities around the construction of workplace knowledge and practices in the context of the changing culture of work.

On the other hand, the goal of the funding body was for us to provide a rational, linear description of the communication skills needed for productive and efficient work and of the training that would lead to these outcomes. The funding body saw the research as a task and product-oriented activity—identifying discrete spoken and written language competencies relevant to communicating in a range of job areas in the food industry and the subsequent development and delivery of relevant training based on the research.

Changing work roles are often regarded as easily understood and able to be learned in short bursts of training, consisting of communication skills (negotiation, conflict resolution, assertiveness training and the like) and/or language and literacy skills improvement (spoken and written language for people with language backgrounds other than English and for people who have literacy 'problems').

The complexities around the reconciliation of the different goals of the various participants in this project will be discussed in the following section. First, however, some further discussion on the intersecting social, economic and political factors that contextualise the significance of collaborative research.

The participation of academics in commissioned workplace research can, in part, be understood in the context of economic rationalist discourse and its blurring of the 'distinction between educational and non-educational discourses and practices'. Educators, in contemporary universities, are not neutral disinterested seekers of workplace knowledge.

Educational institutions, like their research sites, are workplaces. Academics in universities are not simply sociological observers of the effects of economic rationalism on contemporary workplaces and work practices. They are 'in business'—in this case business that involves the commodification and marketing of education.

While academics might analyse or even struggle with the colonisation of education by managerial discourse, they too are in the marketplace. Their business needs more markets in order to be successful in the increasingly competitive global market.

Winning commissioned research contracts has its financial rewards, enabling the employment of academic staff, but also in terms of the higher education funding formulas, where a competitive index is used to distribute research funding. In other words, the previous year's research 'productivity' influences the funding allocation for the following year. Furthermore, academics have been involved in the construction of the workplace as a site of 'learning' and, therefore, a potential recruiting ground for new students. Thus, our complicity in commissioned research workplace projects has its own financial rewards, illustrating the inseparability of workplace reforms, research and educational practice.

This alliance forces us to consider two contrasting positions that are often taken in relation to academic compliance with the government agenda. The first is the critique from the Left that accuses academics engaged in commissioned research of 'selling out' to the economic rationalist agenda. Resistance, it is argued, in the form of non-participation, is needed to subvert the agenda.

The second position is the strategic optimism argument which suggests that academic strategic intervention will make a difference. This position argues that we must exploit the opening provided in the new alliance in order to intervene and, thus, influence the agenda and the products to less performative ends.

We argue that the first position fails to acknowledge the ambiguities and complexities that pull together academics, government and industry into activities centred on the dominance of economic goals. The second position, on the other hand, offers a useful point of consideration—useful in our commentary but also in the development of research tools for intervening in a way that unsettles the otherwise unproblematised realisation of economic rationalist goals.Before examining the details of our project, first a brief discussion on the principle of performativity—a principle that underpins an economic bottom line explanation of productivity and one which makes the alliance between research, economics and the state almost inevitable.

According to Lyotard, performativity is 'the principle of optimal performance: maximizing output (the information or modifications obtained) and minimizing input (the energy expended in the process)'. He further says that where:

... the goal is no longer truth, but performativity—that is the best possible input/output equation. The State and/or company must abandon the idealist and humanist narratives of legitimation in order to justify the new goal: in the discourse of today's financial backers of research, the only credible goal is power.

Lyotard goes on to speak of how a 'legitimation by power takes shape':

Power is not only good performativity, but also effective verification and good verdicts. It legitimates science and the law on the basis of their efficiency, and legitimates this efficiency on the basis of science and law. It is self-legitimating in the same way a system organized around performance maximization seems to be.

Government commissioned research with its emphasis on performativity is an exemplary site, illustrating the way in which the spaces of contemporary educational research have been subjected to:

- Intensification of research work through shorter contracts;
- Greater formal control by state and quasi-state bodies;
- Greater links between policy and research;
- Funding competition which has led to a research economy where the emphasis is on competition and status display.

VALIDITY ISSUES IN QUANTITATIVE RESEARCH

There is an important difference between measurement validity and design validity. The first, measurement validity, estimates how well the instrument measures what it purports to measure. The second, design validity, encompasses internal and external validity. Measurement validity falls under Campbell and Stanley's "instrumentation" (1963). Internal validity is the extent to which any causal difference in the dependent variable can be attributed to the independent variable. External validity is the extent to which the results of the research study can be generalized to other settings or groups.

Measurement and design validity are not independent. A research design is only internally valid if it has measurement validity and reliability. This also is true for the ability to generalize: estimates of the stability of the measurements are needed to estimate external validity. Measurement validity is a subset of internal validity. As discussed, strong measurement validity diminishes the threats to internal validity that come under Campbell and Stanley's category of "instrumentation." We chose to separate measurement validity and design validity to clarify the discussion. Next we discuss internal and external validity as they relate to quantitative research; then we discuss validity in qualitative research.

INTERNAL AND EXTERNAL VALIDITY

We need standards to evaluate research on at least three dimensions: the likelihood of the variables' being causally related; the confidence one would have in being able to generalize the results; and the level of consistency between the researcher's purpose, assumptions, methods, and conclusions. Design validity for quantitative research traditionally has been addressed through the concepts of internal and external validity.

We, along with Goetz and LeCompte, argue that a similar concern should be addressed for those studies that are predominantly on the qualitative end of the continuum. Within the context of our holistic view, however, we subsume all of these consistency questions into the concept of methods validity. The researcher makes decisions about methods, controlling for threats to internal and external validity, and the methods become the research design.

Internal validity is defined as "the extent that one can say the independent variable causes the effects of the dependent variables; in other words, one has the ability to assume causation to the extent that the researcher has control". LeCompte and Goetz (1982) ask this question to get at internal validity: "Do scientific researchers actually observe or measure what they think they are observing or measuring?" To the extent that they are observing and measuring what they think they are, they have validity. The second conceptual area is external validity, defined as "the extent that a study is generalizable to other people, groups, investigations, etc." LeCompte and Goetz (1982) ask this question to assess external validity: "To what extent are the abstract constructs and postulates generated, refined, or tested by scientific researchers applicable across groups?"

Keppel (1973), for one, describes the great amount of effort among quantitative methodologists to achieve internal validity. Such researchers employ controls (*i.e.*, holding constant as many factors as possible that may influence the phenomenon under study) to most efficiently measure the influence of the treatment.

Tests are conducted under the same environmental conditions, using the same instruments, by the same researchers. Factors that are not controllable are allowed to vary randomly across treatment conditions, which work as another control mechanism. Randomization of what Keppel calls "nuisance variables" is a major way of obtaining internal validity, that is, "the elimination of biases which, if present, might invalidate any conclusions drawn concerning the manipulations of the experiment". This randomization removes the effect of bias and variability due to such factors.

Other attempts to achieve internal validity include counterbalancing across the treatment conditions. Called equivalent form, it involves taking two learning tasks, for instance, and giving Group 1 the tasks in A-B order and Group 2 the tasks in B-A order. In this case, the stimulus order is used as an independent variable, and its influence on the variability in the dependent variable can be isolated and measured. Measuring it assists the researcher in obtaining internal validity because its effects can be separated from the treatment effects.

Without internal validity, one can only conclude that the approach being used to answer the question of interest is capable of estimating the relationship, and no statement about causation is possible. Even though there are those among the ranks of qualitative researchers who say they are not interested in internal validity, those who wish to infer causal relationships must be concerned with this aspect of their research.

In fact, even some who dismiss this concern as being only a quantitative researcher's dilemma will admit to processes like triangulation and theoretical sampling, which are conceptual attempts and techniques to get at internal validity.

External validity reflects the extent to which the design and the data match the world. While tight controls over the variables of interest increase internal validity, they tend to do so at the expense of external validity—that is, the more laboratory-like the conditions the more precise and valid are the measures.

However, the world is not as tightly controlled, and the variables operate in the world outside the laboratory. Sampling of subjects across several strata that reflect the world to which the results will be generalized (*e.g.*, age, socioeconomic status, occupation) increases external validity. The inability to control independent variables in ex post facto research (while it tends to decrease internal validity) tends to increase external validity because such variables are more relevant to their real-world distribution.

Diagrams used to illustrate research designs help the researcher plan, interpret, and analyse. Symbols, defined here, are used to depict the components of the research strategy. While the following are examples of symbols commonly used, they do not include all possibilities, nor are they universally used.

X Treatment or experimental treatment; refers to the experimenter's treatment for a group

-X No treatment or absence of treatment (one group might receive treatment, a second group not; second group is commonly called the control group)

Í$ Independent variable, not manipulated and either attributeor assigned variable

O Measurement or observation, frequently some type of test score; can have any number of subscripts

R Random assignment of subjects to groups

M Assignment of subjects to groups using matching

Mr Assignment of subjects to groups by first matching subjects and then randomly assigning each matched subject to group

Based on the classic work of Campbell and Stanley, design validity is limited when an assortment of factors are uncontrolled.

History is a factor that could account for a change in a group. History means any non-treatment, extraneous event that intervenes between the pretest and posttest measurements. For example, a school district investigates the effect of a new set of mathematics textbooks on achievement by measuring achievement at the beginning and at the end of the year.

During that year, however, all the students move to a new building. This is an example of a history factor that might affect the results of the study. The researcher, in this case, would not know if the new books or the new school caused any difference in student achievement outcomes measured in the study.

Another factor that could account for a change in a group is maturation, which means any growth or development that would normally take place independent of an experimental treatment. An example would be an analysis of the impact of a school lunch programme on students' growth. Continued growth normally would occur as part of their maturation. In this case, the researcher's task is to identify what change is due to the lunch programme and what change is due to ongoing maturation. History and maturation are often confused because each is related to something occurring in the time between the pretest and the posttest. The distinguishing point is that historical effects are external, while maturation effects are internal. Other examples of internal changes would be psychological, such as boredom, or physiological, such as fatigue.

Factors associated with measuring devices, testing factors, can also cause change to occur. This can happen when a pretest sensitizes people to an experimental treatment and actually causes them to behave differently during that treatment.

Suppose a teacher is evaluating the impact of a character programme on the moral development of students. If the teacher gives a pretest that asks questions about morality, the pretest could get the students concerned about the topic and thus influence them, making them more receptive to the programme than they might have been without the pretest. This same phenomenon can take place with other factors, such as achievement. Testing effects are the results that the first test has in sensitizing subjects to the treatment, which then affects the posttest.

On the other hand, the term instrumentation refers to the effects that are due to unreliable measurement instruments. If one has an unreliable pretest measurement, any change noted in the posttest measurement might be due to the instability of the measurement device rather than to the treatment.

Instrumentation is a threat to internal validity and is related to the validity and reliability of the data. The data the researcher uses as evidence are gathered through various instruments that measure the variables of interest. The next section describes issues of validity and reliability of such measurements.

Instrumentation

Two concerns of the researcher when collecting data by means of a measuring instrument are the validity and reliability of the instrument. Weaknesses in either threaten internal and external validity in this instrumentation category. In this section, we discuss measurement validity first and follow with a discussion of reliability.

A test or measurement instrument has what is termed face validity to the extent that it appears to the individuals being assessed to be measuring what it purports to be measuring. This is generally considered to be a poor estimate of validity. It might be important because, if a test does not have face validity (credibility), it can decrease the likelihood of people participating or volunteering. When experts in the content areas make subjective judgements about the validity of the instrument, there is said to be expert-judge content validity, which has also been called logical validity and, sometimes, definitional validity. It is similar to face validity, but it is generally estimated by using a table of specifications in which the purported content the test is supposed to measure is listed and assessed by how well and how completely the items represent content areas. How well one assessment instrument correlates with an already-established, valid assessment instrument is known as concurrent validity. Known-group validity is a type of concurrent validity. It is estimated by how well the instrument differentiates between two known groups. If the instrument is supposed to measure successful marriage, the instrument should be able to distinguish between two groups of people who have been identified previously as successfully or not successfully married. To the extent the instrument can do this, it has known-group validity.

An estimate of how well an instrument predicts a future assessment outcome is called predictive validity. The major difference between predictive validity and concurrent validity is that concurrent validity tends to be occurring within the current time span, while predictive validity is future oriented. Sometimes concurrent and predictive validity are combined and are then called statistical, empirical, or criterion validity.

The most important and the most difficult to estimate is construct validity. It is used to estimate is how well the instrument is measuring the underlying construct it is attempting to measure, and it is generally estimated by the use of a combination of the other types of validity mentioned. A statistical technique called factor analysis also is used to estimate construct validity.

Quantitative research studies that lack documented measurement validity have limited truth value; and researchers need to remember that such validity, when it is claimed, is always an estimate, never an actual measure.

If validity is confirmed, having reliability is implicit; however, it is possible to have reliability without validity. The basic framework we are using is that the major purpose of reliability is either to support or to improve validity. Reliability describes consistency.

While validity estimates how well a study or a set of instruments measures what it purports to measure, reliability estimates tell whether the outcomes will remain stable over time (*i.e.*, whether they are "repeatable") or whether they are consistent among independent observers (*i.e.*, whether different observers will report the same outcome).

In quantitative research, reliability in data collection is assured in three ways: measuring internal consistency, applying test-retest correlation coefficients, and using equivalent forms of the instrument. If reliability is not assured, then the scientific assumption of accuracy of measurement is violated. The facts are not repeatable.

Just as reliability is estimated by calculating the internal consistency of a test form, a similar measure can be derived from a structured interview schedule. Control over the timing, the environment, and the question order is possible where no such control is possible with questionnaires. To the extent that these controls enhance validity, they fulfill reliability requirements by definition. For non-structured interviews, no such reliability estimates are possible.

One cannot have validity without reliability and, concomitantly, to the extent that one has validity one need not estimate reliability. For this reason, the predominant effort in this book is issues of validity.

Whenever groups are selected on the basis of extreme scores and for no other reason, a phenomenon called statistical regression occurs. If subjects are selected for a study solely because they score extremely low, at posttest they will tend to score higher, regardless of the treatment. The opposite is also true.

Both are examples of extreme cases regressing towards the mean of the population. Thus, significant differences between pretest and posttest scores can occur because extremes were initially selected.

The loss of subjects between testings is called experimental mortality. If a sample of 100 subjects scores an average of 95 on an IQ pretest and, for some reason, 50 subjects drop out before post testing, then the average IQ of the remaining 50 might be 150. Therefore, the differences between pretest and posttest scores would, in all likelihood, not be due to the treatment but due to the differential loss from pretest to posttest (*i.e.*, mortality).

When subjects are assigned to two or more comparison groups and not all groups are given the treatment, there is selection bias. If these groups are different before treatment, then any difference between pre- and posttest scores may be due to the initial differences rather than to the treatment.

An example would be assigning individualized instruction (treatment) to highly motivated children and traditional instruction to children with little motivation. If the groups were tested for gains at the end of a unit, any difference found might, in fact, be due to initial motivation differences rather than to treatment differences.

These contaminating factors must be considered when evaluating research. They are useful criteria in judging the quality of research.

Bibliography

A.K. Singh: *Modern Trends in Social Work,* Sumit Enterprises, Delhi, 2012.

Chandrashekhar J.: *Modern Social Work Practice*, Cyber Tech Publications, Delhi, 2012.

D K Lal Das and Vanila Bhaskaran: *Research Methods for Social Work*, Rawat Publication, Delhi, 2008.

D.K. Lal Das: *Practice of Social Research : Social Work Perspective,* Rawat Publication, Delhi, 2000.

Edmund Sherman and William J. Reid: *Qualitative Research in Social Work*, Rawat Publication, Delhi, 2013.

Elizabeth A. Segal, Karen E. Gerdes and Sue Steiner: *Professional Social Work*, Rawat Publication, Delhi, 2010.

G.P. Raju: *Role of Development Skills and Social Work*, Manglam Publications, Delhi, 2011.

G.R. Madan: *Radhakamal Mukerjee : An Eminent Scholar, Saint and Social Worker,* Radha Publication, Delhi, 2008.

Ilango Ponnuswami and Abraham P. Francis: *Professional Social Work : Research Perspective*, Authorspress, Delhi, 2012.

Ilango Ponnuswami: *Professional Social Work : Best Practices and Innovations in Teaching Research and Extension*, Authors Press, Delhi, 2011.

Ilango, P.: *Quality Enhancement of Social Work Profession in India : Issues and Challenges*, Allied Publication, Delhi, 2009.

Jainendra Kumar Jha: *Practice of Social Work*, Anmol Publication, Delhi, 2002.

K Narendra Mohan: *Philosophy of Social Work*, Centrum Press, Delhi, 2012.

Margaret Alston and Wendy Bowles: *Research for Social Workers : An Introduction to Methods*, Rawat Publication, Delhi, 2003.

Mohd. Dilshad: *Modernization of Social Work Planning and Administration*, Anmol Publication, Delhi, 2012.

Mukesh Upadhyay: *Personalization in Social Work*, Prateeksha Publication, Delhi, 2011.

Mukesh Upadhyay: *Professional Development in Social Work*, Prateeksha Publication, Delhi, 2011.

P.R. Gautam and R.S. Singh: *Modern Trends in Social Work*, Centrum Press, Delhi, 2011.

P.R. Gautam and R.S. Singh: *Principles and Practices of Social Work*, Centrum Press, Delhi, 2011.

Raj Bala Mathur: *Modernisation of Social Work : Planning and Administration*, Book Enclave, Delhi, 2007.

S.B. Desai and Bharti Joshi: *Research Methods in Social Work*, Alfa Publication, Delhi, 2012.

Shaikh Azhar Iqbal: *Modern Trends in Social Work*, Sublime Publication, Delhi, 2008.

Shaikh Azhar Iqbal: *Principles and Practices of Social Work*, Sublime Publication, Delhi, 2005.

Shaikh Azhar Iqbal: *Problems of Social Welfare and Social Work*, Sublime Publication, Delhi, 2005.

Shweta: *Rural Sociology Human Migration and Social Work*, Kunal Books, Delhi, 2010.

Sudha Datar, Ruma Bawikar, Geeta Rao, Nagmani Rao and Ujwala Masdekar: *Skill Training for Social Workers : A Manual*, Sage Publication, Delhi, 2010.

Sujata Menon: *Principles of Social Work Practice*, Yking Books, Delhi, 2011.

Vijendra Kumar: *Problems and Perspectives on Social Work and Social Welfare*, ABD Publication, Delhi, 2002.

W.R. Mujawar: *Research Methodology in Social Work*, Manglam Publications, Delhi, 2010.

Index